Media Across the African Diaspora

This volume gathers scholarship from varying disciplinary perspectives to explore media owned or created by members of the African diaspora, examine its relationship with diasporic audiences, and consider its impact on mainstream culture in general. Contributors highlight creations and contributions of people of the African diaspora, the interconnections of Black American and African-centered media, and the experiences of audiences and users across the African diaspora, positioning members of the Black and African Diaspora as subjects of their own narratives, active participants and creators. In so doing, this volume addresses issues of identity, culture, audiences, and global influence.

Omotayo O. Banjo is an Associate Professor in the Department of Communication at the University of Cincinnati, USA. She focuses on representation and audience responses to racial and cultural media. Her work has been published in *Journal of Broadcasting and Electronic Media, Communication Theory, Journalism and Mass Communication Quarterly, Journal of Media and Religion,* and *Race and Social Problems.* She most recently coedited a volume on the topics of race, ethnicity, and faith called *Contemporary Christian Culture: Messages, Missions, and Dilemmas.*

Routledge Transformations in Race and Media

Series Editors: Robin R. Means, Coleman University of Michigan, Ann Arbor
Charlton D. McIlwain, New York University

Media Across the African Diaspora

Content, Audiences, and Global Influence

Edited by
Omotayo O. Banjo

Routledge
Taylor & Francis Group

NEW YORK AND LONDON

First published 2019
by Routledge
52 Vanderbilt Avenue, New York, NY 10017

and by Routledge
2 Park Square, Milton Park, Abingdon, Oxon OX14 4RN

First issued in paperback 2020

Routledge is an imprint of the Taylor & Francis Group, an informa business

Library of Congress Cataloging-in-Publication Data
CIP data has been applied for.

ISBN 13: 978-0-36-758854-0 (pbk)
ISBN 13: 978-1-138-06548-2 (hbk)

Typeset in Sabon
by codeMantra

Contents

List of Figures and Tables

Figures

Tables

Foreword

It is always a pleasure and an honor to be invited to write the Foreword to a new volume. It is an even greater pleasure when the book provides a reason to interact with texts you haven't revisited in some time.

Serendipitously, the new trailer for the film *Black Panther* debuted as I began writing this piece. As an avid comics fan, it was a happy coincidence that the movie preview for and a chapter about the *Black Panther* comic series (from which the movie was adapted) came to my computer at exactly the same time. As I watched the highly anticipated trailer on my laptop, I thought to myself that this snippet from the movie aptly illustrated the dominant Western media's troubled relationship to representations of the African continent and people of its diaspora.

The trailer begins with a white interrogator questioning a white male prisoner. Both are being watched, via a two-way mirror, by two people of African descent. The prisoner asks his interrogator:

"What do you know about Wakanda?"

Wakanda is the fictional home of the titular hero, the Black Panther. The interrogator answers by reeling off stereotypes of a premodern, pre-industrial culture:

"It's a Third World country. Textiles, shepherds, cool outfits."

Intercut with his glib response are shots of a rural, lush landscape of a nation in Africa: Wakanda. As the interrogator finishes his description, the prisoner laughs and tells his captor that he has been fooled: Wakanda is much more advanced. As he speaks, the camera takes the viewer over waterfalls and cliffs, then pulls back to reveal a spaceship, skyscrapers, and other technological wonders created by Wakandans; that is, technological wonders designed by and for Black African people.

The juxtaposition of Western assumptions about the "primitive" characteristics of African countries with the "reality" of Wakandan technological advancement provides an interesting launch point for this collection. Professor Omotayo O. Banjo Adesagba and her colleagues deliver an impressive set of chapters that break through the persistent myths and stereotypes of Africa as a land time forgot, a place that does not produce its own industry or narratives, let alone sophisticated modern media.

Media Across the African Diaspora is a welcome addition to works on race, media, and international flows and exchanges of representations of Africa, Africans, and Blackness. The book's chapters deliver subtle insights and introduce new frameworks for thinking not only about media in the context of Africa and its diaspora, but also rethinking standard approaches to global media studies, studies which all too often begin and end with the assumption that the West is the main driver of global flows and the key designer of transnational mediascapes. Our field remains quite U.S.- and Euro-centered in terms of topics and locales. The book calls on readers to reconsider what we mean when we say "global" media, how we study diasporic identities, and how we imagine publics formed in digital spaces. *Media Across the African Diaspora* invites us to expand the scope of our questions about race, media, national identity, media production, and reception in the digital age.

The collection takes seriously the unique historical connections between the African continent and its U.S.-based diaspora, but does not romanticize these connections. Through a breadth of texts, technologies, and geographies, *Media Across the African Diaspora* gives readers an exciting set of introductions to media phenomena rarely discussed, from the Black Press in Canada and Nigeria's booming cinema industry to African immigrant women's understanding of how Western media frame their lives and the online chats of Afrofuturist scientific communities. The authors provide vantage points from which to view the issues of race, gender, and media as technologies accelerate and expand access to multiplying narratives of blackness and African-ness around the world.

What I find refreshing about this book is how it confronts the legacies of racism, the transatlantic slave trade, and imperialism without limiting its scope to how those legacies are portrayed. Rather, with complexity and care, the authors engage with history and sociopolitical realities, charting oppressive and resistant practices. They identify important trends and pose questions that help the reader imagine current and future possibilities for creative responses within African and Black media production and consumption. The book is a welcome "crash course" in media matters in and about Africa and its diaspora. From case studies to audience analyses, interviews and historiography, the wide range of methods showcased here will be a boon to students and instructors who are looking for models for their own work.

While one book cannot cover or represent the vast, long, and complicated history of media for such a diverse continent and peoples, *Media Across the African Diaspora* provides an excellent start. From where I sit, in a metropolitan area that has been transformed over the last three decades by migration flows from Somalia, Eritrea, and other parts of East Africa, we would do well to encourage more students to consider the African continent and its diaspora (rather than limit ourselves to "race relations" within the U.S. or Europe) as a crucial entry point of departure for studies of race, media, and globalization.

Catherine R. Squires
St. Paul, Minnesota
October 2017

Acknowledgements

Many thanks to each contributor to this volume for believing in the project and sharing your ideas. I would like to honor my family for inspiring and supporting my curiosity and passion that led to this project. I would also like to thank my daughter Morayo AdeYara Adesagba for being a renewing source of motivation for me. Lastly, I would like to thank those scholars I met along my journey who dissuaded me from pursuing questions of race and identity on the basis that it was "irrelevant." I say to you, these questions are very much relevant. We are relevant.

Introduction

Omotayo O. Banjo

The global perspective of Black people around the world is generally not positive. In fact, the recent surge in White nationalist movements articulates an opinion that nothing good comes from people of color, especially those of African descent. But of course, these assertions are false as Africans have contributed to knowledge, business, infrastructure, and literary and creative arts for centuries. The purpose of this book is to celebrate the contributions of people of African descent around the world, as well as to capture some of the struggles that people of African descent continue to face in their endeavors to tell stories which reflect their multifaceted experiences and narratives.

This book refers specifically to Black people of African descent as members of the African diaspora. It is noted that the conception of African diaspora has been defined, contested, and articulated by various scholars. For some this definition is limited to those descendents of the Atlantic slave trade which focuses primarily on Black Americans, but Palmer (2000) argues that discussing the movements of African people only within that context dismisses other and also significant movements and migrations of African people including that which led to tribal migrations in West Africa and African presence in Asia, the Middle East, the Mediterranean, and Europe prior to Columbus's Manifest Destiny. Palmer (2000) writes that "the construction of a diaspora, then, is an organic process involving movement from an ancestral land, settlement in new lands, and sometimes renewed movement and resettlement elsewhere" (p. 28). In addition, Clark (2008) notes that African populations are often homogenized and as such the richness within the cultural diversity is often overlooked. In fact, Clark (2008) refers to the movement or migration of Africans to America as "the New African Diaspora" arguing that such a shift redefines and adds depth to terms like "African-American" when describing first and/or second generation Americans who blend the culture of their ancestral and domestic homes. In contrast, the late Richard Iton (2013) described diaspora as "an anaformative and already cosmopolitan impulse or dynamic that recontextualizes attempts to draw tight lines between power and space, gender, sexuality, and governance, and institutionalize and naturalize the logically related hierarchies" (p. 33). Iton approached diasporic communities as a "geoheterodoxy"—one that is no longer limited to an ancestral homeland, but is reconstructed and renegotiated in multiple spaces of blackness as diasporic communities are constantly in motion.

These stories, the experience in the domestic land, the ties to the ancestral land, and the complicated fusion of identities across global borders need to be told and celebrated among scholars of race, ethnicity, culture, and identity because it frustrates the assumptions of homogeneity that we so often make about people of African descent. Moreover, it gives voice to the multilayered experience of Black people around the world worth celebrating, investigating, and learning from. The chapters in this collection cover diasporic communities mostly in North America and West Africa. However, it should be noted that narratives from diasporic communities in Central and South America, and other parts of Africa and the Caribbean are just as valuable. Arguably the ideas presented in this book can be extended to the overall diasporic experience.

This book is organized in five parts: the Contributions to Mainstream Media Culture, Owning Images and Narratives, Bridges Across the African Diaspora, Audiences' Responses and Effects, and an examination of the Digital Diaspora.

Beginning with Ojo's exploration of the Black press in Canada, this chapter demonstrates how Black people used the power of the press to advocate for social justice. More than report on information regarding Black communities, Ojo delineates how the Black press facilitated and managed public discourse which pushed for rights of minority groups.

In the second chapter, Mark Ward describes the progression of the popularity of Black evangelicals. This chapter illustrates the tensions between spirituality, consumerism, and the history of Blacks in America that produces a theology based on economic mobility which provides insight into the appeal of prosperity theology for the Black community. Ward also shows how Black evangelicals are able to surpass the boundaries of federal policies meant to limit the voices of racial minorities through media ownership.

Isaken follows with a thorough discussion of how the writers and producers of the hit series "Blackish" attempts to deconstruct a "Black American experience" and racial inequality in America for mainstream audiences. Offering an analysis of three episodes, she explains how the show uses comedy as a vehicle through which audiences of all racial backgrounds may gain insight into the complexities which racialize an American lived experience. Isaken celebrates the show as one of many programs written and produced by Black people that offer insight into the diverse experience within the Black community not just for Black consumption, but for people of all backgrounds. These chapters identify experiences of Blackness within a North American context.

In Chapter 4, Godfried Asante and Rita Daniels discuss the ways in which YouTube series "An African City" gives voice to Blackness within diasporic communities abroad, focusing on women from different ancestral and domestic homes. In this chapter, the authors argue that the program is one of few which feature Africaness or Blackness outside of African contexts and as such presents conflicts in identities and culture especially as it pertains to patriarchy. Specifically, the authors argue that the show presents a feminism which counters traditional cultural assumptions of femininity in Africa, thus pushing the envelope in African program. Not only does the program showcase a diasporic experience, but also works to both complicate notions of femininity and present a progressive view of femininity for African and Western audiences.

Using Ta'nahesi Coates' comic adaptation of the Black Panther, Brown et al., provide an analysis of how Black creatives fuse African and American aesthetics to present a vision of an unadulterated Pan-African identity. Through the lens of Afro-futurisim, the authors argue in Chapter 5 that the writers of the comic use meaningful symbols and technical strategies to tie Black American identities to its African heritage.

In part III of the book, Chapters 6 and 7 deal with tensions of inclusion and collaboration seemingly influenced by regional context. Specifically, Grammage and Grammage discuss the ways in which some Black American programming subscribes to Western ideals of Africa and as such may disrupt the possible connections between Black Americans and native Africans.

On the other hand, in Chapter 7 Abah writes about the growth of one of the most yielding film industries in the world, Nollywood. She discusses how collaborations between native Nigerian and Black American actors lay the groundwork for storytelling which connects members of differing diasporic societies. By analyzing three films, Abah attempts to identify themes unique to the Nollywood USA genre and argues that the genre should be considered among Black independent films. Doing so arguably not only bridges narratives of communities with similar heritages, but also reinforces a sense of diasporic community in the minds of Black Americans and Africans and global audiences in general.

Whereas an analysis of visual text yield insight into messages about diasporic identities, audience response research help scholars gain insight into how members of the diaspora interpret these messages. In the following chapter, Pindi's critical ethnography of African female immigrants reveals a disconnect between portrayals of Africanness and how these women self-identify. Adams-Bass and Henrici follow in Chapter 9 with a discussion of how young Black men express an oversight of positive Black role models in media. In the following chapter, in a previously published article, I present empirical data which supports anecdotal expressions of anxiety regarding the public presentation of Blackness for non-Black consumption. The findings of an experiment reveal that Black audiences may be concerned that misrepresentations of their social group could negatively influences White audiences. Therefore, this chapter suggests that the presentation of Blackness is critical to lived Black experiences, both domestically and globally, and perhaps has an impact on diasporic communities' sense of pride.

The final three chapters focus on the expression of African diasporic identities in virtual or digital environments. Similar to Ward, Blevins contends that deregulation presents challenges to free expression of minority groups. Based on this reality, the author argues that digital media allow for the free expression of social justice for Blacks in America and abroad and discusses how social media can be used effectively to garner support for Black people. Alzouma writes of the use of digital spaces to cultivate a transnational identity among the African diaspora and contain knowledge which reinforces African contribution to science and technology. Expanding on the concept of an identity without borders, Stanley-Niaah discusses the global transcendence of production technology called "videolight" and the ways in which this technology cultivates a dancehall culture across the globe. These chapters demonstrate the ways in which diasporic Blackness is mediated across geographical and cultural boundaries.

The academic study of the modern African Diaspora is crucial in the deconstruction of monolithic assumptions of peoples of African descent, while at the same time finding points of connection and collaboration that help to foster and strengthen a sense of identity and community within the African diaspora. For example, recent collaborations of actors Will Smith and Jay-Z on the Broadway show *Fela!* helped to open communities, Black American communities especially, to meaningful spiritual connections to a possible ancestral home. This collaboration is said to influence the African aesthetics more visibly presented in Beyonce' s music (Mokoena, 2015). Rappers Drake and Jidenna's collaboration with artists from the African continent such as Wizkid, Tiwa Savage, Maleek Berry, Sarkodie, and Burna Boy are examples of the fusion of African diasporic communities' (i.e., Black Canadian, First Generation, British Nigerian, Ghana, and Nigeria) cultivation of unique creations which connect members of the diaspora to an ancestral home, one that they can be proud of.

References

Clark, M. K. (2008). Identity among first and second generation African immigrants in the United States. *African Identities, 6*(2), 169–181.

Iton, R. (2013). Still life. *Small Axe: A Caribbean Journal of Criticism, 17*(1 (40)), 22–39.

Mokoena, T. (2015, March 26). Beyoncé scrapped entire Fela Kuti-inspired album, says The-Dream. *The Guardian*. Retrieved November 11, 2017 from www.theguardian.com/music/2015/mar/26/beyonce-scrapped-fela-kuti-inspired-album-says-the-dream

Palmer, C. A. (2000). Defining and studying the modern African diaspora. *The Journal of Negro History, 85*(1–2), 27–32.

Part I

Contributions to Mainstream Media Culture

1 The Early Black Press in Canada

Tokunbo Ojo

Historically, Black media have always been important sites of discursive activities and public engagement in the wider sociocultural contexts of political struggles and community building. For instance, in the 19th century, Black newspapers were at the forefront of antislavery and emancipation movements. They fostered critical deliberations and civic dialogue on issues that were of common concerns to Black publics. In the contemporary era, Black media still remain important sociocultural and political institutions in the contexts of Canada's mosaic of multiculturalism (Ojo, 2006). Through their hybridized form of civic and cultural journalism, they chart the connections between notions of citizenship, public service ethos, and communal identities in the mediated context of the Canadian nationhood. In addition to being alternative subaltern public spheres, they have been strategic training 'grounds' for many young and veteran Black Canadian journalists. Among the veteran journalists that have crossed from the Black news media outlets to the mainstream national news outlets are Tom Godfrey (investigative reporter for the *Toronto Sun*), Hamlin Grange (retired celebrated print and broadcast reporter for outlets such as Canadian Broadcasting Corporation), and Royson James (award-winning reporter and municipal affairs columnist for the *Toronto Star*). The young journalists include Maya Johnson, Quebec City bureau chief for the CTV Montreal since February 2016.

But, quite strikingly, within the broader discussions of Canadian journalism history and evolution of news media, the role and contributions of Black press are conspicuously absent. This neglect or lack of consideration in the scholarship is not limited to Black media alone; it also extends to other nonmainstream media such as Aboriginal and native press in Canada. This is also reflected in many journalism programs' curricula and course syllabi where the social history of journalism mainly begins from the era of Johannes Gutenberg's printing press and ends with web 2.0, social media and Mark Zuckerberg's 'Facebook media' with minimal or zero attention to nontraditional mainstream media that are not in the canon of the "elite journalism." As articulated in Osler's (1993) seminal work on the evolution of journalism in Canada, newspapers such as the *Globe and Mail* and *Le Devoir* exemplified the elite journalism in the Canadian context.

> In radio and television, elite journalism is narrowly restricted to some news and public affairs components of such state-owned or sponsored organizations as the Canadian Broadcasting Corporation (CBC), the provincial educational television authorities ... and the news and public affairs contents of virtually all North American privately owned broadcasting organizations.
>
> (Osler, 1993, p. 78)

Against this backdrop of the scholarship gap, this chapter examines the development of Black press in Canada. It provides an analysis of the multifaceted roles of early Black newspapers and their contributions to journalism as a cultural act. Of particular interest is these early newspapers' journalistic orientation of public service and social responsibility, albeit ideological lens of Black political consciousness.

Development of Black Press in Canada

Historically, the evolution of Black newspapers in Canada began in March 1845 in Toronto with *The British American* newspaper (Winks, 1997). But, in the historical rendition of the evolution of Black press in Canada, *The British American* newspaper is not often included because it only existed for less than a month. Consequently, the *Voice of the Fugitive*, which was established almost six years after *The British American* newspaper, is often regarded as the first Black newspaper in Canada. While *The British American* indeed folded prematurely and was ephemeral in the historical contexts of Black press in Canada, it still remains the first Black newspaper in Canada. However, in terms of the historical impact and legacy, both the *Voice of the Fugitive* and the *Provincial Freedman* were the standard-bearers for the Black expression and concerns in the 19th century, despite the existence of other Black Canadian newspapers that included *The Voice of the Bondsman* (ran by J.J.E. Linton, a Presbyterian abolitionist), *The British Lion*, and Windsor-based *The True Royalist and Weekly Intelligencer* that Reverend A.R. Green of the New British Methodist Episcopal Church published. Both newspapers remain the bastion of advocacy community journalism, as far as Black communities were concerned in the 19th century.

The sociopolitical contexts of the era made them an important institution for the Blacks in Canada as well as those on the south of the border. Socially and politically, Blacks were considered "outcasts" in the Anglo-Saxon modern nation-state of Canada. Like Jews, Asians, and Native people, they did not fit into 19th-century Canada's national visions, which were codified around Anglo-Saxon cultural heritage and allowed for a deeply entrenched moral racial superiority in the political discourse and rhetoric of every prime minister that ran for office between 1870 and 1940 (Mathieu, 2010). Up till 1940, "every prime minister, whether running on the Liberal or the Conservative ticket, insisted that the Dominion of Canada would be a White man's land toiled by brawny Europeans and Americans, without elbow room for people of color" (Mathieu, 2010, p. 14). The divisive political rhetoric of racial supremacy of White Canadians also fueled derogatory and racist commentaries about Blacks in the mainstream White-owned newspapers such as *Kent Advertiser, Toronto Colonist, Hamilton Spectator*, and *Brantford Expositor*, especially with a new wave of migration of Black entrepreneurs and professionals from the United States to Canada from 1877 onward (Cooper, 2016; Mathieu, 2010; Silverman, Bellavance, & Rudin, 1984). In the backdrop of all these were ongoing legal and illegal transatlantic slave trades in which several Blacks were forcefully taken from Africa and sold as slaves across Quebec, Atlantic, and Central Canada, in particular (Mensah, 2010; Winks, 1997).

Such harsh sociocultural realities and political climate led to the formation of these newspapers as both key communicative infrastructure for civic consciousness and also a counter-hegemonic vehicle of political engagement for social justice. At the 1850 Sandwich Colored Convention, a mutual resolution passed for the establishment of Black press in Canada. As Cooper (2016) documented, the resolution from convention delegates stated:

> *Whereas*, We as a people, have a great work to accomplish and we have no instrument that we can use with more effect than the public press – as we struggle against opinion, our warfare lies in the field of thought, embodying ourselves to field, we need a printing press – for the press is the vehicle of thought – the ruler of opinions. We need a press, that we may be independent of those who have always oppressed us – we need a press that we many hang our banners on the outer wall, that all who pass by may read why we struggle, and what we struggle for.
>
> *Resolved*, that we make immediate effort to have a newspaper established in our midst, which shall be the advocate of the colored people of Canada West.
>
> (p. 137)

The following year, Henry Bibb[1] and Mary Bibb established the *Voice of the Fugitive* as a bimonthly newspaper for audiences in Canada, the United States, and England. In 1853, Mary Ann Shad Cary founded *The Provincial Freeman*, a weekly newspaper. As was the norm at the time in the newspaper industry, it was a four-page broadsheet newspaper. Both newspapers had their own printing press platforms.

In fact, the *Provincial Freeman*'s became the official printing press[2] of the town council of Chatham, Ontario (Murray, 1959). They published a variety of news stories that were specific to the Black communities as well as general national and international public affairs news stories. They were also repositories for public knowledge, banal lists of community events, information, and concerns of everyday life.

Unlike in the United States where there were at least three daily Black newspapers and scores of weekly Black newspapers between 1827 and 1860, there was no single Black daily newspaper in Canada (Simmons, 1998; Winks, 1997). Combined, Canada had less than 12 Black newspapers, which were published weekly, biweekly, monthly, or even quarterly between 1827 and 1860. The absence of Black daily newspaper was primarily due to the limited financial resources[3] to support such an enterprise. Second, with a low Black population in the country at the time, the readership base was small and scattered across the country. As an example, out of Toronto's population of 50,000 in early 1850s, only about 1,000 were Black (Bearden & Butler, 1977; Rhodes, 1998). In Montreal, there were also about 1,000 Blacks among the city's population in 1840 (Austin, 2013). Based on multiple accounts from government and nongovernment sources, the aggregated population of Blacks across in places such as Chatham, Halifax, Windsor, Charlottetown, Newfoundland, Pine Creek, Vancouver Island, and St. John's was estimated to be less than 100,000 out of Canada's population[4] of about 4.1 million in the 1860s (Krauter & Davis, 1978; Mensah, 2010; Williams, 1997; Winks, 1997). In addition to all these, the literary level was also low across country.

Nonetheless, newspapers were still important outlets for opinion and public debates for Canadian Blacks, many of whom were freeborn Black Canadians, African-Americans who fled the United States during the slavery trade era, indentured laborers from Britain, and Canadian Pacific railway workers/porters. In particular, newspapers were influential forums for community debates on slave trade abolition as well as on the socioeconomic and political empowerment education of Blacks in Canada. As an integral platform of the communal communication ecology, the *Voice of the Fugitive* and the *Provincial Freeman* drew on contributors and writers from Canada, the United States, and across the Atlantic Ocean to sensitize their readers to structural inequality of the period. Though varied in style, length, tone, and expressed points of views, all were related in different ways to the specific set of lived relations, or what Raymond Williams (1977) called "structure of feelings," that underpinned the broader "Black transnational antislavery awareness and culture, in respect not only to Canada and the United States, but beyond" (Cooper, 2016, p. 136). The collage of contents on the transnational Black experiences not only animated discrete interests and viewpoints that were part of constitutive voices of the civil publics of broader Black communities, but these contents also alluded to a shared sense of urgency in the struggle for equality and Black freedom in Canada and other places that spanned the frontiers of Americas, Africa, Europe, and the Caribbean.

Both newspapers through the community activism of their publishers/editors linked up with other Black institutions such as churches and community-based activist groups to press for social justice, equality, and Black empowerment in Canada. These community-based activist works included intense lobby for access to education and schools for Blacks.

> To many Blacks, education was key to freedom, a privilege denied in slavery. It served as a way to combat charges of racial inferiority and would produce a generation of skilled men and women who would, leaders hoped, foster the development of a self-reliant community.
>
> (Rhodes, 1994, p. 65)

In the same vein, both newspapers also aligned with White abolitionists such as George Brown (editor of the influential Toronto based *Globe* newspaper) and William King in the political advocacy for "safer resettlement homes" for Blacks in Canada, following the passage of 1850 Fugitive Slave Act in the United States (Cooper, 2016; Harrell, 2008; Paul, 2011; Yee, 1997). Conversely, in the backdrop of absence of full rights of citizenship and political participation, Black readers of these newspapers were activated into social and political relations with non-Black readers, who were not among the newspapers' primary audiences,[5] and the activist groups that were part of the solidarity 'fight' for social justice and racial equality in the society.

Black Press as the Subaltern Counterpublic Sphere

As the communicative network infrastructures that were socially and politically connected with other community institutions, they forged multiplicity of Black public spheres in 19th-century Canadian society. The Black public sphere[6] as forged by these newspapers, in concert with collectives of other Black subgroups and institutions, was not uniquely different from Habermas' idea of public sphere in terms of its purpose as the locales for the exploration of ideas and issues that were relevant to greater number of Black people in the communal sense. However, structurally, the established Black public sphere had the features and coloration of Fraser's (1992) conceptualized subaltern public *spheres* because of the multiplicity of dialectically diverse perspectives on racial prejudice, social injustice, and antislavery movement on the pages of these newspapers. Specifically, while *Voice of the Fugitive* and the *Provincial Freeman* coexisted under the broader rubric of the Black public sphere and engaged in the progressive political actions, they did not share the same counter-ideologies and perspectives on the internal dynamics of affairs and politics within the Black settlements. As an example: though both newspapers were united in the struggle for Black freedom and empowerment amidst the racial inequality oppression in the traditionally state-sanctioned sociopolitical and economic spaces, their publishers/ editors had different views on the direction that the Black education should take in practice. The different views on the direction of Black education became a "war of words" between both publishers on the pages of their newspapers. Shadd ferociously opposed government-sponsored public school for Blacks, while Bibb welcomed the government-sponsored public schools for Blacks in addition to the Black privately-run schools (Yee, 1997). But, in spite of their ideological difference on the form of ownership and the direction that education should take in the Black settlements, both still deemed education as important and lobbied for improved access to education for Blacks.

To this end, the Black public sphere was a plurality of subaltern counter-publics in the 19th century (Dawson, 1994; Squires, 2002). Fraser (1992) defined counterpublics as "parallel discursive arenas where members of subordinated social groups invent and circulate counter-discourses to formulate oppositional interpretations of their identities, interests and needs" (p. 123). As the courtrooms of public opinion, both newspapers did not shy away from debate or pretend to be casual neutral observers of the events. They were incubators of ideas and active platforms for alternative voices. The contents of the *Provincial Freeman*, in particular, were first and foremost a radical departure from the entrenched Victorian age doctrine of separate spheres for women and men's expression (Rhodes, 2007). For the *Provincial Freeman*'s editor, Mary Ann Shadd Cary, the fight for liberty and equality was for all individuals (Van Brenk, 1988). To this end, she rejected the Victorian age dichotomy of rights between sexes and used her editorial writing to advocate for equality of all people. Needless to say, the pages of the *Voice of the Fugitive* also featured contents and stories from women. The major difference in this context was that Shadd Cary was among the handful of female editors in the male-dominated 19th-century media institutions and also an influential voice in an era when women were predominately deemed the "weaker sex" (Rhodes, 1998; Van Brenk, 1988; Yee, 1994).

That said, the pages of the *Provincial Freeman* were not just filled with critical deconstruction of issues, mentalities, and psyche of the broader society, but they were also a public arena where issues such as corruption, religion, education, and political leadership within the Black communities were examined and discussed. Specifically, it put a spotlight on the complicity of a cross section of Black leaders and White abolitionists/clergymen in the marginalization and enslavement of Black Canadians. For example, in a series of articles between 1854 and 1856, the paper exposed how community and church leaders misappropriated money raised through fundraising and donation for the resettlement and education of escaped slaves from the United States to Canada. Following the "exposé" series of the misappropriation of funds and donation, one of the paper's editorials in December, 1856, made the following clarion call to its readers and the broader Black public:

> Speak through papers not in the begging interest, to the generous donors whose pockets are being relieved of gold, and whose generosity is thus abused by the horde of long-faced pretenders of piety and brotherly regard for the 'poor colored man,' who make incessant appeal to help this 'mission' or that other 'institution'.
>
> (The Provincial Freeman, p. 1)

The call was part of the subtext message of the paper's mission statements of being the 'voice of the voiceless,' while preserving self-dignity of all Blacks in Canada. Overall, the degree of the paper's social and political activism illuminated the strategic importance of the counterculture communication and advocacy journalism to the emergence of multiple subaltern Black public spheres within the national political scene.

Whereas the *Provincial Freeman* was unabashedly radical in its advocacy community journalism as a way of energizing civil action and consciousness, the *Voice of the Fugitive* maintained moderate and conservative perspective of the 19th-century Black press (Hutton, 1993; Simmons, 1998). The *Voice of the Fugitive* was not the odd one in this case. Several Black newspaper editors and publishers took the moderate conservative perspectives as a conscious decision of "providing straight news and opinion about racial problems without any sensational flair. The idea was to provide the news with dignity and honor reflective of the newspaper's solid position in the black community" (Simmons, 1998, p. 6). Additionally, a cross section of them took a moderate and conservative perspective to avoid being lynched by the slave owners who were profiting from the slave trade and racial structural order of 19th-century America. As Washburn (2006, p. 20) observed, prior to the American civil war, outspoken Black editors were most likely to be "attacked" or "killed" and their newspapers "destroyed" at the same time. Bibb, an escaped slave from the United States, was aware of these dire consequences, which partly might have shaped his newspaper's[7] moderate conservative perspective.

In spite of different political perspectives and fierce rivalry[8] between the *Voice of the Fugitive* and the *Provincial Freeman,* both newspapers had similar end goals, which were essentially about Black empowerment and social justice. The difference in perspectives and approaches underscored the polysemy of views on empowerment and social justice within the Black communities. As sites of cultural nationalism and sociopolitical expression, both newspapers' editors, and contributors[9] appropriated diverse communicative genres—news stories, sermons, editorials, op-ed articles, public lecture addresses, letters, poems, essays, and long-narrative form of explanatory journalism—to engage in public deliberation and discussions relating to Black empowerment, civil rights issues, and social justice. The readers-generated contents, particularly letters and opinion pieces from contributors and readers outside the province of Ontario where both papers were based, enabled a notion of cultural citizenship and imagined communities for Blacks that were geographically separated. Whereby the imagined communities were fostered by the unity in the time and space via communication, the cultural citizenship, in this context, is based on the sense of common experiences expressed in diverse genres of cultural idioms and voices that cultivated both communal social capital as well as individual's capacity for action (Ojo, 2006; Stevenson, 2003).

Thus, while political and legal bounded territorial nation-states might be bureaucratically exclusionary, the pages of the *Voice of the Fugitives* and the *Provincial Freeman* provided the autonomy and choice for expressions. In this vein, the convergence of diverse communicative genres on the pages of these newspapers not only showcased discrete interests and viewpoints that were part of constitutive voices of the civil publics of Black communities, but it also underscored the crucial roles of these newspapers and other Black newspapers in the United States as the "advocate, facilitator of Black community bond and transmitter of cultural heritage" (Wilson, 2014, p. 11) during the pivotal era of racial segregation, political oppression, and sociocultural inequality in North America.

Conclusion

As mediated public forum, the *Voice of the Fugitives* and the *Provincial Freeman* allowed readers and contributors to deduce their own meanings of being Black in Canada through print conversation. In the ritual sense of communication, the journalism of conversation, as practiced by both newspapers, was both a sociocultural act of community building and a service to public life—that is, a form of journalism where the press is connected to the struggle, everyday life, and experience of its audience (Carey, 1974). It was the John Dewey-type of journalism that the late James W. Carey envisioned for any democratic society (Carey, 1987). This form of journalism was a direct opposite of the information-based journalism, which is presumably characterized by hierarchical structure of professionalism and telegraphic writing formula of *5Ws and 1H*[10] whereby the events and issues of the day are explained and interpreted through the lens of subject experts/elite opinion leaders.

In sum, both in the institutional sense and in practice, the *Voice of the Fugitives* and the *Provincial Freeman* were an embodiment of expression of Black imagination, temperament, consciousness, and cultural ethos within the sociopolitical and cultural spaces of 19th-century

Canada. They existed primarily for the Black publics and were not handmaidens of corporate power, political elites, and government. As other Black newspapers of the era, they uplifted, educated, informed, and imbued their readers "with a sense of cultural identity while fighting the forces of social injustice" (Wilson II, 2014, p. 149). They were not merely "conveyor belts of observations," but active facilitators, monitors, participants, and originators of public conversation in regard to Black experience in the racially divided societies of the time. They also laid the foundation for other Black media that came after them from the turn of the century onward.

Notes

1 Henry Bibb was one of the delegates who drafted the resolution, which called for the establishment of Black press in Canada.

2 The ownership of its own printing press is an attestation of the entrepreneurial dimension of the *Provincial Freeman*'s journalism. Before it finally settled down in Chatham, Ontario, the *Provincial Freeman* started its operation in Windsor, Ontario and then relocated to Toronto due to high Black population in Toronto (Rhodes, 1998).

3 The newspapers depended heavily on the revenues from individual subscriptions, advertising, publishers' personal resources, and good-will donation from friends.

4 There was no accurate data on the number of freeborn Black Canadians due to a combination of poor data collection and the official government' inadequate census data for Blacks in the country (Williams, 1989; Winks, 1997).

5 The primary audiences were Blacks, irrespective of their geographical locations in and outside of Canada.

6 It was detached from the national Westphalian public sphere, which also correlated to the sovereign power. As such, the Black public sphere drew "energy from the vernacular practices of street talk and new music …and church voices, entrepreneurship and circulation" to challenge exclusionary violence and practices in the public space (Black Public Collective, 1995, p. 3).

7 Ironically, the *Voice of the Fugitive* went out of business in 1854, following the burning down of its office in October 1853. The loss from the fire included the all printing equipment, personal records, archives, and the building (Cooper, 2016). Though the fire was believed to be an accident—act of nature—Afua Cooper whose PhD dissertation was on Bibb's works indicated that arson was also suspected (Cooper, 2016). Bibb and the newspaper never recovered from the loss. Less than a year after the fire incident, Henry Bibb died at the age of 38, and that 'officially' marked the end of the *Voice of the Fugitive*. He died from illness.

8 There are well-chronicled bitter exchanges between Bibb and Shadd Cary that later developed into fierce rivalry between both newspapers (Murray, 1959; Rhodes, 1998; Ripley, 1986; Winks, 1997).

9 Public participation and deliberations included common individual citizens and members of the civil society groups.

10 The telegraphic writing formula of *5Ws and 1H* refers to inverted pyramid news reporting style of the contemporary journalism, in which *5Ws* stand for "Who, Where, What, When and Why" of the news story and *1H* stands for "How."

References

Austin, D. (2013). *Fear of a Black nation: Race, sex, and security in sixties Montreal*. Toronto: Between the Lines.

Bearden, J., & Butler, L. J. (1977). *Shadd: The life and times of Mary Shadd Cary*. Toronto: NC Press Ltd.

Black Public Sphere Collective (Ed). (1995). *The Black public sphere*. Chicago: University of Chicago Press.

Carey, J. W. (1974). Journalism and criticism: The case of an undeveloped profession. *The Review of Politics, 36*(2), 227–249.

Carey, J. W. (1987). The press and the public discourse. *The Center Magazine, 20*(2, March/April), 4–32.

Cooper, A. (2016). The *voice of the fugitive*: A transnational abolitionist organ. In K. S. Frost, & V. S. Tucker (Eds.), *A fluid frontier: Slavery, resistance, and the underground railroad in the Detroit River borderland* (pp. 135–153). Detroit, MI: Wayne State University Press.

Dawson, M. C. (1994). A Black counterpublic?: Economic earthquake, racial agenda(s), and Black politics. *Public Culture, 7*(1), 195–223.

Fraser, N. (1992). Rethinking the public sphere: A contribution to the critique of actually existing democracy. In C. Calhoun (Ed.), *Habermas and the public sphere* (pp. 109–142). Cambridge, MA: MIT Press.

Harrell, W. J., Jr. (2008). "Thanks be to God that I am elected to Canada": The formulation of the Black Canadian Jeremiad, 1830–61. *Journal of Canadian Studies, 42*(2), 55–79.

Hutton, F. (1993). *The early Black press in America, 1827 to 1860*. Westport, CT: Greenword Press.

Krauter, J., & Davis, M. (1978). *Minority Canadians: Ethnic groups*. Toronto: Methuen.

Mathieu, S. (2010). *North of the color line: Migration and Black resistance in Canada, 1870–1955*. Chapel Hill, NC: University of North Carolina Press.

Mensah, J. (2010). *Black Canadians: History, experience, social conditions* (2nd ed.). Halifax: Fernwood Publishing.

Murray, A. L. (1959). The provincial Freeman: A new source for the history of the Negro in Canada and the United States. *The Journal of Negro History, 44*(2), 123–135.

Ojo, T. (2006). Ethnic print media in the multicultural nation of Canada: A case study of the Black newspaper in Montreal. *Journalism, 7*(3), 343–361.

Osler, A. M. (1993). *News: The evolution of journalism in Canada*. Toronto: Copp Clark Pitman.

Paul, H. (2011). Out of Chatham: Abolitionism on the Canadian frontier. *Atlantic Studies, 8*(2), 165–188.

Rhodes, J. (2007). At the boundaries of abolitionism, feminism, and Black nationalism: The activism of Mary Ann Shadd Cary. In K. K. Sklar, & J. B. Stewart (Eds.), *Women's rights and transatlantic antislavery in the era of emancipation* (pp. 346–366). New Haven, CT: Yale University Press.

Rhodes, J. (1998). *Mary Ann Shadd Cary: The Black press and protest in the nineteenth century*. Bloomington, IN: Indiana University Press.

Rhodes, J. (1994). Race, money, politics and the Antebellum Black press. *Journalism History, 20*(Autumn-Winter), 95–106.

Ripley, C. P. (1986). *The Black abolitionist papers, volume II: Canada, 1830–1865*. Chapel Hill, NC: The University of North Carolina Press.

Silverman, J., Bellavance, M., & Rudin, R. (1984). 'We shall be heard!': The development of the Fugitive Slave Press in Canada. *The Canadian Historical Review, 65*(1), 54–72.

Simmons, C. A. (1998). *The African American Press: With special reference to four newspapers, 1827–1965*. London: McFarland & Company Inc.

Squires, C. R. (2002). Rethinking the Black public sphere: An alternative vocabulary for multiple public spheres. *Communication Theory, 12*(4), 446–468.

Stevenson, N. (2003). *Cultural citizenship: Cosmopolitan questions*. Maidenhead: Open University Press.

Van Brenk, D. (1988). She was the Freeman: Mary Ann Shadd as editor. In H. Hiscox (Ed.), *Essays in journalism* (pp. 103–121). London, ON: Graduate School of Journalism, The University of Western Ontario.

Washburn, P. S. (2006). *The African American newspaper: Voice of freedom*. Evanston, IL: Northwestern University Press.

Williams, D. W. (1989). *Blacks in Montreal 1628–1986: An urban demography*. Cowansville: Les Editions Yvon Blais.

Williams, R. (1977). *Marxism and literature*. Oxford: Oxford University Press.

Williams, D. W. (1997). *The road to now: A history of Blacks in Montreal*. Montreal: Vehicule Press.

Wilson, C., II (2014). *Whither the Black press? Glorious past, uncertain future*. Bloomington, IN: Xlibris LLC.

Winks, R. W. (1997). *The Blacks in Canada: A history* (2nd ed.). Montreal: McGill-Queen's University Press.

Ye, S. J. (1994). Gender ideology and Black women as community-builders in Ontario, 1850–70. *The Canadian Historical Review, 75*(1), 53–73.

Ye, S. J. (1997). Finding a place: Mary Ann Shadd Cary and the dilemmas of Black migration to Canada, 1850–1870. *Frontiers: A Journal of Women Studies, 18*(3), 1–16.

2   Increase Your Faith

The Domestication of Black Televangelism

Mark Ward Sr.

When the 2016 Oscar nominations yielded no African-American candidates in the top award categories, a grassroots "#OscarsSoWhite" Twitter campaign became the voice of a global backlash. Yet the proliferation of social and digital media platforms, which enabled #OscarsSoWhite to be an effective "flash" protest movement, has also produced fragmentation among media audiences (Webster & Ksiazek, 2012) and a "winner-take-all society" (Frank & Cook, 1995) in which only the most popular discourses receive general attention. Nevertheless, many niche media play important roles in various sectors of American life—including televangelism, which remains a decisive arbiter of the evangelical subculture and has, in fact, leveraged digital technology to expand far beyond its 1980s incarnation. One in four adults in the United States identifies as an evangelical Christian (Pew Research Center, 2015), while one in five consume religious media on a daily basis (Barna Group, 2005). As such, racial progress and polarization in the "electronic church" are phenomena that merit study—even if today's media proliferation and audience fragmentation mean that televangelism "is distributed via religious channels consumed almost entirely by religious audiences" and "televangelists are no longer public figures but primarily celebrities of the evangelical subculture" (Ward, 2016a, p. 1).

In any given month, more people consume religious media than attend a church and, in particular, 45 percent of adults report watching a religious television program (Barna Group, 2005). In reaching this vast audience, Black televangelists in the 21st century have achieved mainstream acceptance as preachers T. D. Jakes, Creflo Dollar, Frederick Price, Tony Evans, and Bill Winston are nationally syndicated on the highest-rated evangelical TV networks, Trinity Broadcasting and Daystar Television. These two networks alone reach a potential audience of 100 million households, carried by all major satellite services (DirecTV, Dish Network, AT&T U-verse, Verizon FiOS) and cable operators (Bright House, Cablevision, Charter, Comcast, Cox, Mediacom, Suddenlink, Time Warner), as well as on-demand via streaming apps for iPhone, iPad, Android, Amazon TV, Kindle Fire, Roku, and PlayStation (Ward, 2016b).

This mainstreaming of Black televangelism is undeniably a remarkable development. Historically, "Many white mass media religious celebrities came to the fore during the early part of the twentieth century... [while] African Americans did not have the same kind of access to radio as their white counterparts" (Martin, 2014, pp. 3–4). Thus, midcentury Black preachers did not build a broadcasting infrastructure, either as personalities or station owners. The first Black-owned local religious radio station did not air until 1978 and the first local TV station the same year (Ward, 1994). Even today, only a single Black radio preacher is nationally syndicated (Ward, 2018), while Black Gospel music is played on its own radio stations rather than on Contemporary Christian Music outlets. After the advent of television, Black televangelists were relegated for decades to the fringes of religious broadcasting. During the 1970s and 1980s when Oral Roberts, Rex Humbard, Jerry Falwell, Jimmy Swaggart, and Robert Schuller reaped spectacular success in first-run syndication, impressions of Black televangelism centered on the controversial Frederick "Reverend Ike" Eikerenkoetter whose "flamboyant lifestyle... and questionable fundraising practices drew criticism" and "was repudiated by mainstream Christian churches" (Melton, Lucas, & Stone, 1997, p. 279). Today, however, the mainstreaming of Black televangelism has occurred alongside the ascendance among both White and Black evangelicals of "prosperity theology." One of its early popularizers, Black Los Angeles preacher Frederick Price, helped set the pace when he debuted on the Trinity Broadcasting Network in 1978, became the nation's tenth-highest rated televangelist by 1990 (Melton et al., 1997), and advocated prosperity theology as a key to Black upward mobility. As the nation's middle class has steadily shrunk since the 1970s, the "prosperity gospel" has resonated with Black and White audiences alike. One in six Christians of all races now identify with the prosperity gospel movement, 31 percent believe God materially blesses those who give, and 43 percent believe faith produces health and wealth (Bowler, 2013).

Yet the mainstreaming of Black televangelism has come at the cost of its "domestication" or, as African-American scholar Paula McGee (2017) observes, its "Wal-Martization." She sees in the rise of Black celebrity televangelists a paradigm shift toward a "New Black Church" in which Black believers, a generation removed from the civil rights era, embrace commodification of spirituality and pursue liberation within a capitalistic framework. Similarly, African-American scholar Marla Frederick (2016) rhetorically asks, "Is the 'black church' itself undergoing a particular type of metamorphosis given the demands inherent in the business of broadcasting?" (p. 4). These and other observers have looked, with justification, at the *message* of Black televangelism. Yet the present study argues that the *medium* is also a vital factor.

Ownership in the religious media industry has, like other mass media, become highly concentrated since the late 1990s due to media deregulation (Ward, 2009, 2012). As will be seen, the nation's evangelical TV networks are largely owned by White founders who possessed the capital and connections, then unavailable for Black religious broadcasters, to launch cable and satellite channels when these media were new. Now deregulation and the resulting concentration of media ownership has enshrined a relative handful of White-owned and often family-controlled evangelical networks as the gatekeepers that control access to religious viewers. Preachers, Black or White, who would reach these viewers must play by the rules of these gatekeepers. Because purchasing program time on a national scale is only possible by monetizing spirituality, the result is a "domesticated" message that is sufficiently homogenized for broad appeal. The present study reviews the history of televangelism and then offers portraits of three preachers who were each the leading Black televangelist of their respective generation. Their careers illustrate the larger narrative of Black televangelism: its inception as a distinctively Black aesthetic in the 1960s and 1970s, its move toward the mainstream in the 1980s and 1990s through a message of Black economic empowerment, and its fully-fledged "Wal-Martization" in the 21st century.

A Brief History of Televangelism

Though commercial television service debuted in 1939 and the Federal Communications Commission (FCC) enacted technical standards in 1941, the new medium was abruptly put on hold by the outbreak of World War II. The war ended in 1945, but the technology to link local stations into national networks that could "simulcast" the same programs at the same times did not exist until the end of the decade. Syndicated radio preacher Walter Maier aired the first made-for-television religious program when he simulcast his weekly *Lutheran Hour* for New Year's Day 1948 over national radio and his hometown St. Louis TV station (Ward, 1994). A year later, in 1949, popular radio evangelist Percy Crawford mounted the first weekly network religious telecast with his *Youth on the March* (Crawford, 2010). The highest-rated radio preacher, Charles Fuller, followed in 1950 with his *Old Fashioned Camp Meeting* weekly program (Fuller, 1972). Yet these early efforts at televangelism soon failed. Since relatively few American cities had TV stations and few American households owned TV sets, donations from viewers could not cover production costs (Ward, 2017). A few religious programs supported by national church bodies thrived in the 1950s, most notably *Life is Worth Living* with Catholic bishop Fulton J. Sheen. Otherwise, independent televangelists—including pioneers Oral Roberts, Rex Humbard, and Jerry Falwell—honed their media skills on local television.

Several developments in the 1960s literally changed the picture. Historically, the major networks refused to sell airtime for religious radio and television programs. Instead they donated time to the nation's representative

Jewish, Catholic, and Protestant bodies (Hangen, 2002; Ward, 2013). The Federal (later National) Council of Churches controlled this donated time on behalf of mainline Protestants, thus excluding independent evangelicals. The latter formed a lobby, the National Religious Broadcasters, which by the end of the 1950s convinced the networks to drop their bans on paid religious programs. Then in 1960, the FCC ruled that radio and TV stations could meet their requirements for serving the public not only by donating time for religious programs but also by selling such time. Paid-time evangelical programs quickly outpaced their competition, and within 20 years mainline programs on donated time were largely off the air.

In 1964, to open local television to more competition and increase viewer choices, the FCC mandated that all new TV sets must receive the entire spectrum of TV channels. Because many existing sets only received the part of the spectrum dominated by the three major TV networks, the mandate was a boon to independent stations. Also in the 1960s, the invention of broadcast-quality videotape allowed producers to easily copy their programs and ship them to stations around the country. And as use of videotape increased, the price of editing equipment came down to a level that independent producers, such as televangelists, could afford. Thus, the 1970s saw a boom in televangelism as Roberts, Humbard, and Falwell put their weekly programs into national syndication by each purchasing airtime on more than 300 stations and attracting weekly audiences of between 1 million and 7 million viewers (Melton et al., 1997).

The boom went bust in 1987–1988 when prominent televangelists Oral Roberts, Jim Bakker, and Jimmy Swaggart were each embroiled in financial or sexual scandals that received intense news media coverage. All preachers were impacted by the fallout and the televangelism genre lost three-fourths of its audience (Winzenburg, 2005). Yet this loss arguably had as much to do with the coming cable revolution (Ward, 2016c). In the 1980s, most households did not have cable TV and received only a handful of over-the-air channels, mostly affiliates of the three major broadcast networks plus a few local independent stations. In such a media environment, televangelists could hope to win a share of the national Sunday night audience. By the 1990s, however, the audience share for traditional over-the-air television declined as most households signed up for cable and gained access to dozens of channels. The national TV audience became "fragmented." Televangelism was no longer about competing for a share of the masses but about attracting a loyal niche audience among viewers with multiple channel choices.

The new model for televangelism was pioneered by the Trinity Broadcasting Network (TBN) and its founder, Paul Crouch, who debuted over a single low-power Los Angeles station in 1973 (Ward, 2016d). Yet Crouch was intrigued by a new technology, satellite transmission. The major networks were then stymied by an FCC rule that, to protect local over-the-air stations, barred satellites from relaying first-run major network programs or repeats. All satellite-delivered programming had to be live and original—which TBN featured in abundance with its live worship services, concerts, and studio talk and variety shows. Once TBN in 1977 acquired a satellite uplink facility, it could distribute programming via satellite to local stations nationwide faster and more cheaply than competing religious programs that shipped videotapes. This proved an advantage with the rise of cable television in the 1980s. To protect traditional stations from losing their audiences to cable, the FCC required cable systems to also carry local over-the-air channels in their markets. By supplying programs via satellite to local stations, TBN guaranteed itself access to the emerging cable market. By the 1990s, many local cable systems included TBN as the religious offering in their basic channel packages. As a result, televangelists moved their syndicated programs away from local stations and instead purchased time on TBN and other evangelical cable channels. At the same time, deregulation ultimately changed the cable industry from a hodgepodge of small local franchises to a handful of large conglomerates that today operate cable systems nationwide and dominate the industry. The payoff is that syndicated televangelists are carried today on systems that can reach up to 100 million TV households. Yet the religious channels on which these televangelists appear exist in a fragmented media universe of more than 900 channels (NCTA, 2017).

The 1990s was a decisive decade for religious television in other ways. In 1994, the FCC authorized direct-broadcast satellite TV service, thus permitting households to receive television programming directly from satellites. Then in 1996, the agency mandated that all TV stations must switch from analog to digital broadcasting within ten years. At the same time, the FCC also eliminated most restrictions on how many stations any one broadcaster could own. Since most independent local religious stations could not afford digital conversion (Schultz, 2000, 2005), many sold out to TBN, which today claims to be the nation's third-largest broadcast TV group with more stations than NBC, CBS, ABC, and FOX.

TBN further illustrates how the nation's evangelical television networks were established by White founders with the capital and connections to get in on the ground floor of cable and satellite TV, and who are now in the dominant position as these technologies have matured. The network now controls more than 100 local over-the-air TV stations, plus carriage on some 8,000 cable and satellite systems, that potentially reach 100 million American households. Digital broadcasting also permits local TBN stations in 35 markets to "multicast" or send five affiliated channels over the same airwaves that could carry only one channel in analog. Further, TBN programs some three dozen English- and foreign-language channels that are beamed around the world on more than 80 satellites with a claimed reach of 1 billion households. Founders Paul and Jan Crouch, both White, were the faces of Los Angeles-based network for 40 years until Paul died in 2013 and his wife Jan died three years later.[1] Today their son Matt

Crouch and his (White) wife Laurie are "the next-generation leadership of the Trinity Broadcasting Family of Networks" (Trinity, 2017).

Daystar Television Network (2017) was founded by Marcus Lamb, who is White and formerly owned local religious TV stations in Alabama and Texas before launching Daystar in 1997. Six years later, the Dallas-based network moved into a 90,000-square-foot International Ministry Center. Daystar currently operates more than 70 local over-the-air television stations in the United States and is carried by all major cable and satellite systems with a potential reach of 100 million households. Since 2004, Daystar has secured space on eight international satellites that, it claims, cover "the entire footprint of the world reaching over 200 countries and 680 million households globally."

INSP (2017) launched as the Inspiration Network in 1990 after White evangelist Morris Cerullo purchased Jim Bakker's scandal-ridden PTL Television Network from bankruptcy court. Based near Charlotte, North Carolina, INSP is led today by David Cerullo, son of the founder, and claims a potential reach of 80 million households via 2,800 local cable systems and nationally via the DirecTV and the DISH satellite services.

SonLife Broadcasting Network (2017) debuted in 2009 as an outreach of Jimmy Swaggart Ministries in Baton Rouge, Louisiana, and now claims a potential reach of 80 million households through satellite carriage on DirecTV, the DISH Network, Verizon FiOS, and Glorystar. The programming is all Swaggart, all the time, featuring Jimmy Swaggart (who is White) plus his wife Frances, son Donnie, grandson Gabriel, and nine associate pastors—all White—of his Family Worship Center church.

TCT (2017) was founded by White businessman Garth Koonce and his wife Tina in 1977 as Tri-State Christian Television. The couple started with a single Illinois station, acquired other small-market Midwestern stations, and later secured satellite space to feed other local stations and cable systems. Rebranded as the TCT Network, the channel is carried today by DirecTV and Sky Angel to a claimed potential reach of 60 million households.

TheWALKtv (2017) debuted in 2010 and provides a satellite feed of syndicated evangelical programs to 250 local independent television stations nationwide. Originally founded as Legacy TV by (White) partners Buddy Winsett and Jim West, the network is now headed by West and claims a potential reach of 54 million households.

NRBTV (2017) was established in 2005 by the National Religious Broadcasters (NRB) association. Carried by DirecTV, the Washington-based network claims a potential reach of 48 million households. NRBTV president and CEO Troy Miller is White, as is NRB president Jerry Johnson and all but four members (three Black, one Asian) of the 90-member NRB board of directors.

Golden Eagle Broadcasting, or GEB America (2017), is a division of Oral Roberts University (ORU) in Tulsa, Oklahoma. The institution's namesake, White televangelist Oral Roberts, passed away in 2009. Today, GEB America is carried by DirecTV and claims a potential reach of 34 million viewers. As a division of the university, GEB America is led by (White) ORU president William Wilson, an all-White administration, and a board of trustees led by four White officers and 35 additional board members of whom only half a dozen are non-White.

GOD TV (2017), based near Orlando, Florida, is carried in the United States by DirecTV and in 2009 claimed a potential reach of 20 million American households (Christian News Wire, 2009). Founders Wendy and Rory Alec, who are White, began in the United Kingdom in 1995 and added studios and satellite uplinks in continental Europe, Jerusalem, Africa, and Asia (CBN, 2004), before debuting in the United States in 2006. Rory Alec left the network in 2014, and in 2016 Wendy Alec announced she would focus on her own GOD TV telecast and appointed Ward Simpson, who is White, as president and chief executive officer (Charisma News, 2014, 2016).

Sky Angel (2017), which debuted in 1996, is carried by the DISH Network and claims a potential reach of 14 million households. Based in Naples, Florida, the network does business as FaveTV ("Family and Values Entertainment"). Founder Robert Johnson Sr., who was White, died in 2004 and was succeeded by son Rob as chief executive officer.

Family Entertainment Television (2017) is programmed by the LeSEA Broadcasting Network—named for the Lester Sumrall Evangelistic Association—and carried via satellite by the DISH Network and AT&T U-verse. Sumrall was a (White) Pentecostal evangelist based in South Bend, Indiana, who launched a TV ministry in 1972 and died in 1996. Son Peter Sumrall followed his father as president and CEO until his own passing in 2015 and was then succeeded by his brother Drew. In addition to Family Entertainment Television, LeSEA owns about ten local television and radio stations and claims to reach 90 percent of the world's population through terrestrial and shortwave radio and via over-the-air and satellite television.

The Word Network (2017) is based near Detroit and was founded in 2000 by White father and son Franklin and Kevin Adell. The network is carried via satellite by DirecTV and Verizon FiOS and via cable by several major operators—though discontinued in 2017 by Comcast, a cable operator with 22 million subscribers nationwide (Hinds, 2016). Even so, Word claims a potential reach of 93 million households plus a satellite footprint that reaches 200 countries. Though White-owned, Word has striven to carve out a competitive niche as "the largest African-American Religious Network in the world" by featuring a lineup of mostly Black preachers and music artists. Kevin Adell, since the passing of his father, has continued to head the network.

The lone exception to White ownership is The Impact Network (2017), also based near Detroit and founded in 2010 by husband-and-wife megachurch pastors Wayne and Beverly Jackson. Since replacing The Word Network in the Comcast channel lineup, plus its carriage by other cable operators and by the DirecTV and DISH satellite services, Impact bills itself as "the only African-American owned and operated faith-based national TV network, broadcasting urban ministries and gospel life-style entertainment to over 75 million homes across the world!" (Bishop Wayne T. Jackson, 2017).

While the claimed potential reach of the top White- and Black-owned networks seem roughly equivalent, yearly revenues tell a different story. In their 2014 tax filings, Daystar reported assets of $233 million, while TBN reported an income of $177 million and Pat Robertson's Christian Broadcasting Network (now a program production company rather than a TV channel) reported $288 million (National Public Radio, 2014). By contrast, The Impact Network reported a 2014 income of $1.59 million (down from $1.66 million the previous year) against expenditures of $2.6 million (Campbell, 2016). Table 2.1 summarizes the gatekeepers of televangelism.

Table 2.1 Founders and Executives of Evangelical Television Networks

Network Name	Founders	Chief Executive	Claimed Reach (HHs)[a]
White-Owned Television Networks			
Trinity Broadcasting Network	Paul and Jan Crouch	Matt Crouch	100 million
Daystar Television Network	Marcus and Joni Lamb	Marcus Lamb	100 million
INSP	Morris Cerullo	David Cerullo	80 million
SonLife Broadcasting Network	Jimmy Swaggart	Jimmy Swaggart	80 million
The Word Network	Franklin and Keith Adell	Keith Adell	71 million[b]
TCT	Garth and Tina Koonce	Garth Koonce	60 million
TheWALKtv	Buddy Winsett, Jim West	Jim West	54 million
NRBTV	Troy Miller	Troy Miller	48 million
GEB America	Oral Roberts	William Wilson	34 million
GOD TV	Wendy and Rory Alec	Ward Simpson	20 million
Sky Angel	Robert Johnson Sr	Rob Johnson	14 million
Family Entertainment TV	Lester Sumrall	Drew Sumrall	Not available
Black-Owned Television Networks			
The Impact Network	Wayne and Beverly Jackson	Wayne Jackson	75 million

[a] No networks self-reported actual viewership or ratings; all networks reported only potential reach in millions of households. The business model for religious television is less dependent on ratings because revenue is primarily generated not through sale of advertising availabilities but through sale of program time. Thus, what networks are offering televangelists is potential reach.

[b] The network claims a reach of 93 million but in 2017 was dropped by Comcast, a national cable operator with 22 million subscribers.

In contrast to the 1970s and 1980s when televangelists bought airtime on local over-the-air stations and could scale their media buys up or down—or to the 1990s when cable access was fragmented among thousands of locally operated franchises—televangelism today is the province of syndicators who can afford to purchase airtime on a national scale. Yet as Table 2.1 illustrates, access to audiences is controlled primarily by networks established a generation ago by White founders who had the resources to enter the nascent cable and satellite TV industries and who have kept control of their networks often by keeping ownership within their families. Thus, hundreds of millions of dollars for program time is exchanged each year between syndicated televangelists and a relatively small coterie of mostly family-controlled, mostly White media gatekeepers.

Three Portraits of Black Televangelism

The stories of three Black televangelists tell the larger story of Black televangelism across five decades of change in media and popular culture. Starting in the 1960s, when Oral Roberts and other White televangelists were promoting a prosperity gospel through their "Word of Faith" movement, Frederick "Reverend Ike" Eikerenkoetter launched a parallel development as he "combined the metaphysical and Pentecostal threads into a single prosperity gospel" of his own. In so doing, he "gave the prosperity gospel its first black spokesman with a national platform" (Bowler, 2013, p. 67). Eikerenkoetter's beginnings, however, were conventional. The son of a Baptist pastor in South Carolina, he earned a 1956 degree at the American Bible College in Chicago and served two years as an Air Force chaplain. Yet after his discharge, Eikerenkoetter left the Baptist faith and embraced New Thought, a religious philosophy that promoted spiritual and material progress through the powers of the human mind. He founded a storefront church, moving it from South Carolina to Boston and, finally, to New York. By 1969 he had renovated an abandoned theater into a 3,500-seat worship center and broadcast facility, organized his own United Christian Evangelistic Association, and founded a Science of Living Institute. As "Reverend Ike," he debuted in 1969 on radio over a network of more than 50 stations. Four years later, his *Joy of Living* program went on television and was ultimately syndicated on more than two dozen stations. During the 1970s, Eikerenkoetter's network grew to 89 stations, weekly services at his United Church Center Palace Auditorium averaged 5,000 worshipers, and his *Action!* magazine boasted a million subscribers (Erickson, 1992; Melton et al., 1997). Yet rather than pursue mainstream acceptance, Eikerenkoetter reveled in his attempts to cultivate a distinctively Black aesthetic.

> Reverend Ike's flashy jewelry, conked hair, and tailored suits reinforced his expansive message of abundance, summed up in

catchphrases like "you can't lose with the stuff I use," and "the lack of money is the root of all evil." ... His evolving theology took on a metaphysical fervor, setting aside Pentecostal messages for a New Thought-inspired "Science of Living" [with] ... glittering promises of material wealth, channeling mind-power toward tangible rewards. He implored believers to change their circumstances for the better rather than rely on heavenly reward, aptly summarized in his famous saying, "Don't wait for your pie in the sky by and by; have it now with ice cream and a cherry on top."

(Bowler, 2013, pp. 67–68)

With a reported weekly clothing budget of $1,000 and a taste for luxury cars, Eikerenkoetter modeled what he preached: affirming one's own abundance by visualizing, and then manifesting, what one desires. "Dressed exquisitely in the finest apparel and driving different colored Rolls Royces to match his various outfits, Ike preached possibility thinking" (Rouse, Jackson, & Frederick, 2016, p. 197). His flamboyance "was as much about creating a narrative of possibility for colored people as it was about the fashion and egoism of the preacher" (Frederick, 2015, p. 11). Eikerenkoetter once summed up his Black-oriented message:

Black people, many of the masses of colored people, did not believe they should be anything, do anything, or have anything. God forbid money; money was evil... And then this Rev. Ike comes along, because, you see, the Bible says "the love of money is the root of all evil." This Rev. Ike comes along and gets right into people's faces on radio and television and in these big meetings and says, "No." It's not the love of money that's the root of all evil, it's the lack of money that's the root of all evil.

(quoted in Rouse, Jackson, & Frederick, 2017, pp. 197–198)

Other televangelists and mainstream churches may have repudiated "Reverend Ike" as a huckster, while civil rights leaders criticized his emphasis on private gain over social reform. However, perhaps because Eikerenkoetter was the only Black televangelist of the 1970s with a national following,

otherwise responsible news organizations debated over whether he was sincere or a charlatan, while talk show hosts invited him to exclaim, 'I want my pie with ice cream on top!' and then proceeded to treat him with the same deference as they would a mainline minister, priest, or rabbi.

(Erickson, 1992, p. 151)

Thus, even as other prosperity preachers distanced themselves from Reverend Ike, "no one forgot his dramatic promises of material wealth for right-thinking Christians," and his "popular message served as a sturdy bridge, across which subsequent preachers and participants carried a metaphysical—and heavily instrumental—Christianity into the future" (Bowler, 2013, p. 67). Eikerenkoetter's star faded by the 1980s, though he continued a thriving mail-order business until his death in 2009. Yet in their study of Black televangelism, Rouse et al. (2016) see Eikeren-koetter as a "connectional figure" who linked African-American reli-gious practices with the emerging economic emphasis of the post-civil rights era.

> Eikerenkoetter's flamboyant style and dress rebuffed civil rights leaders with their demure black suits. And, yet, it was precisely the emphasis on financial gain that Eikerenkoetter believed civil rights advocates missed.... [His message] operated to turn black people's attention inward instead of outward.
>
> (pp. 51–52)

Reverend Ike thus served as a bridge to the next era, as Black televan-gelism in the 1980s "coincided not only with the decline in civil rights activism but also with the rise in conservative religious broadcasting and the entrenchment of neoliberal economic policies" (Rouse et al., 2016, p. 52). The development is aptly illustrated by the leading Black televan-gelist of the day, Frederick Price, a Los Angeles native who was raised a Jehovah's Witness but converted to Pentecostal Christianity at a 1953 tent meeting. The experience "pulled him away from the traditional black denominations and toward the white prosperity circles" (Bowler, 2013, p. 89), where White Word of Faith preachers had "managed to create an easy alliance of diverse preachers, facilitating a high degree of racial mixing at conferences" (p. 203). As a protégé of televangelist Kenneth Hagin, Frederick Price was the Word of Faith movement's ris-ing Black star. He served several congregations until founding his own Crenshaw Christian Center and debuting on local radio in 1973. Five years later, Paul Crouch put Price's weekly *Ever Increasing Faith* telecast on TBN and its satellite feed.

From the start, the smiling and telegenic Price, clad in convention-ally businesslike suit and tie, cut a more reassuringly "domesticated" figure than the frenetic Reverend Ike. "It is not unusual for Price to smile, laugh, shake people's hands, give encouragement, tell humorous personal anecdotes, and even jest with the congregation during the ser-mon" (Melton et al., 1997, p. 266). Rather than echo Eikerenkoetter's esoteric "science of living," Price took his message down to earth as he "implored his... congregation to use prosperity theology to overcome barriers to black upward mobility" (Bowler, 2013, p. 5). In further con-trast to the unapologetically flamboyant Reverend Ike, Price stated he was "surprised that God wanted him to be wealthy" after being raised to think that African-American life "was supposed to be defined by financial struggle" (Frederick, 2016, p. 80). Thus, he was almost apologetic about his own personal wealth: "I'm only doing it so that you can see that there's somebody the same color as you are... and I'm prospering because of the Book" (quoted in Bowler, 2013, p. 134). In this way, "Price successfully linked social injustice to structural racism in the context of a highly individualistic gospel" by preaching that "Black Christians had been denied their God-given right to determine their own destinies: holiness, wisdom, and increase" (p. 203).

In 1981, Price purchased the former downtown Los Angeles campus of Pepperdine College and built a 10,000-seat auditorium on the 32-acre site. Three years later his Crenshaw Christian Center moved again to its present South Central Los Angeles campus. By 1989, when other televangelists were retrenching in the aftermath of the Bakker and Swaggart scandals, Price opened a new $10 million "Faithdome" whose 15,000 seats made it the nation's largest worship center at the time. *Ever Increasing Faith* by then was syndicated on nearly 70 television and 70 radio stations, while Price was the tenth-highest rated televangelist in America (Erickson, 1992). By the end of the 1990s, the TV network for *Ever Increasing Faith* stood at 125 stations and Price was recognized as "the most successful African American evangelist in the history of religious broadcasting" (Melton et al., 1997, p. 90). *Ever Increasing Faith* continues to be widely viewed over the Trinity, Daystar, TCT, and Impact networks, while Fred Price Jr. now pastors the 28,000-member Crenshaw Christian Center.

If the idiosyncratic Eikerenkoetter was the first Black spokesperson for the prosperity gospel, and the conventional Price first "domesticated" that gospel with his message of economic empowerment, T. D. Jakes has become the leading Black televangelist of the present generation by being in tune with today's emphasis on self-empowerment and emotional healing. From his base at the 30,000-member Dallas megachurch called The Potter's House, Jakes serves his flock as one of "America's counselors [and] self-help advisors as trusted as professional therapists," a man who once "appeared easily alongside Dr. Phil on the psychologist's hit television show, two relationship experts with cures for country's ills" (Bowler, 2013, p. 6). After founding a church in his native state of West Virginia, Jakes burst on the national scene with his self-published 1993 book, *Woman, Thou Art Loosed*. A surprise best seller that dealt frankly with sexual abuse, the book paved the way for his nationally syndicated *Get Ready* radio and television program—which now air as *The Potter's Touch*. Three years later, Jakes moved to Dallas with 50 church families, bought a large church campus, and founded The Potter's House.

A recent study (Bowler, 2013, p. 253) illustrates the evolution in the messaging of Price and Jakes. The former fully deployed the entire range of coded terms shared by Word of Faith preachers: *to speak faith, positive confession, divine wealth, divine health, sowing and reaping, divine favor, destiny, rhema* (Greek for "utterance"), *hundredfold blessing, Jehovah Jireh* (an Old Testament name for God that is popularly interpreted as "The Lord Who Provides"), and *seed faith.* By contrast, while Jakes frequently used the terms *divine health, destiny,* and *Jehovah Jireh,* he employed the other Word of Faith codes, used by Price, much less often or not at all. Though he holds that economic prosperity is a key to African-American empowerment, he is a "soft prosperity" preacher.

> In a media environment that had learned to mistrust overwrought emotional preaching and beseeching figures, new faces... replaced flamboyant stereotypes with a suave, business-like image. By the mid-1990s, these postmodern prophets would not beg but rather focus on the returns. They would offer "tools" in the form of relationship guides, financial principles, or family reconciliation. The new generation set aside much of the hard prosperity that had characterized [the 1980s] in favor of the therapeutic inspiration of *soft prosperity.* They were now preaching to a less credulous, more cynical generation, who tended to put little faith in institutions but were willing to invest heavily in relationships and personal emotion.
>
> (Bowler, 2013, p. 110, emphasis in original)

Jakes' soft prosperity, however, is served up with high energy. Where Price "sees himself more as a teacher providing knowledge than as a preacher giving inspiration" (Melton et al., 1997, p. 266) and his sermons are "marathons of mental agility and digital dexterity... [as he] challenged his flock to look up the biblical passages" (Erickson, 1992, p. 74), Jakes offers a megachurch multimedia "experience" that imparts awe and transcendence. Meetings "feature weeping, dancing in the aisles, speaking in tongues, and ecstatic dashing around the sanctuary" while Jakes "address[es] topics that range from drug addiction, rape, incest, failure to attain personal goals, and low self-esteem" (Melton et al., 1997, p. 161). His conferences—Woman Thou Art Loosed, Manpower, Mega Youth Experience, and MegaKidz—grew wildly until, in 2004, they were combined into a massive Megafest that annually draws more than 100,000 attendees with the slogan "It's More than a Festival... It's an Experience!" Jakes has mastered today's digital media, enjoying a global reach through his half-hour daily telecast over the TBN, Daystar, Word, and Impact networks, plus 30 books and eight theatrical films including the sleeper hits *Woman, Thou Art Loosed* (released in 2004), *Jumping the Broom* (2011), *Sparkle* (2012), *Heaven is for Real* (2014), and *Winnie Mandela* (2014). As media become increasingly convergent, such content is easily digitized and repurposed to generate additional revenues at relatively low distribution costs through on-demand streaming over smartphones, tablets, gaming consoles, and smart TVs.

That Black televangelism has been "domesticated" is attested in several recent studies. Frederick (2016) observes that, while the "religious dandyism" of early Black televangelists "hinged on financial windfalls, elaborate houses, or expensive cars," contemporary Black televangelists "speak more often today of a type of relative prosperity... [and] have added greater nuance to their measure of prosperity" (p. 59). McGee (2017), as noted earlier, argues that T. D. Jakes is a type of the "Walmart-ization of African American Religion" (p. 2). Rouse et al. (2016) interpret Black religious media as a kind of "televised redemption" by which African-Americans have claimed the same God-given endowments and potentials for blessing as White Americans. Yet the new concepts and tools for participating in society that Black prosperity preachers have provided their audiences have also exerted an assimilating effect. Nationally syndicated Black televangelists have "overwhelmingly emphasized that not protest, but faith... is central to redemption" (p. 54) and promoted "a revival of sorts built around an attention to the individual, not the structures" (p. 120). As a result, "the strategy for redeeming black life has been radically altered by the emergence in the past thirty years of a different type of black religious ethos, one marked by hyper-individualism and a radical commitment to capitalist possibility" (p. 52). Programs such as *Ever Increasing Faith* and *The Potter's Touch* will likely never, in a fragmented "winner-take-all" media culture, draw as many viewers as the annual Oscar Awards telecast. Yet niche media, such as religious television, continue to fundamentally shape and reflect important sectors of American life.

Note

1 All individuals referenced in this study were depicted in photographs published online by their respective organizations, although no one named their racial self-identification. Thus, it would be more accurate to say "White-appearing" instead of "White" and "Black-appearing" instead of "Black" or "African-American." For ease of reading, however, the terms "White" and "Black" are used without the qualifiers.

References

Barna Group (2005). *More people use Christian media than attend church.* Retrieved July 19, 2017, from www.barna.com/research/more-people-use-christian-media-than-attend-church

Bishop Wayne T. Jackson (2017). *The Impact Network.* Retrieved July 19, 2017, from www.bishopwaynetjackson.com/impact/

Bowler, K. (2013). *Blessed: A history of the American prosperity gospel.* New York: Oxford University Press.

Campbell, R. (2016). Bishop Wayne T. Jackson: Five facts you need to know. *Heavy,* September 3, 2016. Retrieved July 19, 2016, from http://heavy.com/news/2016/09/bishop-wayne-t-jackson-great-faith-ministries-detroit-impact-network-net-worth-family-wife-house-kwame-kilpatrick/

CBN (2004). *Rory and Wendy Alec: GOD TV.* Retrieved March 11, 2017, from www1.cbn.com/700club/rory-and-wendy-alec-god-tv

Charisma News (2014). *Citing moral failure, GOD TV co-founder Rory Alec resigns.* Retrieved March 11, 2017, from www.charismanews.com/culture/45615-citing-moral-failure-god-tv-co-founder-rory-alec-resigns

Charisma News (2016). *Two years after Rory Alec's moral failure, GOD TV appoints revival-minded CEO.* Retrieved March 11, 2017, from www.charismanews.com/opinion/watchman-on-the-wall/60290-two-years-after-rory-alec-s-moral-failure-god-tv-appoints-revival-minded-ceo

Christian News Wire (2009). *GOD TV tops 20 million homes in the USA.* Retrieved March 11, 2017, from www.christiannewswire.com/index.php?module=releases&task=view&releaseID=11004

Crawford, D. D. (2010). *A thirst for souls: The life of evangelist Percy B. Crawford, 1902–1960.* Selinsgrove, PA: Susquehanna University Press.

Daystar Television Network (2017). *Daystar.* Retrieved March 11, 2017, from www.daystar.com

Erickson, H. (1992). *Religious radio and television programs in the United States, 1921–1991: The programs and personalities.* Jefferson, NC: McFarland.

Family Entertainment Television (2017). *FETV.* Retrieved March 11, 2017, from http://fetv.lesea.com/

Frank, R. H., & Cook, P. J. (1995). *The winner-take-all society: Why the few at the top get so much more than the rest of us.* New York: Penguin.

Frederick, M. F. (2016). *Colored television: American religion gone global.* Stanford, CA: Stanford University Press.

Fuller, D. P. (1972). *Give the winds a mighty voice: The story of Charles E. Fuller.* Waco, TX: Word.

GEB America (2017). *GEB.* Retrieved March 11, 2017, from www.gebamerica.com

GOD TV (2017). *Basis of faith.* Retrieved March 11, 2017, from www.god.tv/about

Hangen, T. J. (2002). *Redeeming the dial: Radio, religion, and popular culture in America.* Chapel Hill, NC: University of North Carolina Press.

Hinds, J. (2016). The Word Network files complaints against Comcast with FCC and FTC. *Detroit Free Press,* December 6, 2016. Retrieved July 19, 2017, from www.freep.com/story/entertainment/2016/12/06/word-network-comcast-impact-network-fcc-complaint-carriage-dispute/95058350/

The Impact Network (2017). *Impact.* Retrieved July 19, 2017, from www.watchimpact.com/

INSP (2017). *INSP.* Retrieved March 11, 2017, from www.insp.com

Martin, L. A. (2014). *Preaching on wax: The phonograph and the shaping of modern African American religion.* New York: New York University Press.

McGee, P. L. (2017). *Brand® new theology: The Wal-martization of T. D. Jakes and the New Black Church.* Maryknoll, NY: Orbis.

Melton, J. G., Lucas, P. C., & Stone, J. R. (1997). *Prime-time religion: An encyclopedia of religious broadcasting.* Phoenix, AZ: Oryx.

National Public Radio (2014). *Thirty leading religious broadcasters.* Retrieved July 19, 2017, from www.npr.org/2014/04/01/297331252/thirty-leading-religious-broadcasters

NCTA: The Internet and Television Association (2017). *Industry data.* Retrieved March 11, 2017, from www.ncta.com/industry-data

NRBTV (2017). *NRBTV. Think deeply. Live differently.* Retrieved March 11, 2017, from http://nrbtv.org/?refresh

Pew Research Center (2015). *America's changing religious landscape.* Washington, DC: Pew Research Center. Retrieved March 11, 2017, from http://assets.pewresearch.org/wp-content/uploads/sites/11/2015/05/RLS-08-26-full-report.pdf

Rouse, C. M., Jackson, J. L., Jr., & Frederick, M. F. (2016). *Televised redemption: Black religious media and racial empowerment.* New York: New York University Press.

Schultz, B. E. (2000). The effects of digital environments on religious television stations. *Journal of Communication & Religion, 23,* 50–71.

Schultz, B. E. (2005). The economic response of religious television stations to digital implementation. *Journal of Communication & Religion, 28,* 307–325.

Sky Angel Faith and Family Television (2017). *FAVE TV.* Retrieved March 11, 2017, from www.skyangel.com

SonLife Broadcasting Network (2017). *SBN: SonLife Broadcasting Network.* Retrieved March 11, 2017, from www.sonlifetv.com

TCT (2017). *TCT.* Retrieved March 11, 2017, from www.tct.tv

Trinity Broadcasting Network (2017). *Matt Crouch.* Retrieved March 11, 2017, from www.tbn.org/people/matt-crouch

TheWALKtv (2017). *TheWALKtv.* Retrieved March 11, 2017, from https://thewalktv.wordpress.com/

Ward, M., Sr. (1994). *Air of salvation: The story of Christian broadcasting.* Grand Rapids, MI: Baker.

Ward, M., Sr. (2009). Dark preachers: The impact of radio consolidation on independent religious syndicators. *Journal of Media and Religion, 8*(2), 79–96.

Ward, M., Sr. (2012). Consolidating the gospel: The impact of the 1996 Telecommunications Act on religious radio ownership. *Journal of Media and Religion, 11*(1), 11–30.

Ward, M., Sr. (2013). Air of the king: Evangelicals and radio. In R. H. Woods Jr. (Ed.), *Evangelicals and popular culture: Pop goes the gospel* (Vol. 1, pp. 101–118). Santa Barbara, CA: Praeger.

Ward, M., Sr. (2016a). Introduction. In M. Ward Sr. (Ed.), *The electronic church in the digital age: Cultural impacts of evangelical mass media* (Vol. 1, pp. 1–28). Santa Barbara, CA: Praeger.

Ward, M., Sr. (2016b). Major networks and personalities. In M. Ward Sr. (Ed.), *The electronic church in the digital age: Cultural impacts of evangelical mass media* (Vol. 1, pp. 255–284). Santa Barbara, CA: Praeger.

Ward, M., Sr. (2016c). Televangelism, audience fragmentation, and the changing coverage of scandal. In H. Mandell & G. M. Chen (Eds.), *Scandal in a digital age* (pp. 53–68). New York: Palgrave Macmillan.

Ward, M., Sr. (2016d). What if? A counterfactual reconsideration of the electronic church. In M. Ward Sr. (Ed.), *The electronic church in the digital age: Cultural impacts of evangelical mass media* (Vol. 2, pp. 1–28). Santa Barbara, CA: Praeger.

Ward, M., Sr. (2017). *The Lord's radio: Gospel music broadcasting and the making of evangelical culture, 1920–1960.* Jefferson, NC: McFarland.

Ward, M., Sr. (2018). Segregating the dial: Institutional racism in evangelical radio. In O. O. Banjo & K. M. Williams (Eds.), *Contemporary Christian culture: Messages, missions, and dilemmas* (pp. 45–56). Lanham, MD: Lexington.

Webster, J. G., & Ksiazek, T. B. (2012). The dynamics of audience fragmentation: Public attention in an age of digital media. *Journal of Communication,* 62, 39–56.

Winzenburg, S. (2005). *TV ministries use of air time, Fall 2004.* Retrieved March 11, 2017, from http://faculty.grandview.edu/swinzenburg/tv_ministries_study.pdf

The Word Network (2017). *The Word Network.* Retrieved March 11, 2017, from www.thewordnetwork.org.

3 Wrestling with Races

When Sitcoms, Families, and Political Struggles Meet

Judy L. Isaksen

In historian James Clifford's (1994) work on diaspora, he argues that within the United States' national ideology of assimilation, clear distinctions lie between immigrants and diasporic people. While immigrants may, indeed, experience nostalgia and even loss, these sensations are "only en route to a whole new home in a new place" (p. 307), for assimilation and integration are the goals for immigrants. This is, however, not the case for diasporic people; their sense of identity is "centrally defined by collective histories of displacement and violent loss," and they experience pain that cannot simply be "cured" by melding into a new national community. This is especially the case, Clifford argues, when the displaced are "the victims of ongoing, structural prejudice" (p. 307). Clifford perceives the term *diaspora* as more than a signifier of simply movement but one of "political struggles" (p. 308).

Drawing from Clifford's perspectives, it follows then that if North American Black media art—that is, media created by Blacks—wrestles with "political struggles," then such media are inherently inscribed with a diasporic vision, one that weaves together layers and layers of interrupted stories and fractured histories, oppressions and resistances, nations and cultures. These diasporic forms of mediated art, which originated in slavery and displacement but result in survival and remembrance, play a distinct role in the construction of not only Black diasporic identities but also a wider cultural understanding of those identities by folks who are not diasporic. Simply put, the origins, memories, and discourses of the past never stop bleeding into the present, for everyone.

A key venue of Black mediated art comes to us through our TV screens, whether broadcasted or streamed; indeed, TV is both pleasurable and at times mind-numbing. But since the inception of this medium more than a half-century ago, it remains a crucial site for the slow-drip teachings of ideologies and the normalizing of views on race relations and racial inequities. Indeed, shifts of racial discourse on television have taken place over the decades, and along with those shifts, our cultural identities have likewise transformed. As Leonard and Guerrero (2013) state, the history of Black American TV is "a space of both racialization *and* resistance, both empowerment *and* demonization" (p. 8), positioning these strategies and outcomes into the binary poles of "containment and resistance" (p. 12). TV indeed functions both as a vehicle to advance the message of the dominant status quo, yet also as a space for opposition to push back against and resist the dominant hegemonic ideologies.

This chapter explores the ways in which the television sitcom black·*ish* regularly wrestles with "political struggles," particularly about matters of race, and intentionally positions itself on the resistive end of the binary role that television plays in our culture. Using a critical cultural studies methodology, I will conduct a textual analyses of the show through an aspect of communication theory referred to as critical rhetoric, an orientation that examines how a text "creates and sustains the social practices which control the dominated" (McKerrow, 1989, p. 92). My argument unfolds in three parts. First, I introduce the Johnsons and the dynamic racial and class tensions that they explore as a Black upper-class family that is flourishing in the Obama Era. The bulk of my argument unfolds as I next explore these tensions as articulated in the "Hope" episode, where the parents wrestle with "the Talk"—that is, how to both protect and prepare their children for their racial reality. And the final section maps the sitcom's bold response to our cultural shift from Obama to Trump, returning to the theme of hope and inviting White viewers to recognize their own complicity as our nation's racial formations move forward.

Wrestling with the Political Struggle: black·*ish*

The Black American sitcom has enjoyed a protracted history that began in the 1950s and has developed over the decades, meandering through distinct stylistic periods. Some shows valued cultural assimilation while others valued Black subjectivity, and still others relied upon a color-blind sensibility while others cemented cultural stereotypes (Acham, 2004; Bogle, 2001; Coleman, Mclwain, & Matthews, 2016; Gray, 1995; Jhally & Lewis, 1992; Leonard & Guerrero, 2013).

black·*ish*, a 30-minute sitcom which began in the Fall of 2014, is successfully carving out a new style for the Black American sitcom as it quite intentionally focuses on what it is like to be Black in present-day White dominant culture. The show was conceived, developed, and debuted on network television in the midst of the Obama Era under the creative vision of showrunner and head writer Kenya Barris. black·*ish* is built largely from Barris' own experience as he tries to unpack how his childhood in the 1980s differs from children of the Obama Era—that is, this generation of youth who are familiar with only a Black president and who have been surrounded by the prevailing cultural narrative of color blindness. Anthony Anderson who plays Dre Johnson, the father, is modeled after Barris, as are Bow, the mom (Tracee Ellis Ross), and their family of children, ages 16 to infant, modeled after Barris' family members. The Johnsons are an upper-middle-class family who are leftist in politics and worldview and hip in swagger and style. Their comedic rapport with one another is fast, smart, and entirely voluntary; this is a family that loves and enjoys one another.

The energy that drives the show is rooted in matters of race and class, and when the writing is at its best, this energy can cut through with the precision of a surgeon's knife. While the show is set in the present, through the use of both flashbacks to Dre's youth along with regularly drawing upon the history of Black life in the United States, there is a pulsing diasporic vibe as the parents routinely instill in their children a sense of racial pride that stabilizes the narrative from week to week. And yet, that stability is routinely called into question as the show continuously ponders the notion of "What actually constitutes Blackness?" The pursuit of this understanding creates movement and tensions that force the family to regularly revisit race, particularly as it intersects with matters of class. Such contradictory fluidity is cast into the show's dye as we first meet the Johnsons, who are enjoying a quite comfortable lifestyle in the predominantly White suburbs of LA, yet we learn that Dre grew up in inner-city Compton. We watch the parents push at these points of disequilibrium as they both enjoy successful careers, yet Dre is disappointed at being promoted to head the "urban" market at the advertising firm. We are privy to the parents' floundering at their parenting gig as they try to honor and teach their kids Black cultural signifiers—like "the nod," attending an HBCU, and the appropriate use of the n-word—while raising them in White suburbia. The show also routinely makes interesting gestures about the complexity of multiraciality; while Dre's parents are both Black, Bow is biracial, so notions of what constitutes Blackness are fluid in both the parents but also in their five children. Dre's folks—Ruby and Pops (Jenifer Lewis and Laurence Fishburne)—who came of age and were active in the Civil Rights Era have a large role in the family dynamic as well. So, the combination of three generations, movement across time, upward class mobility, along with multiraciality provides viewers with a window into the various ways in which each of the characters, both individually and in relation to one another, experiences Blackness—some very Black, some Black-*ish*. Bolstered by its comedy, black-*ish* very seriously holds up a mirror to not only the complex nuances and tensions of the intersection of race and class in our nation but also the cultivated view of a so-called "post-racial America" while simultaneously demonstrating that we are not post-racial at all.

Can We Talk about Hope?

To bring these dynamics into sharper focus, I turn now to the episode poignantly entitled "Hope" (Barris, 2016), which aired in February 2016. As if a one-act play, the entire episode is shot in the living room with all family members present—again three generations. In fact, Barris states that he wanted an eavesdropping audience to literally be the "eighth member of the family" (as cited in Fretts, 2016). With Marvin Gaye singing "makes me wanna holler the way they do my life" in the background, the opening scene shows the family huddled around the television news which is broadcasting tense street protestors, and young Jack, age six, innocently asking, with a confused look on his face, "Why are these people so mad?"

The family is watching the news and awaiting the grand jury's decision on yet another case, this time near their home, of police brutality against a Black man. And although this is a fictional incident, viewers know fully well the facts that surround the very real recent unjustified murders of Michael Brown, Tamir Rice, Eric Garner, Sandra Bland, and others. Moreover, we have the scorching research of sociologist Michelle Alexander (2012) and film director Ava DuVernay (2016), which provides us with endless evidence of our nation's protracted history with racialized social control in the United States, particularly concerning our criminal justice system. So, while the episode may be pivoting on a fictional case, this is not an ahistorical incident.

In response to Jack's innocent question, the faces of all four adults register heart-wrenching despair, and the parents look at each other knowing they just entered a tragic crossroad. Pops responds to his young grandson by calling the police "damn thugs," which sparks Bow's maternal instinct to protect Jack and his twin sister by guiding them to the other side of the room to look at takeout menus. Bow believes that her young children are not ready for the next step in racial socializing, and she is intent on refocusing the conversation. Racial socializing is a developmental parenting process in which parents intentionally cultivate within their children not only positive self-pride but also awareness and pride of their racial and cultural heritage (Ferguson-Peters, 1985; McAdoo, 2007; Peck, Brodish, Malanchuck, Banerjee, & Eccles, 2014). Dre and Bow demonstrate incredible efforts in racially socializing their children; in fact, this show is premised on exactly this style of parenting as each episode unpacks how the kids consume Black culture while living in a dominant White neighborhood.

But there exists another darker aspect of racial socializing beyond racial pride that the show hadn't yet addressed—that is, until Jack's confusion genuinely surfaced. Racial socializing also includes teaching children how to protect themselves from the negative psychological effects of racism, biases, and prejudices as well as the hostile environment they will undoubtedly encounter (Stevenson & Arrington, 2009). This necessary component of racial socializing is frequently referred to as "the Talk," when parents pass down protective measures from generation to generation "like a grandmother's recipe for cornbread" (Whitaker & Snell, 2016, p. 304). Parents must explain that the rules of society are not always the same for Black and White children and that the consequences for behaviors will also differ, especially involving interactions with authority figures, particularly the police. "The Talk" can be a harrowing and distressing aspect of racial socializing for parents because they know that they are powerless to protect their children, which indicates their "own impotence at creating a better, safer world" (Whitaker & Snell, 2016, p. 305). And yet, despite how painful this discussion may be, not addressing these issues would amount to parental negligence that would render their children vulnerable (Peck et al., 2014; Thomas & Blackmon, 2015).

While the Johnson children are distracted with supper options, the parents step aside to privately discuss their next move, but they have differing opinions. Dre emphatically insists that the children must be told "the truth"—that it's time for "the Talk." Bow agrees intellectually, but feels they are still too young, especially Jack who is quite immature. Research on the intersection of gender and race may offer support to Dre and Bow's differing opinions, for African-American boys experience discrimination, racism, and profiling much more frequently than do girls (Fisher, Wallace, & Fenton, 2000; Seaton, Caldwell, Sellers, & Jackson, 2008). In fact, when former Attorney General Eric Holder (2013) was making public comments about the Trayvon Martin case, he called "the Talk" about racial profiling a "father-son tradition." Moreover, research also bears out that parents' specific instances and remembrances of experiences of racism from their youth, in turn, influence the socialization practices that they later provide to their own children (Hughes & Chen, 1997; Thomas, Speight, & Witherspoon, 2010). Undoubtedly, Dre's childhood experiences with racism in Compton influences this pivotal moment. Determining the age, depth, and timing of initiating "the Talk" is a question that hounds Black parents across the nation. For as this scene articulates, parents are often forced to "*insist* that their children are capable" of a level of decision-making and control that is "beyond their development grasp" (Whitaker & Snell, 2016, p. 307).

The young twins hear the family members conversing and point blank ask: "Is anyone gonna explain to us what's happening?" Their mom attempts to explain and praise the value of our nation's judicial system. But when the newscaster announces the grand jury's decision that once again the White policeman is found innocent, even the mom no longer attempts to shield her babies from the truth; the children are fully brought into the family conversation as they try to make sense of what Pops calls "the same story told a different way." How then, as a parent, do you balance the material realities of being Black in America while also maintaining a sense of hope? That is the question this episode seeks to address.

The audience bears witness to the "father-son tradition" as the three generations—Pops, Dre, and teen son Junior—draw upon influential social and cultural critics to help make sense of our nation's persistent institutional racism, particularly pertaining to the criminal justice system. Pops, all too familiar with this master narrative, draws upon James Baldwin (1966), who in discussing the impunity of the police department in the "Occupied Territory" of Harlem considers police "the hired enemies" (p. 41), unaccountable to the community who pays them (p. 42). Sadly in line with the happenings of today, Baldwin pointed out that should Blacks be so bold as to question the brutal behavior of the police, the questioners first risk being beaten as well as being labeled a "cop hater" (p. 39). Dre, likewise, acknowledges the influences of Malcolm X who continually expressed concerns about police brutality both during his time with the Nation of Islam and after becoming a more traditional Muslim. Just days before his assassination, speaking in Detroit, Malcolm X (1965) remarked: "Right now in New York we had a couple [of] cases where police grabbed the brother and beat him unmercifully—and then charged him with assaulting them." And while the black-*ish* episode never explicitly mentions Black Lives Matter, this movement's demand for both acknowledgement and justice clearly echoes Baldwin (1966) who, over 50 years ago, articulated "a plea for the recognition of our common humanity" (p. 40) as well as Malcolm (1965), who warned us of the "trickery" of systemic racism.

Teen son, Junior, listens to his elders and takes in the wisdom of Baldwin and Malcolm with whom he is unfamiliar, but he also adds to the conversation. He had just read *Between the world and me* by contemporary Black writer Ta-Nehisi Coates, someone both his grandfather and father are unfamiliar with. Junior shares Coates' view "that the violence and police brutality isn't new…it's just that the cameras are." Picking up where Baldwin and Malcolm left off, Coates (2015) speaks about his youth in Baltimore where he felt "naked before the elements of the world," clarifying that the nakedness is "not an error, nor pathology. The nakedness is the correct and intended result of policy, the predictable upshot of people forced for centuries to live under fear" (p. 17). Coates discusses how, as a teen, he was mindful of the choices he made as he moved through the world, always knowing that his Black body was vulnerable. This book-length letter to his own teen son resonates deeply with Junior. Coates' book—providing cautionary words to his own son—also adds to this essential conversation that is happening in the Johnson family; as we watch this tri-generational discussion draw upon cultural critics from different eras, the audience is witnessing multiple layers of "the Talk."

It's noteworthy that Pops approves of Junior's appreciation for Ta-Nehsisi, stating, "Well, this fella Coates sounds like he knows what he's talking about." But Dre, Junior's father, has a less favorable reaction to "Ta-Nehisi whatever his name is," claiming that he himself has been saying similar things but no one pays attention to him. Clearly, part of Dre's response is in service to comedy which is splashed throughout the episode. For example, Junior asks to turn up the TV so they can hear Don

Lemon interviewing Coates, and after Dre listens for a few seconds he spouts "where is CNN when I'm saying that stuff?" Without missing a beat, Junior wryly responds: "The same place Def Jam is when you're rapping in the shower," as they cut to a sudsy Dre lamely flowing to his bar of soap. Yet despite the comedy, it is apparent that Dre is troubled—perhaps threatened—by Coates, complaining that "the boy reads one book, and all of a sudden, he's an expert on all things Black." Dre pushes hard on his son, telling him that "just having a little knowledge can be a dangerous thing." It's a fleeting moment, but astute audience members are left wondering if Dre's masculinity or perhaps his parenting is being challenged. After all, he and Coates are both Black men about the same age with Black teen sons about the same age; perhaps Dre is unnerved that his son is turning to Coates for guidance rather than to him. Perhaps Barris is addressing the insecurities Black men—especially Black fathers—face in our culture, giving voice to not only the perils of conducting "The Talk" but also to the fact that Black men do not always know what to do with such emotions (Hill & Kelly, 2016; Majors & Billson, 1992).

Ruby, the grandmother, who is typically feisty, chimes in and tells her grandchildren that there are only seven words that they can use when they are dealing with the police: "Yes, sir"; "No, sir"; and "Thank you, sir." Bow fully agrees. When counseling psychologists Thomas and Blackmon (2015) did situation-specific research on racial socialization by parents after the Trayvon Martin shooting, one of the primary instructions parents gave to their children in order to diffuse any possible tension and avoid any possible violence was "demonstrating respect and answering questions directly" (p. 84). Whitaker and Snell (2016) add further texture to the instructive behavior that parents and grandparents share with their kids: "the Talk" is not about teaching children to avoid "criminal behavior; rather, it is about avoiding the *perception* of criminal behavior" (p. 304). So, when Ruby limits her grandchildren to the usage of these seven words, she isn't warning them to be mindful of their *own* actions; rather, she is warning them to "take responsibility for the actions of the adults [they] may encounter" (p. 304).

Even with all of these charged nuances of "the Talk," including Dre's definitive statement that the "system is rigged against us," Bow maintains her position that she wants her children to be free to live in a world where they can still have hope, both in themselves as Black Americans and in our criminal justice system. Flummoxed at his wife's position, Dre, in a tremendously riveting scene, tenderly says to his wife, with the rest of the family—and us—listening in:

> Oh, so you want to talk about hope, Bow?
> Obama ran on hope.
> Remember when he got elected, and...and we felt like maybe, just maybe, we got out of that bad place and made it to a good place?

That the whole country was really ready to turn the corner.

You remember that amazing feeling we had during the inauguration?

I was sitting right next to you.

And we were so proud.

And we saw him get out of that limo and walk alongside of it and wave to that crowd. (cut to images of Barack and Michelle walking in the 2009 inaugural parade)

Tell me you weren't terrified when you saw that.

Tell me you weren't worried that someone was gonna snatch that hope away from us like they always do.

That is the real world, Bow.

And our children need to know that that's the world that they live in.

As the show cuts to commercial, this scene leaves Bow sitting with her own recognition and agreement that her husband speaks the truth; young Jack, who is just a silly little kid, has heard the voice of despair and looks at his father with the concern of a grown man. Dre, in this poignant scene, indeed, articulates aloud what most people were too fearful to utter in 2009, but what so many of us felt in our heart. Instantly the scene went viral with overwhelming approval on social media outlets.

Despite the power of this scene, the episode, however, does not end in a sense of hopelessness; in fact, the ending bifurcates in two powerful, but equally important, directions. On the one hand, we witness the family moving forward. Bow, who clearly doesn't view the world "as broken" as her husband, suggests that they "as a family" go down to the protest and get involved, which is a major departure from her protective stance at the episode's start. As a montage of hopeful images—Obama being sworn in; peaceful protestors; a Black kid high-fiving a White policeman, an African boy holding a sign that reads simply "HOPE"—are digested by the audience, the parents and teenage kids head off to join the activism with a sense of agency and positivity, working toward what Obama frequently refers to as our "more perfect union."

Meanwhile, as the grandparents—at Dre's request—stay home with the young twins, the closing scene moves the narrative in a completely different direction, boldly commenting on the racial reality of the past and an unwavering acknowledgement that our racial struggles still exist. Drawing upon an incredible mix of late-1960s Black Consciousness movement rooted in the "Say It Loud: I'm Black and I'm Proud" era (Brown, 1968) coupled with artistic elements of hip-hop culture, Ruby, the deliciously ornery grandmother, protests in her own way. The second the family car pulls out of the driveway, a scratching backbeat drops as the audience watches Ruby grab a spray paint can; first we hear that distinctive rattle as she shakes the can and then the whooshing sound of graffiti. The closing scene cuts to Ruby sitting defiantly in a lawn chair in front of the closed double-sized garage door, tagged with large black letters, BLACK OWNED, and challenging any takers, she snarls, "Bring it on, boys." Although Ruby could certainly handle any protestors or troublemakers, she isn't actually expecting any in this swanky neighborhood; rather, she is bringing to bear, to all—both her immediate neighbors and the viewing audience—a broader message that defies the existence of a post-racial narrative. Despite the dignified Blackness that their family brings to this White neighborhood, she is proclaiming the material reality that racism still exists, and on her watch, no one will forget it.

By ending the episode in this bifurcated manner—simultaneously working hopefully toward resolution yet boldly defying any attempts at papering over our racial reality and our political struggles—black·*ish*, though a comedy, seriously addresses the tensions that fill our cultural landscape, reminding us that our work toward racial equity is far from over.

From Lemonade to Lemons

While every episode of black·*ish* addresses racial matters in our country, the "Hope" episode arguably stands as one of the show's most impactful, at least during the Obama Era. But the winds of our political climate, and therefore our political struggles, have radically shifted, and we are currently experiencing a forceful White backlash against all of the Black progress that the Obama Era afforded.

Since the 2016 U.S. presidential election and triumph of Donald Trump, we as a nation are forced to reconsider all matters concerning race as White supremacists now have an influential voice in our President's administration. Throughout our nation's history, Whiteness has always been an unmarked normative default, an invisible privilege (Baldwin, 1962; Ellison, 1952; hooks, 1997; Morrison, 1992; Roediger, 1999), but since the rise of Trump, we are experiencing a seismic paradigm shift in that now Whites are not only the dominating culture, but many are brazenly dominating specifically *as* Whites, and their unleashed racial hatred is being normalized.

Trump himself boastfully broadcasted his personal views on racial formation when he tweeted about the show when it first debuted: "How is ABC Television allowed to have a show entitled 'Blackish'? Can you imagine the furor of a show, 'Whiteish'! Racism at highest level?" (Trump, 2014). Early fans immediately educated Trump: Redenbacher responded, tweeting "'Whitish' has been on for years. They called it 'Friends'…or 'The Big Bang Theory' or 'Seinfeld'" (2014). A tweeter who goes by simply X tweets @realDonaldTrump, asking him "Do you even know the definition of racism?" (2014). Trump's ill-informed 2014 tweet about the show resurfaced in January of 2017 when Tracee Ellis Ross won the Golden Globe award for her role as Bow; once tweeters realized Trump's tweet wasn't a *SNL*-style parody but, in fact, real, the weight of his comments in light of his victory felt suffocating, as expressed by one fan's tweet: "This is a terrifying glimpse into the shallow mind of America's incoming president" (Penebaker, 2017).

Kenya Barris, not surprisingly, set out to capture the emotional turmoil our country was feeling as a nation divided, and three nights after the Golden Globe ceremony and just before the 2017 presidential inauguration, Barris (2017) delivered yet another powerful episode of black·*ish* entitled "Lemons" as he incisively reflects the postelection adjustment period that our nation experienced. With echoes of the "Hope" episode, "Lemons" likewise opens with Marvin Gaye's evocative voice, but now Gaye isn't hollering; he's anxiously questioning, "What's going on?" It has been two months since the election, and everyone in the Johnson household is still reeling from the traumatizing election results. Bow, looking like "an NPR commercial," is wearing head-to-toe clothes from all the progressive causes she has contributed to. The kids describe school as a "pressure cooker about to blow" as they cut to a classroom scene where a White student is boldly disrespecting his Latina teacher with "They're about to ship you back to your country." And concentration and production at Dre's office is practically nonexistent as his crew is repeatedly distracted by the latest news, twitter beefs, and petitions, as they, like 50 percent of America, are trying to make sense of what happened.

Though Barris accurately mirrors both the "anxiety and elation" that Americans were feeling, the show takes the opportunity to engage in serious racial formation. Sociologists Omi and Winant (2015) cogently argue that the meanings of race are not fixed, and thus existing racial meanings can be contested and new racial meaning can be constructed. This episode directly exposes and contests the invisible White privilege to which Trump's tweet so blindly referred. But the show isn't addressing solely those Whites who voted for Trump and might think about race as does he. No, more importantly, and in my estimation, more brilliantly, Barris is also reaching out to rattle progressive Whites, those who clearly didn't vote for Trump, but yet they, like the Trump voters, may also be unknowingly blinded by their own privilege.

After yet another nonproductive afternoon at work where the only order of business is outrage that Trump won, Dre boldly disrupts the White outrage by forcing a new perspective on the aggrieved. With the haunting anger of Billie Holiday's "Strange fruit" in the background, Dre delivers a stinging speech to his coworkers, particularly addressing his White boss, explaining how the system in our country has never worked for Blacks, and yet despite the continuous despair, Blacks carry on because they are quite accustomed to not getting their way. Looking at his whiny privileged coworkers, and by extension White progressives in the viewing audience, Dre calls them out for suddenly being so upset now that they didn't get their way. Dre apologizes that not winning the election is "blowing your mind," but where, he wonders, was all of your "outrage when everything was happening to all of my people since we were stuffed on boats in chains." He boldly points out that the sick feeling that started when the election was called is exactly how it feels to be Black every day. Barris is forcing Whites to look at the world through the eyes of Blacks, to recognize that these new feelings of distrust and fear are the emotions Blacks have lived with since our country's birth. In the "Lemons" episode, black·*ish* takes a unique tact in asking Whites not to solely blame Trump supporters but for progressive Whites to turn their gaze of Whiteness upon themselves. Barris' disruption of privilege simultaneously pushes Whites to be self-reflexive about not only their emotions but also forces them to make visible the blind spot they may have had about understanding the day-to-day realities of Blacks. Being woke about Blackness intellectually, which is the case for many progressive Whites, is radically different from actually experiencing that gut-level visceral sickness that progressive Whites felt on November 9th. This episode literally invites Whites to contemplate waking up with that feeling *every* morning. After jolting his White coworkers, and in parallel fashion, his White viewers, Dre ultimately insists that for the well-being of our country, we must stop the complaining and name-calling and attempt to have genuine and honest conversations about everyday matters of race, difference, and identity. Only then can we work through the uncertainty that plagues us all.

Barris, fully shooting for the "healing effect" of his creative power, wrote this script in a weekend and altered the production schedule to get this on the air directly before the inauguration. Barris states that the "Lemons" episode was purely an "emotional response" and the only time the show's storyline was "ripped from the headlines" (as cited in Demby, 2017). Not surprisingly, Barris (2017) cites this episode as one of the "most important" scripts he has ever written.

Conclusion: Colorful, Collaborative, Courageous

Television is a collaborative art, and the formula for success begins with a visionary showrunner and courageous writers who are willing and critically conscious enough to tackle heavy subjects while simultaneously entertaining the masses. black·*ish* has indeed proven itself as a progressive and intelligent comedy that is rooted in honest and respectful storytelling about everyday Black life. As a comedy writer, Kenya Barris knows that if he can make folks laugh first, then he has a greater chance of his audience hearing and accepting ideas in different ways.

Alongside its comedic appeal, the show has also been a standout for honoring not only the historical racial pain but also the current growth as well as struggles of diasporic people. For example, Barris fully admits that "Obama made this show possible." But, Barris laments, while Obama was in the White House, unfortunately we as a country "were talking about race publically less than ever." His mission with black·*ish* is to intentionally counteract that trend; Barris is motivated to unpack "those things that makes us uncomfortable" and whether viewers "agree or not, at least, maybe they'll start a conversation" (as cited in Demby, 2017). And looking forward, the show has clearly positioned itself to bravely confront what lies ahead within the Trump presidency; this will enable the conversations to continue as we, as a nation, wrestle with racial tensions and work to understand better our racio-cultural identities.

In the last few years, we have undoubtedly enjoyed a Renaissance of Black television. Not too long ago, showrunner Shonda Rhimes stood alone as a creator of Black TV, but black·*ish* is now in the company of an array of amazing shows in all genres—*Queen sugar, Empire, How to Get Away with Murder, Power, Being Mary Jane, Luke Cage, Scandal, Atlanta,* and *Insecure*—with talented colorful people both in front of and behind the camera. This explosion of creative energy is providing accurate representations of diverse people and ideas. Barris is relishing in the fact that people are now "opening their minds up to different voices." In fact, Barris concludes, Blacks "are now defining our culture in a very unique way, a proprietary way, but it's for everyone" (as cited in Demby, 2017).

References

Acham, C. (2004). *Revolution televised: Prime time and the struggle for Black power.* Minneapolis, MN: University of Minnesota Press.

Alexander, M. (2012). *The new Jim Crow: Mass incarceration in the age of colorblindness.* New York: The New Press.

Baldwin, J. (1962). *The fire next time.* New York: Dial Press.

Baldwin, J. (1966, July 11). A report from occupied territory. *The Nation, 203,* 39–43.

Barris, K. (Writer & Director). 2016. Hope. [Television series episode]. In A. Anderson (Executive producer), black·*ish*. Los Angeles, CA: ABC.

Barris, K. (Writer & Director). 2017. Lemons. [Television series episode]. In A. Anderson (Executive producer), black·*ish*. Los Angeles, CA: ABC.

Barris, K. (2017). *Commencement address to the class of 2017: Tufts.* Tufts University. [Transcript]. Retrieved September 2, 2017, from https://now.tufts.edu/commencement2017/speeches/barris

Bogle, D. (2001). *Prime time blues: African Americans on network television.* New York: Farrar, Straus, and Giroux.

Brown, J. (1968). *Say it loud—I'm Black and I'm proud [album].* Los Angeles, CA: Vox Studios.

Clifford, J. (1994). Further inflections: Toward ethnographies of the future. *Cultural Anthropology, 9*(3), 302–338.

Coates, T. (2015). *Between the world and me*. New York: Random.

Coleman, R. R. M., Mclwain, C. D., & Matthews, J. M. (2016). The hidden truths in contemporary black sitcoms. In M. M. Dalton & L. R. Linder (Eds.), *The sitcom reader: America re-viewed, still skewed* (2nd ed.). (pp. 279–294). Albany, NY: SUNY Press.

Demby, G. (Producer). (2017, May 9). Talking black-*ish* with star Yara Shahidi and creator Kenya Barris. *Code switch* [Audio podcast]. Retrieved September 2, 2017, from www.npr.org/sections/codeswitch/2017/05/09/481159422/talking-black-ish-with-star-yara-shahidi-and-creator-kenya-barris

DuVernay, A. (Director). (2016). *13th* [Documentary]. Available from Netflix, Los Gatos, CA.

Ellison, R. (1952). *Invisible man*. New York: Random.

Ferguson-Peters, M. (1985). A racial socialization of young Black children. In H. P. McAdoo & J. L. McAdoo (Eds.), *Black children: Social, educational, and parental environments* (pp. 159–173). Beverly Hills, CA: Sage.

Fisher, C. B., Wallace, S. A., & Fenton, R. E. (2000). Discrimination distress during adolescence. *Journal of Youth and Adolescence, 29*(6), 679–695.

Fretts, B. (2016, February 24). 'black-*ish*' show runner Kenya Barris on police brutality and 'The Cosby show.' *The New York Times*. Retrieved December 15, 2016, from www.nytimes.com/2016/02/25/arts/television/-kenya-barris-police-brutality-episode.html?_r=2

Gray, H. (1995). *Watching race: Television and the struggle for "Blackness."* Minneapolis: University of Minnesota Press.

Hill, S. A., & Kelly, J. (2016). From *Good times* to black-*ish*: Media portrayals of African American fathers. In. L. Tropp & J. Kelly (Eds.), *Deconstructing dads: Changing images of fathers in popular culture* (pp. 187–212). Lanham, MD: Lexington.

Holder, E. (2013, July 16). Remarks on Trayvon Martin at NAACP Convention. *The Washington Post*. Retrieved February 1, 2017, from www.washington-post.com/politics/attorney-general-eric-holders-remarks-on-trayvon-martin-at-naacp-convention-full-text/2013/07/16/dec82f88-ee5a-11e2-a1f9-ea873b7e0424_story.html?utm_term=.0d005a1f29ca

hooks, b. (1997). Representing whiteness in the Black imagination. In R. Frankenberg (Ed.), *Displacing whiteness: Essays in social and cultural criticism*. (pp. 165–179). Durham, NC: Duke University Press.

Hughes, D., & Chen, L. (1997). When and what parents tell children about race: An examination of race-related socialization among African American families. *Applied Developmental Science, 1*(4), 200–214.

Jhally, S., & Lewis, J. (1992). *Enlightened racism: The Cosby show, audiences, and the myth of the American dream*. Boulder, CO: Westview.

Leonard, D. J., & Guerrero, L. (2013). Introduction: Our regularly scheduled program. In Leonard, D. J., & Guerrero, L. (Eds.), *African Americans on television: Race-ing for ratings* (pp. 1–15). Santa Barbara, CA: Praeger.

Majors, R., & Billson, J. M. (1992). *Cool pose: The dilemmas of Black manhood in America*. New York: Lexington.

Malcolm, X. (1965, February 14). After the bombing/speech at ford auditorium. *Malcolm-x.org*. Retrieved January 28, 2017, from www.malcolm-x.org/speeches/spc_021465.htm

McAdoo, H. P. (2007). *Black families*. (4th ed.). Thousand Oaks, CA: Sage.

McKerrow, R. E. (1989). Critical rhetoric: Theory and praxis. *Communication Monographs, 56*(2), 91–111.

Morrison, T. (1992). *Playing in the dark: Whiteness and the literary imagination.* Cambridge, MA: Harvard University Press.

Omi, M., & Winant, H. (2015). Racial formation in the United States. (3rd ed.). New York: Routledge.

Peck, S. C., Brodish, A. B., Malanchuck, O., Banerjee, M., & Eccles, J. S. (2014). Racial/ethic socialization and identity development in Black families: The role of parent and youth reports. *Developmental Psychology, 55*(7), 1897–1909.

Penebaker, K. (2017, January 8). [Tweet]. Retrieved March 5, 2017, from https://twitter.com/kharyp/status/818295421525229568

Redenbacher, R. (2014, October 1). [Tweet]. Retrieved February 20, 2017, from https://twitter.com/rustymk2/status/517322526721318912

Roediger, D. R. (1999). *Black on White: Black writers on what it means to be White.* New York: Schocken.

Seaton, E. K., Caldwell, C. H., Sellers, R. M., & Jackson, J. S. (2008). The prevalence of perceived discrimination among African American and Caribbean Black youth. *Developmental Psychology, 44*(5), 1288–1297.

Stevenson, H. C., & Arrington, E. G. (2009). Racial/ethnic socialization mediates perceived racism and the racial identity of African American adolescents. *Cultural Diversity and Ethnic Minority Psychology, 15*, 125–136.

Thomas, A. J., & Blackmon, S. M. (2015). The influence of the Trayvon Martin shooting on racial socialization practices of African American parents. *Journal of Black Psychology, 41*(1), 75–89.

Thomas, A. J., Speight, S. L., & Witherspoon, K. M. (2010). Racial socialization, racial identity, and race-related stress of African American parents. *The Family Journal: Counseling and Therapy for Couples and Families, 18*, 407–412.

Trump, D. J. (2014, October 1). [Tweet]. Retrieved February 20, 2017, from https://twitter.com/search?l=&q=Blackish%20%20Whiteish%20from%3ArealDonaldTrump&src=typd&lang=en

Whitaker, T. R., & Snell, C. L. (2016). Parenting while powerless: Consequences of "the talk." *Journal of Human Behavior in the Social Environment, 26*(3–4), 303–309.

X. (2014, October 1). [Tweet]. Retrieved February 20, 2017, from https://twitter.com/XLNB/status/517422527497252864

Part II

Owning Images and Narratives

4 "(Re) defining Images of African Women"

A Postfeminist Critique of the Ghanaian YouTube Series "An African City"

Godfried Asante and Rita Daniels

Women of the global south are represented as homogenous, primitive, and unchangeable in Western movies, documentaries, and TV shows (Cole, Manuh, & Miescher, 2007; Grewal & Kaplan, 1994; Mikell, 1997; Mohanty, 1988; Shome, 2014). Particularly, African women have been represented in the West in ways which align their bodies with "nature" and "subordination" (Shome, 2014). However, movies and TV shows produced by African women have sought to represent themselves as empowered, modern, and cosmopolitan. The multiple media representations about the African woman have produced different and sometimes competing ideologies. One particular discourse that has gained international and local resonance is "empowerment." This discourse emanates from international development projects initiated by the World Bank and the UN with private corporations who export particular modes of entrepreneurial subjectivity. For instance, the Bill and Melinda Gates Foundation and UNICEF promote the notion of "girl power" borrowed directly from the UK pop singers, Spice Girls. These discourses are interpolating young African women as a decontextualized and ahistorical consumer subject whose entry into the global economy relies solely on their entrepreneurial ambitions. In this constraining context, women who are not able to succeed in a patriarchal society could be personally held responsible for not having much entrepreneurial skills and ambition. This research seeks to explore similar discourses of empowerment used to represent the new/modern "African woman" by African women writers and producers of African TV shows. Notably, how is the new African "woman" represented in TV shows produced by African women themselves?

Christopher Prendergast (2000) explained the term representation in two folds. First, he wrote that the term representation "is the sense of represent as re-present, to make present again, in two interrelated ways, spatial and temporal" (p. 4). Second, he notes that representation is to delegate presence. Aware of its complicated process, Stuart Hall (1997) argued that representation works as a system consisting of the different ways of establishing complex relations between concepts. Drawing from Prendergast and Hall, we conceptualize representation as a *doing*, a form of construction which adds something to the already constructed context. Thus, the representation of new/modern images of African women through a transnational medium (YouTube) and in a transnational space (Ghana) is *adding* to the already constructed neoliberal economic and political context.

YouTube has offered the digital space for new ideas to be tested before reaching mainstream media distributions and TV Stations. Particularly relevant to this study is the popular YouTube Series *"An African City."* Nicole Amarteifio, a Ghanaian-born U.S. citizen who lives in New York, wrote and coproduced the show. This YouTube TV series gained prominence and popularity because it resonated with Black/African audiences, and especially Black/African women in the diaspora. A key aspect of this show is the dilemma of the "returnees-" someone who has lived in the West for a long period of time and eventually relocates to his/her country of origin. Though previous Ghanaian TV shows in the late 1990s and early 2000s had characters who were returnees, they were mostly males. They hardly portrayed the struggles of women "returnees." *An African City* highlights the experiences of women returnees as they navigate two oppressive structures—racism and whiteness in the West and patriarchy in Ghana.

The representation of their struggles appealed to a wide range of audiences in continental Africa and those in the diaspora. Published on YouTube in 2014, the first season of *"An African City"* has been viewed more than 927, 454 times on YouTube as of April 22, 2018. Although *An African City* received admiration from U.S. media outlets such as NPR, New York Times, Vogue, and CNN, it has also received criticism from human rights activists working with NGOs in African countries and media commentators. For instance, Akinyi Ochieng from *OkayAfrica.com* criticized the glamorized fanciful portrayal of characters as "a narrow elite feminist fantasy." The core of the criticism is whether *An African City* is showcasing new images of African women that are quite distant from the realities.

Drawing from feminist media studies and postcolonial studies, this study shifts the focus of criticism from whether it portrays the "true" experiences of African women or modern African women to what kinds of discourses of empowerment about the new/modern "African woman" are emerging in the YouTube series. We argue that although the new images of African women are giving rise to new representational modes of African women empowerment, such representations are imbued with neoliberal and postfeminist sensibilities. Postfeminism offers an analytical lens to examine how particular discourses of empowerment, sexual subjectification, and consumerism become the signifying modes through which the new/modern African woman is represented in African diasporic produced TV shows. Describing the discourses used to rationalize skin toning in Ghana, Asante (2016) found that African women empowerment discourses are linked to neoliberal ideologies of individual choice and consumerism. He encouraged scholars "to further research how [African] women are decoding and internalizing the meaning of women empowerment and liberation" (Asante, 2016, p. 15). Discussions of women empowerment raise questions about agency within the context of increasing global inequality, growing poverty in Africa, and constraining reproductive and sexual rights in many African countries. Therefore, analyzing the discourses of empowerment represented in *An African City* shows the particular kinds of women empowerment discourses are (re)produced in a transnational space. The authors are not of the opinion that the new ways of representing African women in *An African City* are erroneous. Rather, we are drawing attention to the frailty of emerging discourses about African women empowerment. In what follows, we describe the show, *An African City*. Then we explore postfeminism and hybridity as theoretical concepts of this study. Finally, we reveal the findings of the study and outline the implications.

An African City

Although the show is written and coproduced by a Ghanaian-born U.S. citizen, the main characters are not from one country in Africa; they are from Nigeria, Liberia and Ghana. Drawing from the diasporic desires to return "home," this TV show capitalizes on Africa as a place of "rest," where all diasporic subjects must return to give back (Arthur, 2000). For instance, in a scene where Nana Yaa, the main character is asked why she came back to Ghana, she responds, "I returned to give back to my homeland." The setting of the TV show is quite significant. While the characters have lived in the US and the UK for a significant amount of time, they all return to Ghana. Ghana becomes the "home"—a place to return after spending time in the West. Ghana is also considered the homeland of many Africans in the diaspora whose ancestors were transported through the slave ports in Ghana. Thus, Ghana symbolically represents a place of diasporic return, a resting place for those displaced in the West. In this purview, the bodies of the characters transcend colonial borders that divided Africa.

The first episode of *An African City* debuted on January 24, 2016. This series follows the lives of five single women: Nana Yaa, Sade, Zainab, Makena, and Ngozi. These women are "returnees"—a name given to those who leave the country and return with a so-called "returnee savior syndrome." The characters depict an unseen side of African women on the African continent, which is usually depicted with footage of war, famine, and poverty. Instead, *An African City* struts into the lives of well-off African women. Makena is an Oxford-trained lawyer and Sade graduated from Harvard Business School. Zainab sits atop a growing shea butter empire and Nana Yaa's father is Ghana's Minister of Energy.

Ngozi works for a development agency in Accra. Through the narratives of the five women, *An African City* explores what it means to be a Westernized young African woman readjusting to the culture and surroundings of her home continent. In what follows, we discuss the two theoretical constructs that guide this study.

Postfeminism

Postfeminism as a concept has been used vaguely to denote an epistemological break from the second wave of feminism. It is also constituted as a theoretical positioning of a regressive political era (Gill, 2007). Feminism has seen multiple and contradictory trends in its activism since the mid-1990s. While some scholars have advocated for a Third Wave activism which questions patriarchy and the gendered, racialized, and heteronormative systems of society (e.g., hooks, 2012; Smith, 2012), others have called for a *post*feminist movement which actively engages in the process of undoing the feminist gains of the 1970s and 1980s for a well-informed response and redefinition of feminism (e.g., Hawkesworth, 2004; McRobbie, 2004). Levine (2008) has documented tensions between these two trends of feminism pertaining to media artifacts directed specifically at female adult consumers.

According to McRobbie (2004), postfeminism appears to be a culmination of feminist and anti-feminist ideas, particularly in the context of feminist cultural studies. In the West, it is a response to second-wave feminism (Budgeon, 2011). It has also been explained as a critique of second-wave feminism ideologies to deconstruct authoritative models and practices that subvert the representations of gender (Gillis & Munford, 2004; Robinson, 2011). Budgeon (2001) argued that the prefix of *post*-feminism denotes a continual and ongoing change within the feminist movement. Postfeminism engages with traditional gender norms while embracing (if not partially) feminist ideas of equal opportunities and female empowerment (Gill, 2007). Gill (2006) recounts three dominant accounts of postfeminism: (a) an epistemological perspective (Alice, 1995; Lotz, 2001); (b) a historical shift (Hollows, 2000; Moseley & Read, 2002); or (c) a backlash against feminism (Whelehan, 2000; Williamson, 2003). Without any analytical bend to the current conceptualization of postfeminism, Gill (2007) called for a reconceptualization of postfeminism as a distinct sensibility, made up of a number of interrelated themes. These include the notion that

> femininity is a bodily property; the shift from objectification to subjectification; an emphasis upon self-surveillance, monitoring and self-discipline; a focus on individualism, choice, and empowerment; the dominance of a makeover paradigm; and a resurgence of ideas about natural sexual difference.
>
> (p. 149)

By implication, the focus of a scholar in any postfeminism work should be on the media content as the object of critique through which one examines the contemporary manifestations of gender identities. As posited in the quotation here, postfeminism is concerned with those interrelated themes which are structured by inequalities and exclusions pertaining to identity (e.g., gender, race, ethnicity, and religion).

Postfeminism is also closely linked to neoliberalism and its ideals of free markets and consumerism. As Harvey (2005) contended "Neoliberalism is, in the first instance, a theory of political economic practices that proposes that human well-being can best be advanced by liberating individual entrepreneurial freedoms and skills within an institutional framework characterized by strong private property rights, free markets and free trade" (p. 2). Scharff and Gill (2011) added that neoliberalism as a political and economic exigence sees the market exchange as an ethic in itself capable of acting as a guide for all human actions. Discourses about individual responsibility and internalized self-transformation, which are common in the current neoliberal era, have become dominant frames within which African subjects are made to engage with the contemporary world (Englund, 2006; Piot, 2010). However, Boyd (2013) noted that this new form of "individualisms" and disjointed acknowledgment of self-autonomy and choice are falsely utilized to assume that individual achievement in a capitalist exchange is achievable while these dreams remain out of reach for most Africans. Neoliberalism is ever expanding its geopolitical reach on the African continent. Although not through coercive means of development initiatives such as structural adjustment policies and the like, it is being perpetuated through local actors who utilize their association with the West as a measurement of success, individual choice, and modernity. In *An African City*, the association of the characters with Western modernity through education, mobility, and access to capital places them in a position where it seems they have succeeded because of their individuality, freedom and choices. Although individuality is made a central tenet of neoliberalism in the West, individuality is coopted through hybridity in the African context—the ability to cohabit in two worlds through the consumption of products is presented as the freedom to make individual choices. In this context, African women can enjoy the benefits of the emerging cosmopolitan markets by making specific individual choices.

Postcolonial Theory and Hegemonic Deployment of Hybridity in African City

Combining postcolonial theory and critical/cultural communication research, Shome and Hegde (2002) contended that postcolonial cultural critique is the reexamination and reconsideration of the effects of colonization such as the appropriation of land and territory, the institutionalization of racism, the destruction of local cultures, and the superimposition of Westernized ways of thinking about race, gender, class, and sexuality. Although postcolonial theory provides the historical context, its focus on the nation limits critical engagement with the contemporary transnational and situated nature of structural forces. Given the changing geopolitical structure of the world and the neoliberal realignment of global relations, there is call for a revisiting of notions of self, nationhood, cultural membership, citizenship, belonging, and identity, as well as the nature of gendered and sexual subjects (Chavez, 2013). Hybridity is especially useful in describing how difference is being reconceptualized within the contours of neoliberal ideologies.

In the realm of global and international communication, hybridity has been theorized in many forms to describe the shifting and contextually contingent subject positions of the postmodern subject. Hall (1996) wrote that "identities are not unified around a coherent self. Within us are contradictory identities pulling us in multiple directions so that our identifications are continuously being shifted about" (p. 598). Thus, hybridity offers the theoretical tools to critique how the identities of the characters oscillate as authentically African and global. Characters embody notions of global multiculturalism and cosmopolitanism, which resonates with the current neoliberal consumer subject. In this process, there is a hegemonic deployment of hybridity in the representation of the African woman.

Kraidy (2005) stated that hybridity is one of the most employed and disputed terms in postcolonial theory. Hybridity has become a master trope of many spheres of cultural research, theory, and criticism. For instance, it has been used to describe mixed genres and identities (Kolar Panov, 1996). Bhabba (1994) celebrated the concept of hybridity as a resilience of the subaltern and the contamination of the imperial ideology, aesthetics, and identity by natives. He described the ability of hybridity to subvert dominant discourses. Appadurai (1996) approached hybridity as a by-product of the transcultural dynamics between tradition and modernity sometimes conceptualized as the local and global. Canclini (2005) formulated cultural hybridity as a realm that crosses from the aesthetico-symbolic to the cultural politics of citizenship. This interpretation of hybridity is echoed in performance studies. Joseph (1999) wrote that hybridity is a "democratic expression of multiple affiliations of cultural citizenship in the U.S" (p. 2). Kraidy (2002) added that performative hybridity "is always in a state of tension with transnational and national political economy" (p. 320). Thus, an analysis of the representation of the new modern African woman must be examined within the transnational and national political economy which gives those representations meaning.

Our definition of hybridity draws its theoretical energy from Kraidy (2002), who employed a critical view of hybridity as not a mere site of mixing of cultures or a celebration of global multiculturalism. He stated that hybridity is a communicative practice "constitutive of and constituted by sociopolitical and economic arrangements" (Kraidy 2002, p 317.). As such, the meanings ascribed to the bodies of the characters are not apolitical but understood within the geopolitical arrangements and historical contexts. As "returnees," the characters are represented as cosmopolitan and borderless. They become decontextualized ahistorical bodies who are just consumers in the global economy. We argue that through a critical view of hybridity as multiple performances of "cultural citizenship" (Joseph 1999), the bodies of the characters in *An African City* become complicit in the perpetuation of neoliberal ideologies of individuality, autonomy, and meritocracy. The characters represented as "returnees" who are redefining the images of African women might do so along power lines where their hybrid identities as "African" women who have lived in the West temporarily position them against other African women who are deemed as "authentic" and unchanging. Thus, hybridity is explored as a mechanism through which postfeminist sensibilities in a neoliberal economy are made intelligible to the viewing public. The in/authenticity of the characters as African and Western create spaces where audiences can identify and dis/identify with the representations of empowerment presented in the show.

Methodology

Building on Gill's conceptualization, we explore how postfeminism is "domesticated" in a television series centered on African women in the diaspora. We examine postfeminism themes present in *An African City* series. By engaging the content of these series using the postfeminism lens, we uncover conflicting images of the African woman and how that contributes to her redefinition. Alasuutari (2008) used the term domestication to argue that "external models are never just adopted; when turned into actual practices and incorporated with local conditions their meaning and consequences are different from the original blueprint" (p. 67). Given that every setting has its peculiarities, it is reasonable to expect that the incorporation of a concept not originally framed in an adopted setting will unveil slightly if not complete different nuances. Our use of the metaphor "domestication" highlights the idea of making familiar what is considered foreign through the complex articulation of a novel interpretation from diverse systems of meanings sutured together.

We chose Nicole Amarteifio's *An African City*, a YouTube series centered on African women, because of its heightened prominence and popularity. Currently, Amertefio has two series of African City, each with ten episodes. Season 1 is showing for free on YouTube with a record of over one million views and subscriptions. The ten episodes are each less than 20 minutes long. Hence, we focus on Season 1 instead of Season 2, which viewers need to subscribe in order to have access. The researchers independently analyzed the data by coding and identifying themes, with the actual approaches ranging from impressionistic, intuitive, and interpretive analyses (Hsieh & Shannon, 2005) while reviewing each other's analysis. Through our subjective reactions and interpretations of the selected episodes of the TV series, our critical content analysis seeks to explore the themes of empowerment in the forms of individualism and self-awareness, and consumerism and sexual subjectification. It also expands the literature on postfeminism in the African context and as posited by Hansen et al. (1998), and Van Zoonen (1994) allows for an in-depth understanding of cultural trends that reflect the reproduction of ideologies and notions of gender. Using the themes mentioned before, we critically examine our data intellectually to identify the authentic and inauthentic elements of the African culture. We also examined the use of language in describing and revealing characters.

Analysis

Two major themes became salient in the examination of the YouTube series, *An African City*. The first theme that emerged explored how African women empowerment is represented through consumerism and sexual subjectification. In the second theme, we analyzed how empowerment is signified as the individualized will of African women to transcend structural constraints even if there is a need to use one's sexuality as a bridge to success. Together, these themes show how the characters of the TV show represent African women empowerment in the contemporary neoliberal economy. While analyzing the text, it became apparent that African women empowerment is a major guiding force tying together the loosely fitted idea of the modern African woman. Our goal is not to prove that African women empowerment is a failed project but to untangle the discourse of African women empowerment from the barrows of neoliberal consumerist culture which benefits a few.

Empowerment through Consumerism and Sexual Subjectification

Gill (2007) noted that postfeminism is not a response to feminism but a "sensibility partially constituted through neoliberal thoughts" (p. 148). Embedded in the TV show is the affirmation of postfeminist sensibilities through neoliberal discourses of empowerment and self-help. In fact, empowerment to resist patriarchal structures has become necessary in many countries in Africa as women's reproductive and sexual rights continue to be restricted through government policies (Ahlberg & Kulane, 2011). African patriarchy and fundamentalist Christian and Islamic doctrines about the gendered roles of men and women have become normalized as "African culture." Considerations of empowerment as African women having control over their bodies through policies and laws evoke anxiety and public panic of moral decadence (Tamale, 2011). Such interpretations of empowerment have been described by African nationalists and Ghanaian Pentecostalist-Charismatic Christians as the expansion of Western feminism, which seeks to erode "African culture." However, alternative discourses of empowerment are hardly offered. Within this context, multiple discourses of empowerment have emerged to resist patriarchy.

Representations of the modern African woman in *An African City* evoke notions of glocalized feminism—a form of feminism tied to global neoliberal circulations of female self-empowerment wrapped in traditional African discourses of womanhood. These representations are problematic; it ties feminism and African woman empowerment to consumerism, self-help, and self-transformation. These forms of empowerment are positioning African women to make personal, individual choices about their body through their purchasing power to overcome patriarchy.

In the TV show, discourses of empowerment are represented through the purchasing of one's apartment and being able to afford necklaces and bracelets. This form of emancipatory politics against patriarchy does not challenge the status quo as it situates resistance primarily in purchasing power. For instance, Nana Yaa, the main character, relocates to Ghana from New York. While in Ghana, she experiences the normalized weight of African patriarchy. For example, she is expected to go on dinner dates and sometimes have sex with the manager or human resources manager of the company before being given a position she is qualified to do. While having dinner, Nana Yaa and her friends discuss the unequal positionings of Ghanaian men and women. As a returnee from the United States, Nana Yaa shows her disdain for the Ghanaian cultural system where men have most of the wealth and women become accessories of men's power and wealth. In their discussion, they all agree that marriage to a wealthy man is a yardstick for women's success in Ghana. In this scene, they showcase how patriarchy is "natural" to Africa through statements such as, "Well...this is Africa," indicating that Nana Yaa is back to the homeland where her ideals of Western feminism should be relinquished if she wants to be successful. This scene also positions the United States and the United Kingdom as nonpatriarchal societies in relation to the continent of Africa.

The materiality of patriarchy on women's social mobility becomes evident when Nana Yaa is introduced to a "sugar daddy." "Sugar daddies" are mostly married men who seek very younger women. They buy them clothes, shoes, and sometimes rent apartments for them. Nana Yaa's sugar daddy buys her everything from clothes to shoes and will even pay for an apartment for her. Although she accepts all the gifts from her sugar daddy, Nana Yaa will not accept his gesture to pay for her new apartment because she wants the freedom to own her space and to buy her clothes, shoes, and bracelets. Eventually, she stops talking to the sugar daddy and rents her own apartment. Her emphasis on being independent of men through the purchasing of her own apartment and clothes shows how her character espouses a particular form of empowerment—an empowerment which positions her as independent through the purchasing of her own space without the help of a wealthy man. For instance, while enjoying the company of her friends, she expressed that renting her apartment without her sugar daddy shows that she can *buy* all the things that the sugar daddy used to buy for her. Nonetheless, Nana Yaa accepted some of the gifts from her sugar daddy. In a close-up screenshot of her looking gleefully at her gifts in her office, she tells herself that she will not return the gifts from the sugar daddy, as they're hers now. For a moment, she feels that she has beaten patriarchy at its own game. She took his gifts, did not sleep with him, and finally got her own apartment. What is problematic about this scene is that overcoming patriarchy is measured through one's ability to purchase the space and products they desire without the help of a sugar daddy. This form of empowerment benefits those who have access to such class privileges. It also equates resistance to patriarchy as refusing gifts from sugar daddies. In this vein, resistance is reduced to what the individual can accomplish through purchasing power rather than a collective effort to resist the very patriarchal structure that positions African women to desire sugar daddies in the first place.

Another form of empowerment represented is the need to resist patriarchy through the exploration of one's own sexual pleasure and freedom. While using female sexuality was repressed by second-wave feminism (Gill, 2007), in the TV show, female sexuality can be used "responsibly" to overcome patriarchy. The modern African woman's body can be used to lure wealthy men while maintaining the ultimate goal of seeking financial autonomy to buy whatever they want. This form of resistance to patriarchy is reductive and places the onus of responsibility on women to change the institution of patriarchy. The representation of empowerment does not critique patriarchy; the characters try to, albeit unsuccessfully, reveal how patriarchy subjugates African women while reinscribing patriarchy as *natural* and *cultural* to Africa. Therefore, to circumvent patriarchy, African women should use their sexuality to get the products they want. As Sade puts it, "It is not prostitution, it's how we do it in Africa." The scenes where Nana Yaa is able to manipulate her sugar daddy into buying things for her while avoiding sex with him shows how the new modern African women can/should cohabit with patriarchal structures without directly threatening it. This analysis echoes Audre Lorde's criticism of Western feminists. She stated "For the master's tools will not dismantle the master's house. They may allow us to temporarily beat him at his own game, but they will never enable us to bring about genuine change" (Lorde, 2003, p. 3).

Gill (2007) argued that the notion of objectification, that media representations help to justify and sustain relations of domination and inequality between women and men, has changed. She further explained that contemporary constructions of feminism in media discourse are maintained around young women as active, desiring sexual subjects. This form of sexual expression is evident in the way the characters explore their own sexuality within the cultural contexts where such explorations of female sexuality are limited. In season one episode two, while having dinner, Zainab mentioned that she is worried about what might happen to Nana Yaa's sex life if she continues living with her parents. The conversation at dinner ensues into conversations about how Nana Yaa needs her independence in order to have more sex. In this scene, being independent through the purchasing of an apartment is linked to the ability to enjoy limitless sexual encounters. This scene constructs a shift from older African women generations with traditional values to the modern cosmopolitan Ghanaian woman who is able to talk about sex and enjoy it as much as she wants through the purchasing of one's independence.

In a discussion about Ghanaian men in season one episode two, Makena alleged that she was disappointed in her date when he asked her to pay half of the bill for dinner. She explained that, in the UK, she was a feminist and would never allow anyone to buy her dinner but in Ghana, she expects men to pay for her. In this scene, there is a hegemonic construction of hybridity, which situates Makena as a dual cultural citizen who can deploy multiple performances of feminism to fit the specific cultural context. Makena stated that she found it shocking that her Ghanaian date who is based in Canada will not pay for her meal. The construction of her feminism in the UK where she was a feminist and will not allow men to pay for her in relation to her current construction of feminism in Ghana, where she needs men to pay for her because she has no job, shows a contradiction in her construction of her feminist politics. She asserted that men have access to wealth in Ghana, so she needs men to pay for her. In this context, she is not directly criticizing African patriarchy but is showing that in Ghana, she succumbs to patriarchy through her sexuality to get what she wants. Thus, African women who expect men to pay for them when on dates should not feel bad because it's not about rejecting men's gifts because of feminism; rather, it's the new form of feminism in Africa.

When Ngozi asked if using female sexuality to lure men to buy clothes and apartments is akin to prostitution, Sade quickly responds that it does not make her a prostitute; it makes her a woman. Sexual subjectification is represented through Sade's use of her sexuality to attract older men's attention to get financial support. Concurrently, she is represented as repressing her desire for a "real" relationship with her sugar daddies, positioning emotional connectedness to them as a weakness. In episode four, she sees one of her sugar daddies with another woman in a restaurant and immediately becomes sad and leaves their table for the bathroom. Realizing that Sade has seen her sugar daddy with another woman, Nana Yaa follows Sade to the bathroom. They begin a heartfelt conversation about the men in their lives. She tells Nana Yaa, "I am with them to just get what I want, right?" Thus, her desire for a "real" relationship with some of the "sugar daddies" is downplayed as feminine weakness as she is just using her female sexuality for personal gain. What is ostensibly shown as a better figure to depend on is her vibrator. For instance, in episode four, Sade imported her belongings, including her vibrator, from the United States. But her belongings got stuck at Ghana Customs. In the episode, Sade's frustration with not having access to her vibrator is shown through her anger with the customs officer. When she finally gets access to her vibrator, a close-up of her face showing her satisfaction is shown. A voiceover from Nana Yaa says, "The African woman should depend on vibrators rather than a reliance on men." Again, purchasing products to enhance female sexuality is linked to the representation of empowerment in *An African City*.

A critical view of hybridity makes these forms of empowerment intelligible to the viewing public. The bodies of the characters as "returnees" come to represent the new modern African woman who has been adulterated by Western feminism but is still local. The characters occasionally use their hybrid performances to blur the lines between Western and non-Western, sometimes referring to their comfortable lives in the United States or the United Kingdom to juxtapose the patriarchy, corruption, and unnecessary bureaucracy in Ghana. Thus, we argue that it is the deployment of hegemonic hybridity (as women who blur the lines between in/authenticity) that makes their representation of empowerment as consumerist and sexual subjects effective. It shows that if African women want to empower themselves in late capitalism, they need to be hybrids—a mixture of Western and African. This problematic representation of hybridity is reinforced through the characters as returnees and through the costumes of the characters, which are a mixture of Western designs with local fabrics manufactured in Europe and China.

Empowerment as Individualism and Self-Awareness

Season one, episode one begins with the return of Nana Yaa from New York to join her other four returnee friends. The viewer is introduced to the characters' self-expressions and encouragement of pursuit of dreams in Africa. Even though they talk about their romantic relationships now and then, none of them explicitly state their return to Ghana is because of a romantic relationship/marriage breakdown, which is a culturally sensitive topic for young African women of their age. There is an unspoken expectation for most matured African women in their mid-20s, particularly for well-established women like the returnees, to get married. The expectations of marriage are accompanied with the fear of making oneself unapproachable for romantic relationships with men. For Nana Yaa, the expectations of marriage are nonexistent fears, because among her expressed reasons for returning home is that "Ghana is the place of 'home' and the birthplace of her parents and grandparents." Furthermore, she exclaims that her priority is to find a job and work, given that there are more job opportunities, particularly now that her father is a newly elected government official. Nana Yaa is eager to be independent, so she takes out a loan to pay for her own apartment. According to Sade, the purchase of one's own apartment means "you are a financially independent woman, and men will not know what to do with you" but officially single forever per the unwritten norms of cultural expectations of women. In this context, there is an emphasis on individualism and freedom of choice, which are prevalent in the expression of femininity in postfeminist media cultures.

The women engage in a conversation about finding a man (what they refer to as "uncles," "sugar daddies" who provide anything from purses to cars) to bear a lady's cost of living. While these ladies are portrayed as seeking independence, they also express a sense of reliance on men for material gains and payment of bills when they go on dates. Nana Yaa's reason for wanting her own apartment in Ghana is "independence," having lived by herself in New York for ten years. She describes living with her parents as torture because her mother complains about her natural hair every day (her natural hair embarrasses her mother) and her father scolds her for not watching CNN. This torture also reflects a restriction on her sexual life. With the number of men who kept parading in and out of her apartment, that could not have happened if she lived under the roof of her parents. Even though it is acceptable for an unmarried woman of any age to be living with her parents, she speaks of the need to be independent and to make her personal choices.

A goal of postfeminist media culture is to create anxieties about the female body as needing constant change (Gill, 2007). The emphasis on the (im)perfection of the female body is achieved in multiple ways in the TV series. The women use discourses of African female resistance to whiteness such as maintaining natural hair and refraining from skin bleaching to create anxieties about women's bodies as needing self-regulation in order to attract male attention. All the ladies returned home in their natural hair, but two succumbed to the pressure of permed (straight rather than coarse) hair. While Nana Yaa and Zainab are self-conscious about their natural hair and rebuke any conspiracy to make them feel otherwise, Sade, with her plump figure, receives compliments for being fat and Zainab rejects an offer to bleach her skin to be like Beyoncé. Irrespective of Sade's confidence portrayed in her appearance, speech, and knowledge of cultural norms and expectations, she trembles at the sight of a police officer. She associates policing as an institution of the male gender and invokes traditional masculinity that should give her a pass for her trepidation. Conversely, Ngozi refrains from sex until marriage, though she yearns to be wanted. Not knowing how to cook is not a good appraisal for an African woman, but her sense of spirituality won't permit her to lie about her abilities. Zainab throws in an affirmative consolation that cooking does not define a woman; though that should be relieving, Ngozi expresses nervousness for the belly button test (the practice of a male sniffing a woman's belly button for any odor). These ladies are also conscious about their ability to speak their local languages. Nana Yaa, for instance, will take language lessons and they would practice their speech at restaurants.

Finally, the ladies each have and hold their partners to their own prescribed standards for a perfect man. Most of the men the characters were dating were only perfect on paper: (a) a 33-year-old single Harvard graduate who works as a junior partner at a top law firm, (b) a 34-year-old single U.S.-educated returnee, and (c) a 28-year-old single Oxford-educated returnee leading his father's pharmaceutical company. These on-paper perfect men and others who were not profiled were culprits of one of the following: snoring, "taking dumps" in the presence of his date without shame, sweating profusely, pulling the lady's hair during sexual intercourse, and leaving around used condoms anywhere—none of which met the standards of the ladies and so the relationships did not see the light of day. Nana Yaa, however, was unable to let go of her ex-boyfriend of seven years ago, Segun. Undoubtedly, though these female characters are shown to be independent, from a critical perspective, their independence is marked on some insecurities and reinforcement of the very gender roles and expectations they actively appear to overcome.

Conclusions and Implications

New media such as YouTube has become an important outlet to examine emerging ideologies about African women and how such ideologies are represented. In this study, we analyzed the YouTube TV show *An African City* using postfeminism and hybridity as the theoretical framework. Two themes emerged as salient in the examination of the episodes: empowerment through consumerism and sexual subjectification and empowerment through individual autonomy and self-awareness. The two themes reflect how the modern African woman is represented through discourses of empowerment and liberation. Nonetheless, they can be linked to discourses which are distinctively neoliberal and post-feminist (Gill & Scharff, 2011). It is important to complicate the underlying assumptions of empowerment of the modern African woman through consumerism, individual autonomy, and choice. This chapter asks very difficult questions about subjectivity. In doing so, we share our roles with what Ien Ang (2001) calls the "party pooper." She writes "The diasporic intellectual acts as a perpetual party pooper because her impulse is to point to ambiguities, complexities and contradictions, to complicate matters...." (p. 2).

Empowerment discourses are situated in the ongoing enclaves of the neoliberal economy, which is also transnational. Neoliberalism, write Hong and Ferguson (2011), relies on valuing respectability and normativity to subject the racialized (among others) to brutal violence through rhetorics of individual freedom and responsibility. Boyd (2013) argued, "Neoliberal projects of development and economic restructuring have emphasized the individual rather than the state or community as the central actor in projects of social transformation" (p. 700). Ideologies of neoliberalism are linked and articulated with individualism, self-transformation, and free market. Central to postfeminism is the ongoing individuality expressed through discourses of the free will of the individual. This problematic disciplinary regime positions women as autonomous agents no longer constrained by inequalities and power imbalances. This is especially problematic given the growing inequality overwhelmingly affecting African women and the concomitant restraining of sexual and reproductive rights (Ahlberg & Kulane, 2011). Moreover, the notion of choice and access to apartments, clothes, and money avoids the very difficult questions about how socially constructed ideals of African womanhood and femininity are internalized and re-produced. Gill (2007) wrote that the notion of choice is a postfeminist mantra. The idea that women are making their own choices is rampant in numerous media representations. For instance, women choose to have cosmetic surgery, women leave their children and choose to travel to rich countries, and women are making their own choices to be with "sugar daddies." Of course, some women make "choices" like these. However, other women do not make choices in conditions of their own making. To relegate such decisions to the discourse of freedom to purchase any apartment of choice, clothes, and get loans oversimplifies the political exigencies of female empowerment in African contexts.

Describing "flexible citizenship," Ong (1999) stated that in their quest to accumulate capital and social prestige, subjects emphasize, and are regulated by, practices favoring flexibility, mobility, and repositioning in relation to markets, governments, and cultural regimes. The use of hybridity allows the characters flexibility and ambiguity to oscillate between foreign and local, permitting postfeminist discourses of individualism, sexual subjectification, and consumerism to be center stage. The characters are able to represent notions of the new African woman in relation to the old African woman who is traditional and unchanging, using patriarchy as the cultural backdrop. Thus, the representation of hybridity through the characters as returnees who are both local and global shows how their bodies oscillate between global and local forms of women empowerment. In this context, forms of Western feminism are characterized as necessary for African women empowerment in the global economy. However, such feminist moves should be deployed or work in tandem with African patriarchal structures in order not to threaten masculine hegemony. Imelda Whelehan (2000) noted that contemporary postfeminist discourses are often characterized by "retrosexism," the fear of the collapse of masculine hegemony. To end this chapter, we revisit McRobbie's (2004) concerns that current characteristic of contemporary representations of women empowerment feature entanglements of feminist and anti-feminist ideas within them. Therefore, an analysis of empowerment discourses is necessary to open spaces for alternative worldviews that highlight the differential effects of power relations.

References

Ahlberg, B., & Kulane, A. (2011). Sexual and reproductive health and rights. In S. Tamale (Ed.), *African sexualities: A reader* (pp. 312–329). Nairobi, Kenya. Fahamu/Pambazuka.

Alasuutari, P. (2008). The domestication of worldwide policy models. *Ethnologia Europaea, 39*, 66–74.

Alice, L. (1995). What is postfeminism? Or, having it both ways. In L. Alice (Ed.), *Feminism, postmodernism, postfeminism: Conference proceedings*. Auckland. Massey University.

Ang, I. (2001). *On not speaking Chinese: Living between Asia and the West.* London. Psychology Press.

Arthur, J. A. (2000). *Invisible sojourners: African immigrant diaspora in the United States.* Greenwood Publishing Group.

Appadurai, A. (1996). *Modernity at large: Cultural dimensions of globalization.* Minneapolis: University of Minnesota Press.

Asante, G. (2016). Glocalized whiteness: Sustaining and reproducing whiteness through "skin toning" in post-colonial Ghana. *Journal of International and Intercultural Communication, 9*(2), 87–103.

Bhabha, H. K. (1994). *The location of culture* (Routledge classics; Routledge classics). London: Routledge.

Boyd, L. (2013). The problem with freedom: Homosexuality and human rights in Uganda. *Anthropological Quarterly, 86*(3), 697–724.

Budgeon, S. (2001). Emergent feminist(?) identities: Young women and the practice of micropolitics. *European Journal of Women's Studies, 8*, 7–28.

Budgeon, S. (2011). *Third wave feminism and the politics of gender in late modernity.* London: Palgrave-Macmillan.

Canclini, N. G. (2005). *Hybrid cultures: Strategies for entering and leaving modernity.* U of Minnesota Press.

Chávez, K. R. (2013). Pushing boundaries: Queer intercultural communication. *Journal of International and Intercultural Communication, 6*(2), 83–95.

Cole, C. M., Manuh, T., & Miescher, S. (2007). *Africa after gender?* Bloomington, IN: Indiana University Press.

Englund, H. (2006). *Prisoners of freedom: Human rights and the African poor.* Berkeley, CA: University of California Press.

Gill, R. (2006). *Gender and the media.* Cambridge: Polity Press.

Gill, R. (2007). Postfeminist media culture: Elements of a sensibility. *European Journal of Cultural Studies, 10,* 147–166. doi:10.1177/1367549407075898

Gillis, S., & Munford, R. (2004). Genealogies and generations: The politics and praxis of third wave feminism. *Women's History Review, 13,* 165–182.

Grewal, I., & Kaplan, C. (1994). *Scattered hegemonies: Postmodernity and transnational feminist practices.* Minneapolis, MN: University of Minnesota Press.

Hall, S. (Ed.). (1997). *Representation: Cultural representations and signifying practices* (Vol. 2). Sage.

Hall, S. (Ed.). (1996). *Modernity: An introduction to modern societies.* Blackwell Publishing.

Hansen, A., Cottle, S., Negrine, R.,& Newbold, C. (1998). Content analysis. In A. Hansen, S. Cottle, R. Negrine, et al. (Eds.), *Mass communication research methods* (pp. 91–129). New York: New York University Press.

Harvey, D. (2005). *NeoLiberalism: A brief history.* London. Oxford University Press.

Hawkesworth, M. (2004). The semiotics of premature burial: Feminism in a postfeminist age. *Signs, 29,* 961–985.

Hollows, J. (2000). *Feminism, femininity, and popular culture.* New York: Manchester University Press.

Hong, G. K., & Ferguson, R. A. (Eds.). (2011). *Strange affinities: The gender and sexual politics of comparative racialization.* Duke University Press.

hooks, b. (2012). Feminist politics: Where we stand. In S. Shaw & J. Lee (Eds.), *Women's voices, feminist visions: Classic and contemporary readings* (pp. 33–36). New York: McGraw Hill.

Hsieh, H., & Shannon, S. (2005). Three approaches to qualitative content analysis. *Qualitative Health Research, 15,* 1277–1288.

Johnson, B. (2013). Global issue affecting women poverty. www.globalissues.org

Joseph, M. (1999). Introduction: New hybrid identities and performance. In M. Joseph & J. N. Fink, (Eds.), *Performing hybridity* (pp. 1–24). Minneapolis. University of Minnesota Press.

Kolar-Panov, D. (1996). Video and the diasporic imagination of selfhood: A case study of the Croatians in Australia. *Cultural Studies, 10*(2), 288–314.

Kraidy, M. M. (2002). Hybridity in cultural globalization. *Communication Theory, 12*(3), 316–339.

Levine, E. (2008). Remaking Charlie's angels: The construction of post-feminist hegemony. *Feminist Media Studies, 8,* 375–389.

Lorde, A. (2003). The master's tools will never dismantle the master's house. *Feminist Postcolonial Theory: A Reader, 25,* 27.

Lotz, A. (2001). Postfeminist television criticism: Rehabilitating critical terms and identifying postfeminist attributes. *Feminist Media Studies, 1,* 105–121.

McRobbie, A. (2004). Post-feminism and popular culture. *Feminist Media Studies, 4,* 255–264.

Mikell, G. (1997). *African feminism: The politics of survival in sub-Saharan Africa.* Philadelphia: University of Pennsylvania Press.

Mohanty, C. T. (1988). Under Western eyes: Feminist scholarship and colonial discourses. *Feminist Review,* (30), 61–88.

Moseley, R., & Read, J. (2002). Have it ally: Popular television and postfeminism. *Feminist Media Studies, 2,* 231–250.

Ong, A. (1999). *Flexible citizenship: The cultural logics of transnationality.* Durham, NC. Duke University Press.

Piot, C. (2010). *Nostalgia for the future: West Africa after the Cold War.* Chicago, IL: University of Chicago Press.

Prendergast, C. (2000). *The triangle of representation.* New York: Columbia University Press.

Robinson, P. (2011). Mobilizing postfeminism: Young Australian women discuss sex and the city and desperate housewives. *Continuum: Journal of Media and Cultural Studies, 25,* 111–124.

Scharff, C., & Gill, R. (2011). *New Femininities: Postfeminism, Neoliberalism and Subjectivity.* London. Palgrave Macmillan.

Shome, R., & Hegde, R. (2002). Culture, communication, and the challenge of globalization. *Critical Studies in Media Communication, 19*(2), 172–189.

Shome, R. (2014). *Diana and beyond: White femininity, national identity, and contemporary media culture.* Urbana, IL: University of Illinois Press.

Smith, A. (2012). Dismantling hierarchy, queering society. In S. Shaw & J. Lee (Eds.), *Women's voices, feminist visions: Classic and contemporary readings* (pp. 205–207). New York: McGraw Hill.

Tamale, S. (2011). *African sexualities: A reader.* Oxford: Pambazuka Press.

Van Zoonen, L. (1994). *Feminist media studies.* London: SAGE.

Whelehan, I. (2000). *Overloaded: Popular culture and the future of feminism.* London: Women's Press.

Williamson, J. (2003). Sexism with an alibi. The Guardian, Supposedly ironic, even kitsch, ads still keep women in their place. 42 Retrieved from www.theguardian.com/media/2003/may/31/advertising.commen

5 Walking through Wakanda

A Critical Multimodal Analysis of Afrofuturism in the Black Panther Comic Book

Christopher Brown, Brandon McCasland, Mandy Paris, and Sachi Sekimoto

The revival of the *Black Panther* comic book written by African American National Book Award winner Ta-Nehisi Coates and illustrated by African American cover artist Brian Stelfreeze generated much excitement in the first week of its massive launch by Marvel Entertainment. Created by Stan Lee and Jack Kirby, the *Black Panther* appeared in 1966 as the first mainstream Black superhero. The release of Coates' version, *Black Panther: A Nation Under Our Feet*, was a bestseller and received excellent reviews from a variety of news outlets. Having Black writers and artists who use popular culture texts such as a comic book as a medium to provide social and political commentary comes at an important time with heightened racial tensions and divides in policing, immigration, and the criminal justice system. Several scholars have already studied comics to provide attention to their political, cultural, and ideological meanings (DiPaolo, 2011; McCloud, 1993; Meskin, 2007; Skidmore & Skidmore, 1983; Veloso & Bateman, 2013). Yet, it is rare that researchers focus on the use of science fiction tropes and motifs in the comic renderings of Black writers and artists who critique the impact of dominant White institutions. In this study, we will examine how Coates and Stelfreeze carve out an imaginative and speculative space of diasporic belonging—a world reimagined through artistic multimodalities as a place for and of Black subjects.

Coates' storyline focuses on T'Challa (the Black Panther) who confronts the powerful terrorist group from the neighboring fictional nation of Niganda, referred to as The People. The comic book begins with T'Challa returning to a series of chaotic events in his home country of Wakanda. Wakanda is a fictional East African country, south of Uganda and just west of Nyanza, a Kenyan province. This country is ruled by a monarchy and is the most technologically advanced nation on Earth because of its abundance of Vibranium, a valuable, extraterrestrial metal that absorbs vibrations. T'Challa's sister, Shuri, died while serving as Wakanda's queen, leaving their stepmother Ramonda as queen. Upon his return to Wakanda, T'Challa finds a restless nation on the brink of an uprising led by a woman named Zenzi, who has the power to control minds, and a shaman named Tetu, who has the power to control Mother Nature. During this time, the women from the kingdom's elite female guard, the Dora Milaje, rejected the Wakandan government after it had failed to protect them from corrupt tribal leaders who physically and sexually assaulted them. Through it all, T'Challa must consider the role that strength and force play as he strives to be a better leader for his people.

In this chapter, we use Afrofuturism as a theoretical lens to provide a critical multimodal analysis of visual and textual meanings in Coates' superhero comic book. In doing so, the following questions will guide our theorizing and analysis: how do multiple artistic modalities of the Black Panther—images, colors, words, and sequences—construct the Afrofuturistic world of Wakanda? In what ways do these constructions come together to produce a form of speculative fiction rooted in Pan-African identity?

Through the multimodal analysis of this visually rich text, we illustrate how the Afrofuturistic narrative of the *Black Panther* series by Coates and Stelfreeze intertwine multiple spatiotemporal layers—the past, present, and future—that speak metaphorically about the present-day racial and gender politics. Furthermore, the Afrofuturistic narrative resonates with, and feeds into, the diasporic identification with and yearning for "home." Taken together, we conclude that *Black Panther* as an Afrofuturistic cultural expression functions as a narrative of 'what ifs,' portraying an imagined past of a fictional African nation free from colonization and enslavement by the West, and a possible future where the residents of Wakanda struggle towards their self-determination and liberation—while simultaneously demonstrating the inescapability of colonial impact on the diasporic imagination.

In what follows, we first establish the notion of Afrofuturism in its conceptual origin as well as popular cultural manifestations in the context of African Diaspora. Second, we discuss the visual metaphor as a concept that informs our analysis. After briefly explaining the multimodal process of reading comics, we provide our analysis and conclusion.

The Impact of Afrofuturism on the African Diaspora

Afrofuturist studies draw attention to science fiction themes and techniques in the work of Black authors and artists. Dery (1994) coined the term *Afrofuturism* to describe speculative fictional storytelling that addresses African American concerns and encompasses a Black aesthetic of a diverse range of artists who share interests in projecting the future through Afrodiasporic experiences rooted in the displacement of people from Africa during the slave trade and the development of new identities imposed on people of African descent. For example, Yaszek (2006) argued that Ralph Ellison's *Invisible Man* engages in an Afrofuturistic critique by using science fiction motifs that demonstrate the strategies and tactics used by White American institutions to erase Black history and culture from future imaginaries—or even challenging the notion of a color-blind future. The Afrodiasporic experience, therefore, insists on an authenticity of Black subjectivity in Western cultures and brings attention to the historical and cultural dislocation felt by people of African descent (Yaszek, 2006). For an Afrofuturist, time is a fluid rather than linear concept. Womack (2013) viewed Afrofuturism as a way of projecting the future through alternate realities and possibilities of Black cultural expressions encompassing both African diaspora and those still on the African continent. Nelson and Miller (2006) explained that Afrofuturist scholars explore futuristic themes combining realist and speculative modes of storytelling through technological innovations in Black art and culture. Afrofuturism disrupts the notion that a digital divide exists between Blacks and Whites, as Black Afrofuturists have mastered ongoing technological advancements (Elia, 2014). The aesthetic mission of an Afrofuturist is to restore people of the African diaspora in the future imaginary by fusing ancient African cosmology and spirituality with space-age technological advancements (Womack, 2013; Yaszek, 2006).

Afrofuturist artists also project Black future in writing and visual art by combining the narratives and motifs of science fiction with an Afrodiasporic perspective. Hence, Afrofuturism is very much connected to mainstream popular culture via the world of art, entertainment, and fashion. La Ferla (2016) stated that the visual metaphor of empowerment is evident in Afrofuturistic themes underscored in loosely tribal motifs, android-like figures, and regal self-portraits with a futuristic edge in the writings of contemporary Black people like Octavia Butler and Kodowo Eshun and in performances of recording artists like Sun Ra, Beyoncé, Maxwell, and Missy Elliot. Music performers and artists incorporate Afrofuturistic epic imagery and themes in their performances to project Black heroism and empowerment into fantasy-like landscapes. For example, P-Funk legend George Clinton used sci-fi themes in performing the alter ego of an alien called "Starchild," who came down from the mothership to bring funk to the Planet Earth. Similarly, singer Janelle Monáe often displays the flamboyant, android-like, fiery figure in her energetic and fluid musical and dance performances. Erykah Badu also popularized Afrofuturist aesthetics and philosophies of an uncertain future in her music video "Didn't cha know" while outfitted in a futuristic exoskeleton. In essence, Afrofuturism liberates Black people to reimagine and reconstitute their subjectivity through the intersection of the mystical past and futuristic figures and technology.

Visual Metaphor and Afrofuturism

Lakoff and Johnson (1980) posited that metaphors function by allowing one to experience and understand one thing in terms of another.

They also posited that metaphors are not only a poetic way of using an abstract term to represent something literal, but they also are products of thought and action. In other words, human thought processes are metaphorical and connected to our bodily sensorimotor experiences with various entities in the world (Frosh, 2011). Still, communication scholars predominantly examine verbal dimensions of metaphors, leaving out visual dimensions (Arnett, 2001; Brown, 2009; McMillian & Cheney, 1996; Napoli, 1999; Santa Ana, 1999). Therefore, scholars must pay close attention to how visual metaphors function to fuse separate entities that are spatially bounded and produce metaphorical thought and action often expressed in interrelated verbal and visual signs (Bounegru & Forceville, 2011; El Refaie, 2003).

Visual metaphors are images that are abstractly associated with a particular idea or belief. Many studies explored visual metaphors in different genres such as film (Carroll, 1996), cartoons (Bounegru & Forceville, 2011; El Refaie, 2003), photographs (Edwards & Winkler, 1997), politics (Frosh, 2011), comics (Cohn, 2013), and advertising (Forceville, 1996). Scholars of visual communication believe a visual mode can prompt similar complex symbolic meanings as verbal language, albeit differently (Barnhurst, Vari, & Rodriguez, 2004; Frosh, 2011). Multimodality is an approach through which communication is more than about verbal language, but it also includes other elements that people use to communicate such as images, gestures, and gaze (Jewitt, 2009; Sekimoto, 2011). A metaphor is multimodal if the target and source domain are seen in both the verbal and visual model (Bounegru & Forceville, 2011). As E. H. Gombrich (as cited in El Refaie, 2003) once asserted, a metaphor is a "main weapon in the cartoonist's armory [*sic*]" (p. 77). Comics, therefore, are a multimodal medium, drawing on several modes/modalities including thought bubbles, color, font size, nonverbal expressions, shading, and word choice through which visual metaphors manifest. More specifically, we examine how the *Black Panther* comic book produced visual metaphors of Afrofuturistic expression traced to Afrodiasporic experiences of people of African descent.

A Multimodal Reading of Comic Books

Cohn (2013) described "comics" as a network of ideas consisting of themes, characters, readership, history, and other cultural elements. Comic artists use sequential images and/or written language to tell stories that express a variety of symbolic and literal meanings. Comic scholars, who view comic strips as objects of inquiry and study the semiotics of its art form, consider comic artists and their readers as co creators of meaning-making (El Refaie, 2009). These scholars wish to eliminate associations of comic books with trivial fantasy and silly, childlike humor (Cohn, 2013; El Refaie, 2012; McCloud, 1993). In fact, a growing number of comic scholars explore the impact of political and social messages within comic strips. For example, communication scholars, specifically theorists and researchers in political and visual communication, examine the use of visual tropes and imagery in contemporary political and social processes (Barnhurst et al., 2004; Edwards & Winkler, 1997; Frosh, 2011; Griffin, 2001).

While scholars of visual culture focus on interpretation of symbolic meanings within a given text, they increasingly provide critical understandings to visual modes of expression (Barnhurst et al., 2004; Edwards & Winkler, 1997; Eisner, 1985; McCloud, 1993). In fact, McCloud (1993) argued that comics are "juxtaposed [with] pictorial and other images in deliberate sequence, intended to convey information and/ or to produce an aesthetic response in the viewer" (p. 9). Eisner (1985), therefore, suggested that to analyze comics we have to understand them as a literary form with their own grammar, and we must break this grammar down into potential modes of thought and action.

Both Eisner (1985) and McCloud (1993) provide a vocabulary for analyzing visual and graphic elements of comics. McCloud (1993) argued that comics are comprised of multiple modes of art working in concert across static frames. Comic art forms convey meanings such as motion, direction, emotion, interaction, and speed across sequences of comic panels (Veloso & Bateman, 2013). These meanings complement modes of analysis which include imagery, timing, expressive anatomy, gutters, writing, iconography, and even the material on which the comic is printed (Eisner, 1985). In this analysis, first, timing is important in the *Black Panther* comic book; we view single and interrelated comic panels as moments frozen in time (McCloud, 1993). Second, we examine visual imagery in each comic panel, including the use of symbols, color, facial expressions, posture, and thought bubbles (Eisner, 1985). Third, we interpret how these multimodalities influence how the comic is read through an Afrofuturistic lens. A critical multimodal analysis of Afrofuturistic dimensions of the *Black Panther* comic requires an examination of these modes with particular attention to the relevance of the visual expressions derived from the deliberate juxtaposition of elements in a sequence of comic panels. After completing this analysis, we developed two overarching themes where Afrofuturistic imagery in the *Black Panther* highlights: (1) the Pan-African construction of Wakanda, and (2) a yearning for home in the Afrodiasporic imagination.

Afrofuturistic Imagery and the Pan-African Construction of Wakanda

In this section, we explore the *Black Panther* comic's utilization of visual modes that draw upon a Pan-African identity, an identity that makes multiple spatial and temporal references to African cultures. Coates and

Stelfreeze use popularized imagery of African culture that complicates and, at times, reifies stereotypical notions of "Africa." In this theme, we analyze 12 panels that set the scene for the imminent rebellion of former loyalists to the Wakanda monarchy as well as demonstrate the political hierarchy of Wakanda. We will isolate images that juxtapose the spatial and temporal iconography of Africa through which Coates and Stelfreeze co-create meanings about the multimodal Afrofuturistic world of Wakanda. In this case, they fuse various Pan-African visual cues with the artistic modalities of an Afrofuturistic city that simultaneously reimagines a world inhabited and controlled by Black people and prompts homogenizing and exoticizing discourses of Africa.

In the first scene after T'Challa encountered disillusioned people at the Great Mound, Coates and Stelfreeze take the reader to a large circular room within the Golden City, the capital of Wakanda. As an Afrofuturistic motif, the room is gold with an ornate triangular design and a long, narrow window overlooking the Golden City's skyline. Here, an all-important and powerful figure stands in the foreground wearing a floor-length black robe with bold purple linework, signifying her status and power. While facing away from the reader, the figure, the Queen Ramonda (T'Challa's stepmother), is the largest person in the frame. "Ramonda" is a Spanish name meaning protector or counselor. She stands and looks towards the center of the room where two of the cadre of royal guards stand, dressed in full-body black and blue uniforms with small woven headbands wrapped around black headscarves—visually similar to a keffiyeh. The guards wear headwear that might remind readers of Ancient Egyptian headdress. One guard stands and holds a chain that wraps around the neck of a female prisoner, Aneka, who kneels in an orange jumpsuit. The orange jumpsuit resembles U.S. prison garb, eliciting the African diasporic condition where Blackness is contained through literal and metaphorical shackles. Aneka has been found guilty and sentenced to death for killing the tribal Chieftain. The other guard stands upright, seemingly stoic, over Aneka and holds a spear resembling those held by an Ancient Egyptian guard. At the far side of the room stands another woman, Ayo, who defends Aneka by explaining that the tribal Chieftain abused other women and deserved to die. Ayo is a Nigerian name meaning joy or happiness. She wears a white and blue tunic, black pants, and simple tan shoes. She is bald, except for a long ponytail. Queen Ramonda and Ayo visually fuse images of the past, present, and future. Their clothing and hairstyles represent a blend of tribal fashion and modern apparel along with the vibrant, futuristic patterns on Ayo's scalp and Queen Ramonda's robes. Ayo's scalp is decorated with a fuchsia pattern resembling futuristic circuitry—very much like the purple lines on the robe of Queen Ramonda.

Through these illustrations, Coates and Stelfreeze fuse multiple spatial and temporal references to African history and cultures using familiar imagery to communicate the strength of the Wakandan monarchy to the comic's Western audience. In developing this fictional world, they also demonstrate Wakanda's Afrofuturistic motifs of technological advancements and wealth through the metallic skyline, the use of kimoyo bands to project video recordings, the polished and pristine floors, as well as the circuit-decorated robe worn by Queen Ramonda. Within some of these panels, the colors that reflect the Western conception of African landscapes as primarily desert—tans, browns, mud reds, and a little green—juxtaposed with cooler tones such as light blue and gray in the metallic skyline. In another panel frame, in the metallic skyline, we observe T'Challa riding an Afrofuturistic birdlike aircraft with blue metal blades which look like outstretched feathers and with blades positioned around two large drone-like circular pieces of metal, which sit in the same place as an aircraft's wings. The aircrafts' futuristic technology, represented through the birdlike image, still connotes Western associations of Africa with nature and large, exotic animals. The Pan-African world of Wakanda is carefully constructed through multiple visual elements that speak to popularized (and stereotyped) imagery of traditional "Africa," while simultaneously invoking the current state of Black racial struggle for liberation as well as transcending the material reality of Africa and Black America through hyper-futuristic spatial and temporal representations.

In the next sequence of panels, Ayo steals two Midnight Angel armor suits and breaks Aneka out of the prison cells of Fort Hahn. They both renounce the Dora Milaje and vow to take down the Wakandan monarchy. As the scene commences, they stand together wearing the high-tech Midnight Angel suit of armor—a superhero armor that is fully metal with strong angles which maintains midriffs exposed under mesh netting. This Afrofuturistic armor has what appears to be metal breastplates, knee-high boots, and elbow-length gloves, while their heads are covered with metal helmets that hide their eyes and face. In some ways, their uniforms reference African Nguni tribal practices, as they wear gold neck rings usually worn by married women of the South African Ndebele and typically associated with fashionably elongating the neck. Ayo's helmet has one thick tentacle-esque wire which holds her ponytail, while Aneka's helmet is draped with thick cloth cut to look like dreadlocks or braids. Some of the cloths have been pulled back into a ponytail, and others rest down past her shoulders like a headdress. They also wear long one-piece loincloths that drape around their hips and cover their groin. The loincloths resemble those worn primarily by South African Bushmen who cover their genitals while living in places where temperatures are unreasonably high. But, Ayo and Aneka's loincloths appear to subvert the gendered associations of this cloth. Ayo and Aneka, who are both lesbians in powerful—and probably heavy—metal uniforms, become vigilantes against gender violence while challenging perceived Western stereotypes of African women as only maternal figures. Ayo and Aneka are mainly distinguishable by their long staves. Aneka's stave is fashioned like a trident and Ayo's is topped by a smooth, bulbous jewel. This imagery shows that Wakanda exists both within and beyond the Western conceptualization of African countries and people. The use of clothing, landscape, technology, and architecture in the comic all draw upon elements of Pan-African cultures familiar to the Western audience; yet combined with advanced technologies and alien-like visual cues, the reader experiences the Afrofuturistic world of Wakanda as something that transcends and fundamentally reimagines the world lived by Black subjects.

Afrofuturistic Temporality: African Diasporic Yearning for a Metaphorical "Home"

Eisner (1985) stated that comics emphasize the arrangement of pictures and images in which a scene tells a story about a particular moment depicted in the comic panels. Eisner also argued that the rhythm or pace of stories within comics represent movements in time. In this theme of the *Black Panther* comic, there are four key scenes made up of 25 panels forming correspond to a visual metaphor that symbolizes the passage of time in terms of movement through space with the past behind us and the present and future before us. Every panel within this narrative of temporarily enters a relationship with each other. In Coates' version of the *Black Panther*, the rhythms and intersections of time and space are visible in a sequence of panels representing the aesthetic and technical modes of Black cultural motifs of Afrofuturism. Coates' writings combined with Stelfreeze's illustrations underscore tropes of science fiction and Black cultural production demonstrated in Afrofuturistic storytelling. Coates and Stelfreeze weave together a mystical storyline and imagery that fuse the Afrofuturistic worldview with a sense of nostalgia or yearning for the sense of home rooted in the connection with the past and Mother Earth.

For example, T'Challa went to mourn the death of his sister Shuri, the princess of Wakanda, whose body is preserved in Necropolis—the city of the dead. As T'Challa arrives, we see how Coates and Stelfreeze rely on Afrofuturistic imagery to play with supernatural elements of time which speak of Shuri's journey to power. First, Shuri's body is encircled by a barrier and suspended in midair. A bright yellow light shines behind her and on the body of T'Challa, who regretfully holds his head down before her. Visually, Shuri's wardrobe resembles the android-like and loosely tribal motifs of Afrofuturistic code. Shuri's dark muscular skin is exposed as she wears only a bead-like chain around her neck, large white cuffs around her wrist, and a circular object reminiscent of Batman's utility belt situated around her waist and held up by her muscular thighs and hips. Although she is presumably dead, Shuri opens one eye as T'Challa leaves signifying that, in fact, she resides in a liminal space of life and death. In the next sequence of panels, Coates and Stelfreeze demonstrate Afrofuturist tenets of nonlinear temporality by manipulating time and space in moving from the present technical society to African pasts. In this scene, Shuri's Afrofuturistic attire suddenly disappears. She is seated in a meditative state while adorning a white long sleeve shirt and white loose-fitting legwear. Her entire body is now covered. Shuri is in a dream state or cosmic space where she meets an elderly woman who looks like the Queen mother. When we turn the page, we see the panel titled, the *Djalia: The Plane of Wakandan Memory*. In this panel, Shuri sits side-by-side on top of a large rock with elderly woman at the land. Shuri, unaware of her own passage through time, asks the woman "where are we?" The elderly woman gestures forward with her hand and replies "home!" From an Afrofuturistic lens, home appears to be more exemplary and peaceful, a striking contrast from the sci-fi-like technical societies in present-day Wakanda. Home represents a transcendent plane, a replica of the massive and beautiful subtropical regions of places in Africa, with its large savannas, green trees, and still waters underscored in the past collective memories of Wakanda.

As we turn the page, we are brought to another flashback in a sequence of panels titled the *Alkama fields*. In this scene, Tetu stands in the Alkama fields wearing African headgear. Tetu has magical powers to unite with Mother Nature and command her to act according to his will. In this scene, Coates positions Tetu as the voice of the spirit of the Earth, lamenting the plunder of African land by technological advancements. As Tetu walks through the desert-like Alkama fields, he lends an Afrofuturistic voice in thought bubbles that speak nostalgically about the African land—"the sun that woke me up green at dawn, wind [that] combed the branches of my hair, and the rain that washed my limbs." These nostalgic claims function not only to reference the conceptual metaphor of home, but also as a way of revisiting the past to cope with the voids created by the postindustrial and colonialist malaise of Wakanda. In other thought bubbles, Tetu uses the metaphor of "flesh" as a signification of the people who ravaged and stripped of the African land of its natural resources—the flesh "cuts me down and enslaves my limbs, burn[s] me up in flames, listens no more the voice of spirts talking through my limbs." Accordingly, in a sequence of panels, Stelfreeze creates representations of the "flesh" in Afrofuturistic, android-like robotic warriors and sci-fi mutants who launch fire from their hands. The technologically advanced Afrofuturist warriors set fire to the land, killed defenseless and unarmed Black citizenry, and set fire to Natives wearing feathered headdresses. As Tetu tells the story of the destruction of the African land through voice of the Earth, he dances ceremoniously in a sequence of panel while a blue smoke rises and a white, patterned symbolic image appears under his feet signifying his deep connection to Mother Nature.

After a few subplots where T'Challa speaks with the Queen Ramonda about recent defeats and his visions of Shuri, and where Aneka and Ayo plot to form an army, Coates and Stelfreeze, again, emphasize the nonlinear temporality of Afrofuturism as they take the reader from the present to the Djalia, where the soul of Shuri stands amid the forest with the elderly woman. In this moment, we observe the sci-fi themes of Afrofuturism as a bright light shines on the entire body of the elderly woman. The elderly woman reveals herself as the Griot of the Djalia—the caretaker of Wakandan history that has been lost to the "acolytes of machine, and prophets of this Metal Age." This underscores Afrofuturistic discourse in bemoaning the loss of Black culture and history to forms of domination—in this case, the technocrats of postindustrial economies. The elderly griot also stated that she was the collection of all her Queen Mothers, and when the Black Order banished her, they were unware of where her soul would appear. The griot further stated that the Black Order was oblivious of the Djalia, unarmed with "the spear," but with "the drum." Bewildered, Shuri asks "what is that, mother?" The griot responds, "The power of memory, daughter. The power of our song." Visually, we suddenly see sci-fi and tribal-like imagery of Afrofuturistic tenets, as the griot's attire magically morphs into the attire of a queen. Also, what seems to be guardians, or an army, of the elderly griot suddenly appear behind her—some stand with arms crossed and others with their hands on their hips. While the guardians wear blue futuristic clothing and headgear, the elderly griot wears futuristic clothing, gold headgear, and holds a long staff that is eclipsed by the light that surrounds her. This Afrofuturistic transformation signifies the power and nobility of the elderly griot. In this scene, home represents the space where Shuri learns of the power of cultural memory and where the elderly griot unabashedly expresses her concerns on the impact of rapidly evolving technologies on the land.

Conclusion

Through the multimodal analysis, we examined how the world of Wakanda comes together as an Afrofuturist cultural production. As a form of speculative fiction rooted in Afrofuturism, the *Black Panther* uses various visual cues and images that invoke Pan-African identities and meanings, while situating its narrative in a hyper-futuristic city and making reference to contemporary social tensions. On the one hand, the use of Pan-African images may invite familiar critique of potential exoticization and monolithic stereotyping of Africa; on the other hand, the fusion of various African cultures reflect the lived condition of Afrodiasporic subjects whose ancestral and cultural roots were lost in the Middle Passage and the subsequent destruction of Black families during slavery. Carrington (2016) argued that "Every cultural form invented by Black people in diaspora...demonstrates complex and potentially liberatory uses of existing cultural forms...[through which] Black subjects have come to emblematize the generative quality of marginality in the popular imagination" (p. 13). The Afrofuturistic and Pan-African construction of the superhero comic carves out a space to reimagine Blackness by reclaiming the past while seizing the future.

This Afrofuturistic tale is also inherently diasporic, tapping into the generative possibility of reimagined past and mythical memory. As the tumultuous state of the nation unfolds in the story, the memory of a peaceful past—uncontaminated by technological advances and rooted in the connection with the natural landscape of home—provides a sense of sanctuary from the ongoing conflict in Wakanda. The depiction of "home" takes place in the Plane of Wakandan memory, a liminal space between life and death. The Wakandan temporality—where the past, present, and future intersect—resonates closely with the diasporic temporality of Black subjectivity. The Black Panther is a tale of "what ifs"—what if Africa was never colonized? What if the transatlantic slave trade never happened? What if Africa controlled its own resources? What if we could return to this imagined past? As a speculative and realist mode of storytelling, the Afrofuturism in Black Panther demonstrates the power of diasporic cultural production to articulate the "what if" of a world lived and controlled by and for Black subjects. Such speculative imagination is "a subversive way of life for Black Americans, who were determined to self-actualize, forge communities, and experience pleasure on their own terms" (Commander, 2017, p. 6). Black artists and writers of the *Black Panther* reclaim ownership over the construction of Black bodies where multimodal cultural and artistic representations intersect with technology, imagination, and empowerment to unveil creative alternatives and surrealist futuristic endeavors. Singers like Rihanna and Solange Knowles and hip-hop artists like André 3000 incorporate futuristic and science fiction themes in their art, revealing hidden and explicit notions of racial and gender liberation. Afrofuturism, thus, inspires Black people to champion and connect with their sense of self. In the *Black Panther*, albeit in conflict, the pain, pleasure, memory, loss, and progress all belong to Black societies—lived and negotiated by Black leaders and citizens. Both visually stunning and narratively complex, Coates and Stelfreeze's speculative imagining of "what if" is a political act of reclaiming Blackness.

References

Arnett, R. (2001). Dialogic civility as pragmatic ethical praxis: An interpersonal metaphor for the public domain. *Communication Theory, 11*, 315–338.

Barnhurst, K. G., Vari, M., & Rodriguez, I. (2004). Mapping visual studies in communication. *Journal of Communication, 54*, 616–644.

Brown, C. (2009). WWW.HATE.COM: White supremacist discourse on the internet and the construction of whiteness ideology. *Howard Journal of Communications, 20,* 189–208. doi:10.1080/10646170902869544

Bounegru, L., & Forceville, C. (2011). Metaphors in editorial cartoons, representing the global financial crisis. *Visual Communication, 10,* 209–229. doi:10.1177/1470357211398446

Carrington, A. M. (2016). *Speculative blackness: The future of face in science fiction.* Minneapolis: University of Minnesota.

Carroll, N. (1996). A note on film metaphor. *Journal of Pragmatics, 26,* 809–822.

Cohn, N. (2013). *The visual language of comics: Introduction to the structure and cognition of sequential images.* London: Bloomsbury.

Commander, M. D. (2017). *Afro-Atlantic flight: Speculative returns and the Black fantastic.* Durham, NC: Duke University.

Dery, M. (1994). Flame wars: The discourse of cyberculture. Durham, NC: Duke University.

DiPaolo, M. (2011). *War, politics, and superheroes. Ethics and propaganda in comics and film.* Jefferson, NC: McFarland & Company, Inc.

Edwards, J. L., & Winkler, C. K. (1997). Representative form and the visual ideograph: The Iwo Jima image in editorial cartoons. *Quarterly Journal of Speech, 83,* 289–310.

Eisner, W. (1985). *Comics and sequential art: Principles and practices from the legendary cartoonist.* New York: W.W. Norton & Company, Inc.

El Refaie, E. (2003). Understanding visual metaphor: The example of newspaper cartoon. *Visual Communication, 2,* 75–95.

El Refaie, E. (2009). Multiliteracies: How readers interpret political cartoons. *Visual Communication, 8,* 181–205. doi:10.1177/1470357209102113

El Refaie, E. (2012). *Autographical comics: Life writing in pictures.* Jackson, MS: University Press Mississippi.

Elia, A. (2014). The languages of Afrofuturism. *Lingue Linguaggi, 12,* 83–96.

Forceville, C. (1996). *Pictorial metaphor in advertising.* London: Routledge.

Frosh, P. (2011). Framing pictures, picturing frames: Visual metaphors in political communication research. *Journal of Communication Inquiry, 35,* 91–114.

Griffin, M. (2001). Camera as witness, image as sign: The study of visual communication in communication research. *Communication Yearbook, 24,* 432–463.

Jewitt, C. (2009). An introduction to multimodality. In C. Jewitt (Ed.), *The Routledge handbook of multimodal analysis* (pp. 14–27). London: Routledge.

La Ferla, R. (2016). Afrofuturism: The next generation. *New York Times.* Retrieved from www.nytimes.com/2016/12/12/fashion/afrofuturism-the-next-generation.html?_r=0

Lakoff, G., & Johnson, M. (1980). Metaphors we live by. Chicago, IL: University of Chicago.

McCloud, S. (1993). *Understanding comics: The invisible art.* New York: HarperCollins Publishers.

McMillian, J. J., & Cheney, G. (1996). The student as consumer: The implications and limitations of a metaphor. *Communication Education, 45,* 1–15.

Meskin, A. (2007). Defining comics? *Journal of Aesthetics and Art Criticism, 65,* 369–379. doi: 10.111/j.1540-594X.2007.00270.x

Napoli, P. (1999). The marketplace of ideas metaphor in communications regulation. *Journal of Communication, 49,* 151–169.

Nelson, A., & Miller, P. (2006). About Afrofuturism. *Afrofuturism.* Retrieved from www.afrofuturism.ent/text/about.html.

Santa, Ana, O. (1999). Like an animal I was treated: Anti-immigrant metaphor in US public discourse. *Discourse & Society, 10,* 191–224.

Sekimoto, S. (2011). A multimodal approach to identity: Theorizing the self through embodiment, spatiality, and temporality. *Journal of International and Intercultural Communication, 5,* 226–243. doi:10.1080/17513057.2012.689314

Skidmore, M. J., & Skidmore, J. (1983). More than mere fantasy: Themes in contemporary comic books. *Journal of Popular Culture, 17,* 83–92.

Veloso, F., & Bateman, J. (2013). The multimodal construction of acceptability: Marvel's civil war comic books and the Patriot Act. *Critical Discourse Studies, 10,* 427–443. doi: 10.1080/17405904.2013.813776

Womack, Y. (2013). *Afrofuturism: The world of black sci-fi and fantasy culture.* Chicago, IL: Lawrence Hill Books.

Yaszek, L. (2006). Afrofuturism, science fiction, and the history of future. *Socialism and Democracy, 20,* 41–60.

Part III

Bridges Across the African Diaspora

6 Stereotyped Representations of African Cultural Values in Black Media

A Critical Analysis

Marquita Marie Gammage and Justin T. Gammage

African-American culture is influenced by the African worldview and, thus, reflects the core of African cultural values (Kambon, 2004; Nobles, 1997). African cultural values are a combination of several central principles that underpin African peoples' cosmological, onto-logical, axiological, and epistemological understanding of the universe while supporting their way of life (Diop, 1974; Kambon, 2004, 2006). According to scholars, these core principles historically have included a deep sense of spirituality; communalism; respect for traditions/elders; and good human relations (Ani, 2003; Kambon, 2004, Nobles, 1975). Hence, people of African descent in the Diaspora, including the United States, manifest these cultural values in their unique cultures despite environmental changes, systems of oppression, and influence from other cultural groups. Moreover, the core values of African culture serve as a survival thrust for African people (Kambon, 2004) and historically have been used to maintain and defend their humanity (Ani, 2003; Kambon, 2004; Nobles, 1997). Therefore, it is not surprising to find illustrations of African/African-American cultural values situated in Black media pro-ductions. However, there exist an overabundance of stereotyped repre-sentations of African culture (Gandy, 1998; Gray, 1995; Parenti, 1992), African-American cultural values, and cultural practices in the media in general (Gandy, 1998; Gray, 1995; Parenti, 1992), particularly in some Black media content (Gammage, 2015). Representations of African cul-tural values in mainstream media have largely cast Africans as uncivi-lized, savage, ignorant, and morally bankrupt. In an attempt to counter these images, Black media productions seek to create a space that more accurately represents Black reality (Bobo, 1995; Fuller, 2010). As such, Black media productions are consistently challenged for questioning the legitimacy of mainstream White media's portrayals of Blackness (Gray, 1995). According to Entman and Rojecki (2000), in order for Black me-dia productions to reach mainstream audiences, they have to appeal to White Americans, which meant creating similar stereotypical portray-als. As a result, some Black media productions mirrored the approach of mainstream White media and its treatment of African cultural values (Fuller, 2010; hooks, 1992) and began to represent African-Americans through a White cultural lens (Means Coleman, 2002).

In contrast to African cultural values, White American cultural values are derived from the Western worldview and emphasize individualism, materialism, dominance/control, aggression, linear thinking, and opposition (Kambon, 2004, 2006). Contemporary Black television dramas and sitcoms rarely make reference to African culture; however, when represented, we argue that it is often hypercritical of African cultural values. That is to say, mainstream media has historically and contemporarily represented African culture as inferior to White culture and not worthy of maintaining (Entman & Rojecki, 2000; Gammage, 2015; Gandy, 1998; Gray, 1995; Parenti, 1992). Despite attempts to create more culturally informed images of African-Americans, majority ownership of television networks makes it difficult for 21st-century Black television shows to eliminate White cultural biases (Gammage, 2015).

In this chapter, we argue that Black-oriented media is juxtaposed between two dueling realities; on one hand, Black-oriented media must meet the audience appeal to reflect images of Blacks that reinforce stereotyped assumptions of Blackness (Entman & Rojecki, 2000; Gandy, 1998; Gray, 1995; Parenti, 1992), while on the other hand, Black-oriented media seeks to highlight the functionality of African-American cultural values (Bobo, 1995; Fuller, 2010). These dueling realities are in direct opposition to each other and can result in a distortion of reality. This dilemma is what W.E.B Du Bois terms double-consciousness (1903, 1999), which refers to individuals and/or groups viewing themselves from a foreign cultural lens. Du Bois (1903) asserts "This double-consciousness, this sense of always looking at one's self through the eyes of others... two souls, two thoughts, two unreconciled strivings, two warring ideals in one dark body whose dogged strength alone keeps it from being torn asunder" (p. 8). When double-consciousness is present in Black-oriented media, both intentional and unintentional misrepresentation are manifested. As a result of this dilemma, some Black television shows have misrepresentation historical African cultural values as outdated and a thing of the past that have no relevance to African-American lifestyles today. In addition, Africans and African-Americans are represented as separated and lacking any connection. For other Black-oriented media, the misrepresentation of African cultural values or the lack of reference to Africa illustrate a denial of the significance of African cultural values in the everyday lives of African-Americans. These misguided representations of African culture do not take into consideration the historical, social, cultural, or contemporary role of African cultural values in the lives, religion, language, and lifestyles of African-Americans. This chapter will first provide a brief overview of how African-Americans have been stereotyped in the media. Second, a critical analysis of modern television shows including *Black-ish, Empire, Greenleaf,* and *Survivors Remorse* are discussed to demonstrate Black media's stereotyped representation of African cultures, values, and practices. These shows were selected because they are currently leading programs, focused on the Black family, which is argued to be the central hub for maintaining cultural practices (Nobles, 1997). These shows were also selected because they either make direct reference to an African cultural practice or they display some level of African cultural practices. Ultimately, we argue that within some Black-orientated television shows, African cultural values are misplaced, distorted, and reflect century-old stereotypes of Africans, which are not aligned with the actual practice of African cultural values in the lives of African-Americans.

Historical Representations of Blacks in Mainstream American Media

The depiction of African-Americans in theatrical performances finds its origins in the mid 19th century in U.S. history. These depictions served as a form of propaganda to ridicule African-Americans and their cultural customs such as music, dance, language, body type, and moral ethics. To serve its social, political, and economic function, Black depictions in media productions, from its inception until now, have had a pointed purpose of presenting African-Americans as nonhuman, childlike buffoons who threaten the principles of American society (Gandy, 1998; Gray, 1995; Parenti, 1992). Some of the early examples of these depictions are found in minstrel shows. Minstrel shows were theatrical performances that exaggerated and racially demonized African-Americans as intellectually and culturally inferior. These productions became extremely popular during the period of the abolitionist movement to challenge the moral argument to abolish slavery. Minstrel shows, which served as a contradictory depiction of the conditions of slavery and of African-Americans as lighthearted, depended on the rigid structure of slavery (Riggs, 1986).

The popularity of T.D. Rice's depiction of the Jim Crow dance is an example of White mainstream media's attack on African cultural values, serving as an indicator of Whites' common belief in African inferiority. Rice's exaggerated depiction of a crippled African-American doing the Jim Crow dance was the birth of Blackface and the beginning of a theatrical trend geared toward maintaining America's racial order. To illustrate the intent of these depictions, we can observe the correlation between the representation of African-Americans and their culture and the shift in the national political climate. Many of the depictions of African-Americans in early American media productions were portrayals of Blacks as childlike beings, satisfied with bondage. These characters made a case for maintaining the institution of slavery and the acceptance of African servitude by African-Americans themselves

(Gray, 1995; Riggs, 1986). However, after the Emancipation Proclamation of 1865, depictions of African-Americans shifted to characters in need of captivity. African-Americans were regularly depicted as brutes, crime-raved, and threats to order. The silent backdrop to the images that represent African-American culture is that they inform people's perspective about African-Americans to garner support for White racial privilege and institutional racism. Later, media images of Black life began to expand characters of African-Americans to generate a more extensive attack on African-Americans and African cultural values.

Following the minstrel show, the White dominated media industry developed Black characters to depict the stereotyped assumptions of African-Americans in American society. By White dominant media industry, we are referring to an industry where White Americans primarily control the production, filming, and distribution of images while centralizing a European cultural analysis of African-American life (Gammage, 2015). Seven central characters have been recycled in the depiction of African-Americans and their cultural customs, namely the mammy, the sambo, the coon, the zip coon, the uncle, the pickaninny, and the brute. Moreover, through these fictional characters, media outlets have been effective in shaping the world's perceptions about people of African descent and their culture. More importantly, and as stated before, they reinforce the principles of white supremacy in that they depict African-Americans through the lenses of white society for the purpose of establishing a need for social and political control.

The mammy character is a depiction of African-American women as defenders of White authority and the system of slavery in the United States. She was seen as subservient to Whites. In addition, she was presented as a direct contradiction of the American notions of a healthy family structure, playing the dominant figure of the Black family, thus deeming African culture backwards within the context of White cultural norms. The Sambo serves as the lighthearted, docile, and apathetic character that represents African-American males and their neglect for social responsibility. The coon character depicts African-Americans as critical of and distrustful of African-Americans. The zip coon served as the dandy and buffoon possessing an inability to adapt to freedom. The uncle character is a depiction of an elder African-American that had contempt for and severe distrust of African-Americans who challenge the status quo. The pickaninny was the young, unkempt, deviant Black child depicted as victims who evoked the feeling that African-Americans were inhuman. The brute was the menace to society that wreaked havoc on White society with violence.

According to Riggs (1986) "America at the turn of the century experienced unprecedented race hatred. Violence, Jim Crow segregation, mob terror became accepted methods of social control. And always to justify such atrocities was the excuse of the animalistic Black brute."

Therefore, media's creation of characters helped to shape public policy regarding race relations. The philosophical foundations of these characters are the root of contemporary depictions of African people and culture. Today, stereotypes of African-Americans have evolved; that is to say, African-Americans are portrayed in modern-day realities but maintain the same inferior cultural characteristics (Gammage, 2015). Contemporary depictions of African-Americans and their culture are new configurations of the old image produced to demonize African people and culture (Fuller 2010; Gammage 2015; hooks 1992). Thus, the depiction of African people and culture by African-Americans can be analyzed as the proverbial Burt Williams, a leading 20th-century Black entertainer, "of Blacks acting out Blackface." We argue that people of African descent, and their cultural values and practices, are either stereotyped, altered, or criticized in Black-oriented programming.

Stereotyping of African Cultural Values in Black Media

As previously stated, it appears that some Black media productions, whether knowingly or unknowingly, mirror the images depicting African cultural values distributed by White mainstream media, promoting the assimilation of Blacks into mainstream White American culture. Moreover, when Black media productions reference African cultures, they are erroneously presented and stereotyped as uncivilized and out of date. For example, the American television sitcom *Black-ish* focuses on the Johnson family, an upper-middle-class African-American family who has assimilated into the American culture. In its pilot episode, designed to capture mass audience appeal, the family is challenged with the decision to maintain their connection to African cultural practices or abandon them for more Americanized customs. During the episode, when Andre Jr. request a Bar Mitzvah, a Jewish ritual for youth coming of age, for his birthday, his father realizes that his son has adopted a foreign culture and has rejected his African heritage (Season 1, Episode 1). To teach his son that he is African and that African culture has value, Andre Johnson Sr. plans an African rites of passage for Andre Jr. in his backyard. Andre Sr. and his son are dressed in African attire and the backyard is decorated with African decor. His father questions, "Andre what is this mess you are doing?" Andre Sr. responds, "this ain't no mess Pop. This is our culture" His father goes on to state, "This ain't our culture, we Black not African. Africans don't even like us." Andre Jr. then asks if he can leave the ceremony, but Andre Sr. refuses to allow him to leave and proceeds, despite his father's dismissal of the legitimacy of the ritual. When his wife, Rainbow, discovers what Dre is doing, she immediately puts an end to his attempted rites of passage and states: "I will not have you running around torturing my son. What was that? What are you wearing? What are you wearing? Whatever issues you are working through, you need to get over them, now." In the end, Andre Jr. is thrown a Hip-Hop Bro Mitzvah. The Johnson family abandons African cultural practices and disconnects African-American culture from African culture. Electing a modified form of a Bar Mitzvah and rejecting an African cultural practice portrays African-Americans as abandoning their cultural heritage and willingly assimilating into White American culture.

To reinforce the notion that African cultural values are inferior, in season 1 episode 3 *Black-ish* explored the topic of culturally appropriate social behaviors. In this episode, Andre Sr. sought to teach his son about the cultural value of communalism. While aiding his son at school, Andre Sr. notices that Andre Jr. failed to nod his head in acknowledgement toward another Black student and his father. The family discusses this matter, and his wife, Rainbow, discusses the lack of relevance of this practice for Andre Jr.'s generation. The lessons of communalism do not end here, however. Andre Sr. also associates the facial expression of men when "a woman with a big butt walks by" as essential cultural practices. The episode is dedicated to Andre Sr. educating his son on what he argues are critical social behaviors for all Black men. For Andre Sr., communalism is simply portrayed as having Black friends. Andre Sr. invites a Black coworker and his son over for dinner, with the hopes of his son gaining a new Black friend. However, his coworker behaves in a manner that Andre Sr. and Rainbow deem inconsiderate. And when his coworker enters Andre's closet and puts on a pair of his shoes, the night is abruptly ended. Andre Sr. informs his son that their guest must go and that "no other Black kids" can come to his house. However, he realizes that his son and his coworker's son have bonded over a love for science. After lessons don't go as expected, Andre Sr. is willing to adjust his understanding of communalism and states that "Nerd is the new Black." In this episode, communalism is represented as a superficial connection to others based on race and nationality. Thus, being African-American automatically makes you a part of the community, unless you violate Andre's personal space. Perhaps, Andre Sr.'s character embodies Western values of individualism and consumerism, which conflicts with African/African-American values. Thus, this conflict is a form double consciousness and therefore results in a stereotyped representation of the African/African-American cultural value of communalism. According to Constantine, Alleyne, Wallace, and Franklin-Jackson (2006), communalism is "having a sense of responsibility for each other and working together for the betterment of their families and community" (p. 150). This form of communalism is not accurately represented in this episode. What is alarming is the limited examples of African cultural practices, such as rites of passages, within Black television shows. Given this shortage, it appears that assimilation is being promoted in Black media productions, while simultaneously advancing racist ideas about the inferiority of African cultures. Therefore, Black media productions must be careful not to inadvertently participate in the promotion of white supremacy and Black inferiority by situating Black life within white cultural norms and practices.

Shifts Away from African Cultural Values in Black Media

While representations of African cultural values in Black media are stereotyped, there still exists a void of African cultural values in Black media. Generally, Black media productions do not make any direct reference to African culture; instead, altered cultural values are presented as the values of Black families and communities. Although there are indirect references sometimes made to values such as kinship, community, and collectivism, we argue that contemporary Black media almost exclusively erase all references and connection to African culture and values. At best, surface-level illustrations of African cultural values have been displayed such as communal living, communal eating, and communal work. However, even these surface level illustrations have made a mockery of African culture by integrating verbal arguments, physical fights, and intense discussions of immorality.

Greenleaf, for example, is an American television drama detailing the lives of the Greenleaf family, who are a Christian family operating a megachurch in Memphis. Upon first introduction, it appears that the family embraces spirituality, kinship, communalism (also known as the extended family network), and cooperative economics. For example, the bulk of the Greenleaf family all live in the same house and work for the family's megachurch. However, within the first few minutes of season 1, episode 1 (2016), it is revealed that the Greenleaf family has modified their practice of communalism. And while the cultural value is not completely absent, this shift is considered an unhealthy deviation away from the authentic cultural value (Kambon, 2004). For instance, the Greenleaf family does not welcome all members into their close kinship. Instead, daughter Grace returns home after 20 years only to attend the funeral of her sister who committed suicide, and Grace is greeted with unwelcoming comments and stares. When Grace and her daughter arrive at the front door of her family home, her father, mother, and uncle come out to greet them. Grace is embraced by her father and receives and gives an unfriendly hello to her uncle. As Grace steps forward to greet her mother, Lady Mae, her mother asks her "promise me, you are not here to sow discord in the fields of my peace?" When the family sits down for dinner, judgment against Grace begins and discord amongst the family erupts. Viewers soon recognize that the Greenleaf family has wedded its spirituality to American capitalism, in that many are primarily concerned with the economic growth and power of the family and church. Furthermore, each individual in the family is committed to advancing their status and position within the family. When Grace discovers troubling information regarding her family and her sister's death, she decides to expose the family and certain family members for their immoral and criminal acts. Within the first season, Grace's niece and daughter experiment with prescription drug abuse; her brother is having an affair with a woman who works for the church; and her sister's husband is questioning his sexuality. Grace works to collect evidence to incriminate her uncle for sexually assaulting young girls in the church, including her now-deceased sister, and soon discovers that funds from her mother's women's organization were used to cover up the assaults. When Grace's father is introduced to the evidence, he shoots his brother-in-law and is arrested. All of these illustrations represent the Black family structure as dysfunctional and immoral. The African cultural values displayed in the behaviors and attitudes of the Greenleaf family are overshadowed by representations of corruption, individualism, and greed, which corrode the family's name and ministry.

Similarly, *Empire*, an American television drama, showcases the life and business of an African-American family, the Lyons. The Lyons own and operate a successful music company that was largely funded by drug money earned by Cookie Lyons, who was incarcerated for her crimes. In season 1, episode 1, Cookie is released from prison and returns home to claim her place as mother to her three sons and leader in the family music business. However, Cookie does not receive the welcoming reception that she expected. She soon realizes that Lucious Lyons, her former husband, has moved on and so have her children. Within the family, competition for stardom and leadership positions the sons against each other, and physical fights and verbal arguments are a normal occurrence amongst the Lyons. However, the dysfunction does not end there, as murder, theft, and corruption are presented as behavior traits of this Black family. And, all of their actions seem to be justified by their pursuit of stardom, wealth, and power. These criminal and capitalistic behavioral traits contradict the African cultural values of kinship, community, unity, and cooperative economics. On the surface, Black television dramas focused on the Black family seemingly embrace African cultural values; however, upon further investigation, we find distortions of African cultural values in Black media. According to Kobi Kambon (2004), any substantial shifts away from the normal cultural practices of a people constitutes a state of unnaturalness. Thus, the cultural values displayed by these Black families mirror stereotyped portrayals of African-Americans while simultaneously representing Black family values and characteristics as a thing of the past.

Hypercriticism of African Cultural Values in Black Media

When African cultural practices are presented in Black media, they are often criticized as being outdated, impractical, and uncivilized. In the few cases where there is a direct reference to African cultural values and practices, those values and practices are dismissed as irrelevant to the contemporary lives of African-Americans. African cultural practices such as customary ceremonies, healing rituals, and spiritual practices have been heavily criticized in Black media, in particular television dramas and comedies. Within the media, these practices are classified as savage and rooted in incompetent cultural structures, and they are largely advocated against.

Criticisms of African culture in the media often start with disapproval of Africans themselves. Take, for instance, in the television comedy *Black-ish*, African cultural practices and even Africans are dismissed as not worthy of African-American engagement. In season 1, episode 3, attempting to connect his son with other Black kids, Andre Sr. and Andre Jr. browse through a social media site looking for Black kids to befriend. When an African kid at his school is identified, Andre Sr. quickly dismisses the kid as unworthy of befriending. Even after Andre Sr. realizes that there are limited Black kids at his son's school, friendship with the African student is not an option. In some ways, this act portrays African-Americans as disconnected from Africans and illustrates a silent condemnation of Africans as different from or inferior to African-Americans. Dividing Africans and African-Americans challenges the notion of a larger racial community operating under the same worldview system. This act then systematically removes the African-American away from Africa and African cultural values, thereby making it acceptable for Black-oriented media to be hypercritical of African cultural practices. Thus, the dismissal of African peoplehood is used to justify and validate the hypercriticism of African cultural values.

In the television drama *Survivor's Remorse*, the Calloway family is represented as achieving the American dream through athletes and the hard work of Cam Calloway, the star basketball player for a professional basketball team. When the mother, Cassie, loses her brother, she goes on a cultural journey to reclaim her heritage and ancestry (season 3, episode 6, 2016). She discovers through a DNA test that her ancestral lineage is connected to a region of Nigeria and attempts to connect with her culture. It must be noted that no ethnic heritage is ever discussed, only reference to the country of Nigeria, which diminishes the value of the multiple cultural groups in Nigeria. Cassie starts by hanging a Nigerian flag in her front yard, which is met with much contention from her daughter Mary Charles. Mary Charles renders several insulting stereotypes of Nigerians. First, she diminishes the meaning behind the colors of the Nigerian flag, stating

> white for the skin of those who conquered us, green for the cash corrupt kings we got in return. The flag should be a blanket. That flag should be an airline ticket representing how to get the fuck out of Nigeria.

And, when Cassie suggest that they go to the best Nigerian restaurant in town, Mary Charles refers to it as a "food mart at a gas station." She then asks her mother if she is also going to "walk around with your titties out?" These stereotyped assessments belittle and disrespect African cultural groups and their cultural practices. Mary Charles' comments also imply that African cultural practices are savage and irrelevant.

Despite Mary Charles' discontent, Cassie goes to the restaurant with her daughter and niece-in-law, Missy. While in the restaurant, Mary Charles continues to insult the cultural practices of African people and dismisses the connection with Africans in the diaspora. Even the owner of the restaurant, Eka, who is Nigerian, jokes about stereotypes of Nigerian people and speaks about the need to assimilate into American culture. Cassie and Eka, along with Mary Charles and Missy, spend the day indoctrinating Cassie into Nigerian customs in Atlanta. At the end, Cassie offers to share in a cultural exchange and invites the woman to experience African-American culture. Cassie offers to hold a birthday party for Eka's daughter. While at the party, Cassie, Mary Charles, and Missy realize that the party is for the celebrating of the young girl's rites of passage, a coming of age celebrations where she will be circumcised. Immediately, Missy begins to attack this practice and refers to it as "ritual mutilation of the female genitalia" where they will "slice that poor girl's clitoris off." Several insults are shouted at Eka, foreign cultural references, such as the World Health Organization, are used to validate Missy's claim that this cultural practice is savage, unethical, and illegal. The argument is made that most Nigerians have "evolved" and no longer participate in this practice. Feminist arguments are also delivered attempting to persuade Eka away from this cultural practice. Yet when Eka challenges these foreign and misguided cultural assessments and challenges the ladies to evaluate why they accept male circumcision and other American practices as an acceptable norm, Eka's position is quickly dismissed. Despite Eka's compelling arguments, Cassie rejects Eka's position and the party is brought to an end. Cassie takes off her African attire, which could convey that while African-Americans are of African heritage, African cultures and practices are no longer relevant or useful in the lives of African-Americans. It should also be noted that this is the first time any direct reference is made to the family's African heritage, and to date no other discussion of African cultural practices exist. It is also noteworthy to point out that while the women criticize and dismiss female circumcision among Africans, the men attend a Jewish party celebrating and applauding male circumcision. What is problematic here is that within this Black-oriented media production, African cultural practices are portrayed as inferior while White cultural practices are acceptable. Both illustrations provided resulted in the same conclusion, that Africans and African-Americans are disconnected and are irrelevant to each other.

Hypercritical assessments of Africans and African cultural practices in the media are often used to invalidate the usefulness of African culture in the lives of African-Americans (hooks, 1992). This illustration demonstrates not only a dismissal of African cultures in Black media productions, but also a devaluing of African cultures in Black art forms. In addition, representations such as these grossly misrepresent the true practices of African people and thereby undermine their authentic value. These representations give credence to the hypercritical assessments of African cultures. Moreover, the purposeful and/or ill-guided negative portrayals of African culture in the media are used to validate the racist stereotypes about African people. Unfortunately, this practice has been adopted in Black-oriented media and further promotes a disconnect between the African and African-American.

Conclusion

Black media productions present an important opportunity for Black media producers to generate authentic and culturally accurate media representations of Africans and African-Americans and their cultural practices (Bobo, 1995; Fuller, 2010). However, media productions of Blacks have largely been produced by non-Blacks and have overly promoted race-based images of Blackness (Gray, 1995), which have set the standard for all media portrayals of Blacks and African culture. Thus, Black media producers have had to operate within a primarily White-dominated and controlled industry that only promotes and reinforces racist depictions of African people and culture. Therefore, while producers have attempted to provide some realistic cultural references, some Black-oriented media have struggled to avoid stereotyped imagery of Africanness (hooks, 1992). We argue that the current representations of Black-oriented media are challenged with finding a balance in how to represent African-Americans and African cultural practices in an authentic form. The current representation may delegitimize the continued presence of African cultural values in the lifestyles and behaviors of African-Americans (Fuller, 2010; hooks, 1992). By stereotypically representing African cultural values as irrelevant or nonexistent, Black media run the risk of endorsing the abandonment of African cultural values (Kambon, 2003). In all four shows discussed here, each Black family deviates from authentic African cultural values and is portrayed as dysfunctional, unhealthy, and incapable of fully assimilating into an American identity, which further validates the racist assumption that African people are inferior and in need of social control (Gammage, 2015; Kambon, 2003).

Black-oriented media must be careful not to fall into the continued cycle of promoting racist ideas about Blackness (Bobo, 1995; Means Coleman, 2002). It is charged with the task of producing more culturally accurate representations that are attune to the historical and contemporary cultural practices of African people throughout the world (Gammage, 2015). In order to do this, Black media producers must find a way to balance the ever-changing cultural realities of people of African descent and not wed themselves to an industry that has been traditionally beholden to White supremacist ideology that seek to undermine the importance of African cultural values in Black lives. A purpose of Black media productions is to produce media that is reflective of Black life experiences; therefore, adopting White or Western interpretations of Blackness makes this mission impossible (hooks, 1992). Furthermore, the attack on African cultural values in the media cannot go uncontested and must be addressed within Black-oriented media. A hopeful trajectory of Black media is to create content that celebrates the ancestral heritage of Black Americans and demonstrates Black Americans' connections to the African continent and their place within the African diaspora.

References

Ani, M. (2003). To Be Afrikan. In B. Gallman, A. Marimba, & L. Williams (Eds.), *To be Afrikan: Essays by Afrikans in the process of Sankofa: Returning to our source of power* (pp. 14–16). Atlanta, GA: M.A.A.T., Inc.

Bobo, J. (1995). *Black women as cultural readers.* New York: Columbia University Press.

Constantine, M. G., Alleyne, V. L., Wallace, B. C., & Franklin-Jackson, D. C. (2006). Africentric cultural values: Their relation to positive mental health in African American adolescent girls. *Journal of Black Psychology, 32*(2), 141–154.

Diop, C. A. (1974). *The African origin of civilization: Myth or reality?* (M. Cook, Trans.). New York: Lawrence Hill. (Original work published in 1955)

DuBois, W. E. B. (1903). *Souls of black folks: Essays and sketches.* Chicago, IL: A.C. McClurg.

DuBois, W. E. B. (1999). *Darkwater: Voices from within the veil.* New York: Dover Publications.

Entman, R. M., & Rojecki, A. (2000). *The black image in the white mind: Media and race in America.* Chicago, IL: University of Chicago Press.

Fuller, J. (2010). Branding blackness on US cable television. *Media, Culture & Society, 32*(2), 285–305.

Gammage, M. M. (2015). *Representations of black women in the media: The damnation of black womanhood.* London: Routledge.

Gandy Jr., O. H. (1998). *Communication and race: A structural perspective.* London: Arnold, 1998.

Gray, H. (1995). *Watching race: Television and the struggle for "Blackness".* Minneapolis: University of Minnesota Press.

hooks, b. (1992). *Black looks: Race and representation.* Boston, MA: South Ends Press.

Kambon, K. K. K. (2003). *Cultural misorientation: The greatest threat to the survival of the black race in the 21st century.* Tallahassee, FL: Nubian Nation Publications.

Kambon, K. K. K. (2004). The worldviews paradigm as the conceptual framework for Africa psychology. In R. L. Jones (Ed.), *Black psychology* (4th ed., pp. 73–92). Hampton, VA: Cobb & Henry.

Kambon, K. K. K. (2006). *Kambon's reader in liberation psychology: Selected works*. Tallahassee, FL: Nubian Nation Publications.

Lederer, R. S. (Producer). (2015). *Empire* [Television Series]. Los Angeles, CA: Fox.

Marks, P. (Producer). (2014). *Survivor's Remorse* [Television Series]. Beverly Hills, CA: Starz.

Means Coleman, R. R. (2002) *Say it loud! African-American audiences, media, and identity*. New York: Routledge.

Nobles, W.W. (1975). African Roots in Black Families: The Social Psychological Dynamics of the Black Family and Its Implications for Nursing Care. In R.N. Dorothy Luckraft (Ed.), *Black awareness: Implications for black patient care*. New York: The American Journal of Nursing Company.

Nobles, W. W. (1997). African American family life: An instrument of culture. In H. Pipes McAdoo (Ed.), *Black families* (3rd ed., pp. 83–93). Thousand Oaks, CA: Sage Publications.

Parenti, M. (1992). *Make-believe media: The politics of entertainment*. New York: St. Martin's Press.

Riggs, M. (Producer), & Riggs, M. (Director). (1986). *Ethnic notions: Black people in white minds* [Motion Picture]. San Francisco: California Newsreel.

Shockley, L. (Producer). (2014). *black-ish* [Television Series]. Los Angeles, CA: ABC.

Van der Meer, G. (Producer). (2016). *Greenleaf* [Television Series]. Atlanta, GA: Own.

7 NollywoodUSA

Opportunities and Challenges in Forging a Pan-African Storytelling and Identity

Adedayo Abah

Producers, directors, and artists who tell the stories of life from the perspectives of Africans and Black diaspora have found themselves attaining great fame and popularity all over sub-Saharan Africa as well as among Black diaspora groups all over the Western hemisphere in recent decades. This is especially the case in countries with high populations of the African diaspora such as the United Kingdom, Canada, the United States, Australia, and many Caribbean nations. These movies have found great reception with their audiences mainly because of the cultural proximity of the storytelling and the multidimensional portrayal of the lives of Africans within the diaspora. This has created a world of film and video filmmaking that is largely outside the purview of the global networks of cultural industries such as Hollywood. However, cultural proximity cannot be seen as an essential quality of culture or audience orientation, but rather a shifting phenomenon in dialectical relation to other cultural forces (Iwabuchi, 2002). In the last four decades, a major cultural industry that has been largely responsible for this new style of storytelling from the perspectives of Africans and the Black diaspora to other Africans and the Black diaspora is Nollywood. Recently, the industry diversified its mode of production to expand to productions made outside of Africa that tell the stories of the Black diaspora outside of its native Nigeria. These cultural products are important components to the evaluation of Black films in the United States.

Nollywood

In relative terms, Nollywood, the Nigerian video-movie industry, is barely known in the global North but is a global force throughout sub-Saharan Africa and the global African diaspora (Miller, 2016). The nearly three decades old $5 billion industry has thrived and is very popular in different countries across sub-Saharan Africa, as well as with huge populations of Africans and its diasporas including the Caribbean nations, Europe, and North America.[1] Nollywood is known for its melodramatic content as well as its mode of production. Tori Arthur, in a 2016 doctoral dissertation, noted, "Nollywood has been on the rise in the last 20 years and shows no sign of slowing down. The film industry makes up five percent of Nigeria's gross domestic product and eleven percent of the country's non-oil exports."[2]

The Nollywood industry has achieved notable fame in its remarkably resilient history mostly due to its unique storytelling styles that represent the lived experiences of most Nigerians, and in some sense, most sub-Saharan Africans, in a non-patronizing or one-dimensional way. The achievements of Nollywood have been chronicled in the work of scholars such as Hayes (2007, 2016), Ogunleye (2003), Okhai (2008), etc. Its popularity among fans in Africa, the Black diaspora, and other races has spun many trade and academic publications, research papers, theses and dissertations, academic conferences, international film festivals, and copious coverage in global trade and general interest newspapers and magazines.[3]

Despite the achievements of Nollywood within African nations and the global African diaspora, scholars have noted Nollywood's exclusion from dominant global media networks (Miller, 2016). Miller noted Nollywood's lack of international and global connection because it is an industry that was mostly forged by hand by individual entrepreneurs through a labyrinth of informal networks but collectively, these informal networks constitute alternate networks that run counter to and under the radar of the dominant global linkages (p. 120). In

> sub-Saharan Africa networks of cultural product distributions, Nollywood movies are both dominant and ubiquitous: practically unavoidable in networks of popular culture in the region and related diaspora circuits. From another perspective, Nollywood is peripheral in the extreme. In the context of global Hollywood, Nollywood, Nigeria, and indeed, most of sub-Saharan Africa are barely considerations.
>
> (p. 150)

Nollywood is, therefore, a cultural industry that is peripheral to dominant networks but central to alternative networks (p. 150). This insinuates that Nollywood is deliberately reliant on informal networks, which makes it inhospitable to global Hollywood, and draws strength from these informal networks. Marina Tolchinsky (2015), an economic policy researcher in sub-Saharan Africa, suggests that the informality of Nollywood is deliberate, and this is what is keeping foreign investors from engaging with the industry.[4]

Transnationalism and Diaspora Filmmaking

Nollywood "is transnational and glocal for one primary reason: its continuous circulation around the globe" (Arthur, 2017, p. 7). The issue of what makes a production transnational in film studies is multifaceted. Films that invest in a shared cultural heritage and/or geopolitical boundary are often called transnational, as are works on diasporic, exilic, and postcolonial cinemas which aim, through its analysis of the cinematic representation of cultural identity, to challenge the western (neocolonial) construct of nation and national culture (Enwezor, 2007; Marks, 2000; Naficy, 2001). Chris Berry and Mary Farquhar propose an understanding of the transnational as a "larger arena connecting difference, so that a variety of regional, national, and local specificities impact upon each other in various types of relationships ranging from synergy to contest' (Berry & Farquhar, 2006, p. 5). Mette Hjort talks about the plurality of film transnationalism by delineating between strong/weak transnationalism and marked/unmarked transnationalism. Under this guideline, a strong transnational film would have a number of particular transnational essentials in the levels of production, distribution, reception, and the cinematic work itself. Similarly, a film would demonstrably have marked transnationalism when the people involved in the making of the film such as the directors, cinematographers, editors, actors, and producers intentionally direct the attention of viewers towards various transnational properties that encourage thinking about transnationalism. This could be achieved through foregrounding in the camerawork or editing as well as a purposeful use of narrative techniques that allow for full development of transnational themes (worldcinematheory.blogspot.com).

However, a film can be made within a national boundary, oriented toward a national audience, but with a strong transnational theme. Kingsley Okoro's *Osuofia in London* (2003) and Kunle Afolayan's *Phone Swap* (2012) would be examples of Nollywood movies that would fit this profile. After all, "modern popular arts have the capacity to transcend geographical, ethnic, and even national boundaries" (Barber, 1987, p. 15).

> Since the early 2000s, numerous Nollywood films have emerged that combine the narrative aesthetics of the affective Nollywood spectacle with the larger budgets, highly stylized special effects, and production values of Western films to create a new territorialized type of globalized and glocalized transnational cinema.
>
> (Arthur, 2017, p. 7)

Many Nollywood films fit the description of transnational or diasporic filmmaking. The 'new Nollywood' segmentation and, subsequently, NollywoodUSA qualify as transnational cinema because they often have the transnational marked themes of the immigrant experience of cultural tensions, the strong marker of transnational places of production, and sometimes, a transnational network of distribution, and purposeful use of narrative technique.

Diasporic cinema, as noted by Ramona Curry

> refers to a set of films or other media works produced by (and often in the first instance for) members of demographic groups and often their descendants who have experienced collective, sometimes forced, migration from their lands of origin to survive in face of ethno-racial, political, or religious discrimination or displacement due to war or other economic necessity.
>
> (Curry, 2016, p. 1)

The fact that a majority of Nollywood movies made abroad have the African diaspora as the intended audience qualifies them as diasporic as well as transnational. In her study of transnational filmmaking, Hoffmann made note of the fact that Nollywood films shot in the United States are shot in urban spaces such as New York, Los Angeles, and Atlanta, all locations with large African immigrant communities. She noted the movies are also transnational because:

> through diasporic filmmaking, immigrant communities become cinematic manifestations of transnational movements of money, labor, goods, media, and people, and the actual city space, with its building, streets, sidewalks, cars, and other symbols of urbanity, is a place where social actors negotiate the relationship between the local and the global (Hoffmann, 2012, p. 121).

Thus, it would seem that Nollywood, specifically 'New Nollywood'—defined as having transnational thematic focus, "higher production values, use of new distribution windows such as satellite TV, streaming video websites, video-on-demand, in-flight entertainment and theatre releases in Africa and the diaspora, a reach out to transnational and metropolitan audiences," (Ryan, 2015, p. 59), and the use of varied shooting location including sites in Europe and United States—would be considered both diasporic and transnational.

NollywoodUSA—In Search of a Definition

NollywoodUSA is part of a collection of Nollywood video-films that some have termed 'New Nollywood' (Ryan, 2015) but remains within the collection of transnational and diasporic films generally known as Nollywood. NollywoodUSA is a relatively new term and refers to a subsection of the 'new Nollywood' category. The term has been sparsely used. To the author's knowledge, Kevin Onuma first used the term to refer to a category of Nollywood films in 2012 in reference to the film *Stolen*. An entry on Wikipedia on the term also uses Onuma's story as a source. The entry described Nollywood USA as a "broad term" used to refer to Nigerian films made in the diaspora by Nigerian filmmakers living in the diaspora and uses established Nollywood actors alongside up and coming African actors living in the diaspora. In another use of the term, Dennen Brown, staff writer for the *Washington Post,* noted, "Nollywood has swept into Cameroon, the Caribbean and Ghana, which calls its industry Ghollywood. Now Nollywood actors and filmmakers have started making movies in the United States. They call it Nollywood USA."[5] Given Brown's statement, Nollywood USA would seem to refer to Nollywood moviemaking styles using imported Nollywood actors but made in the United States. However, this description would not capture the whole story that Brown was trying to tell in her WP article. The movie in question was not just made in the United States using imported continental Nollywood actors, as the movie's cast included Sarodj Bertin, a runway model and former Miss Haiti Universe, and Jimmy Jean-Louis, another Haitian and a veteran Hollywood actor. Jean Louis was also known for his role on the NBC series, "Heroes." (Brown, 2013).

For the purpose of this chapter, a working definition for Nollywood USA is Nollywood-styled movies made in the United States or North America including casts from the continental Nollywood as well as seasoned and new North American actors. *One Night in Vegas*, the film Brown talked about, was shot in Montgomery County, Maryland, USA, directed by John Uche, and produced by Koby Maxwell. The theme of the movie was quintessentially American, and the cast included actors from both continents.

While the concepts of transnational and diasporic films are tethered to the notions of the local, national, and the global, a few of the NollywoodUSA movies appear to be untethering from these notions and appear to display a desire to blend into the fabric of Black independent films in the United States. With a tie to the notions of transnational and diasporic film, the study uses both a narrative structure and a sociological approach/movie genre to examine some recent samples from NollywoodUSA. As an extension of the Nollywood subsection of transnational and diaspora filmmaking, what themes, narrative style, production values, and genre subversion set NollywoodUSA apart from its continental pedigree? In a documentary about the distinguishing elements of Nollywood USA shot on the set of a 2012 movie called *My Angels Yori Babes*, a member of the cast articulated that Nollywood USA is different because "...they tell our stories about being immigrants and all, and our lives in a foreign country. We definitely live a different lifestyle from people in Nigeria, it is different, our lives are about how to survive..."[6]

Another feature of Nollywood USA movies is that while many of the characters are brought in from Africa, they also use a lot of local talents. One of the characters on the *Yori Yori Babes* cast echoed this sentiment when she said:

> ...we use people who have other jobs, they are not just actors, they might be bankers and other things, and they come to the shooting

after work or when they can. This is not like Africa where they just have the one job of being an actor.

The Nollywood USA movies' first line of distribution is usually a theatre premiere and showings in cities with a large presence of African immigrants. After this, they often go to DVD, though some never even make it to DVD.

NollywoodUSA and Black America Independent Film: An Opportunity for More Global Themes?

Oscar Micheaux is often lauded as the father of black filmmakers. But, according to Nsenga Burton (2010), William D. Foster began producing films nearly a decade earlier than Micheaux's first effort. In 1910, Foster, a sports writer for the *Chicago Defender*, formed the *Foster Photoplay Company*, the first independent African-American film company. In 1912, Foster produced and directed *The Railroad Porter*, which paid homage to the Keystone comic chases, while attempting to address the pervasive derogatory stereotypes of Blacks in film (Burton, 2010, p. 1). Similar to the portrayal of Africans in early Hollywood films, African-Americans in early American film history often had to contend with stereotypical portrayals in mainstream Hollywood films when they make an appearance. Early Black filmmakers such as Micheaux, Foster, and brothers George Perry Johnson and Noble Johnson tried to combat these derogatory images of Blacks in mainstream American films by portraying Black heroes and Black families in storylines and themes that portrayed the full humanity of Black people as a response to the prevailing negative portrayals. Micheaux's films became controversial later for adopting the mainstream portrayal of Blacks in his films. The early 20th-century Black films also included the work of Eloyce Gist, a Black female filmmaker, who made religious films about Black people (Burton, 2010).

The short period between 1970 and 1975 was very significant for African Americans and filmmaking. This was known as the era of Black exploitation—or Blaxploitation as it was known (Lawrence, 2011). The three factors that helped the growth of Black films during this period were the civil rights movement, the continuing misrepresentation of Blacks in motion picture by Hollywood, and Hollywood's financial problems (Lawrence, 2011). White and Black filmmakers who wanted to capitalize on the African-American film audience made Blaxploitation films. Ossie Davis' *Cotton Comes to Harlem* (1970) was one of the first from these series of films. It did very well at the box office and was immediately followed by Melvin Van Peebles' *Sweet Sweetback's Baadasssss Song* (1971). Several more followed. These films were notable for their use of strong Black lead actors, predominantly Black urban locales, and unique musical soundtracks. Hollywood stopped making the Blaxploitation films in the mid-1970s when it went into making blockbusters featuring Black and White characters. Independent filmmakers like Spike Lee shot into fame in the 1990s by making films that were self-consciously about race using Black characters in the lead and telling stories of relevance to Black people. Post-1990s, independent filmmaking using Black lead characters, faith-based, and focusing on social and economic issues affecting Blacks continued to grow in the movies of Tyler Perry, Ava Duvernay, Julie Dash, Rick Famuyiwa, and Christine Swanson, to name a few.

Profit-driven, niche-market Black filmmaking in the United States was concretized presumably with the advent of Spike Lee's movies in the 1980s and 1990s. Move over Lee, when Tyler Perry busted unto the scene with his 2005 film debut *Tyler Perry's Diary of Mad Black Woman*. As noted by Eithne Quinn, the commercial focus of these Black independent films is based on a "keen understanding of the (American) film industry's under-resourcing of black productions and the need to 'circumvent industry exclusion.'" Tyler Perry,

> makes films for a domestic black audience, with relatively low production values. Where the average big-budget Hollywood film costs $100 million, Perry's budgets range from $5 million to $20 million. He joint finances, produces, directs, scripts, stars in, and owns his films
> (Quinn, 2013, pp. 198, 204)

Repeatedly, Quinn argues, "race was both an impediment and impetus" (2013, p. 203) to the career development of Perry. Race is an impetus because the "historic and continuing experience of racism in America acts as a complex resource and spur, priming...creative individuals to surmount Hollywood's possessive investment in whiteness" (Lipsitz, 1998 as cited by Quinn, 2013). Race is an opportunity because conglomerate Hollywood, though its growth since the 1980s seems overwhelming, is not all absorbing or monolithically efficient—its racist assumptions present some opportunities for minority cultural producers. Indeed, when such corporate fault lines are combined with the rich performative and subcultural resources of Black America in an increasingly synergistic, celebrity-fronted industry environment, the opportunities presented can be substantial (Quinn, 2013, p. 204).

Historically, Black American cinema has been inextricably linked to social issues (Burton, 2010); however, the narrative style, use of melodrama, themes, style, and economics of independent Black filmmaking have shared familiar terrain with Nollywood, especially in the areas of early low production value, themes, and financing. Black cinema in America continues to evolve and sometimes dissolve in Hollywood, but independent Black filmmaking continues to thrive.

Given the nature and premise of most of Nollywood USA movies, potential opportunity exists to create a synergistic form and medium of Black films that adds to independent Black films in the United States, such as the Tyler Perry lines of movies which some have described as similar to Nollywood, given that, by Hollywood standards, they are relatively cheap and message-driven, with religion and morality driving the narratives (Obenson, 2014). Along the same line of small-budget, straight-to-DVD independent movies shot in digital rather than celluloid are movies directed by Cora Anne such as: *Do You Know Where Your Man is?* (2013), *Love and Football* (2013), and *Rich in Spirit* (2007). While most Nollywood movies, including 'new Nollywood' and NollywoodUSA, are apolitical, a huge part of their popularity is based on their ability to tell stories of Africans within the continent and in the diaspora that that are relevant and affective to their audiences.

Recent Nollywood USA movies such as Tony Abulu's *Doctor Bello* (2013), John Uche's *One Night in Vegas* (2013), and Robert Peters' *Stolen* (2011), blatantly profit-oriented, have broadened their vision on storytelling and the global Black audiences by trying to expand their audience base through the use of a more global cast. The casts of these films included names that most African-Americans and diaspora Africans will recognize. *Doctor Bello*'s cast included Isaiah Washington of *Grey's Anatomy* fame; Vivica Fox, a renowned African-American dramatic artiste from iconic Hollywood movies such as *Independence Day*; and Jimmy Jean Louis, a veteran American TV and Hollywood actor. This use of casting to reach out to domestic African-American audiences corresponds with Adejunmobi's summation that "as long as producers in these industries do not derive their primary, though limited profits from global corporations but from relatively small companies operating on distribution platforms that cater mainly to domestic and diasporic audiences," they will continue to "exhibit a high degree of creative and financial autonomy with respect to dominant global media" (2014, pp. 75–76).

In an attempt to discern the place for NollywoodUSA in the Black film landscape in the United States, the study examines the prevailing themes in the NollywoodUSA movies, the cast, the setting for these movies, the production values, the intended audience, and the distribution methods. Three samples of NollywoodUSA films (*Stolen, One Night in Vegas*, and *Doctor Bello*) were chosen for analysis because of the varied themes addressed, the variety of shooting locations in the United States, the narrative style, and the cast of characters used.

Stolen

Stolen (2012) consists of cast members from Nigeria, Sierra Leone, Democratic Republic of Congo, and the United States. Shot in Atlanta, United States, the storyline revolves around a woman named Laura, married to David Okonto. David is portrayed as the archetypal African man who believes that marriage is meaningless without children. Unfortunately, Laura is unable to carry a pregnancy to term and has suffered four miscarriages. Finally, Laura succeeds in convincing David to hire a surrogate named Gia. After the baby was delivered, Gia and David disappeared with the baby who was named Destiny. Laura was devastated as a result of the betrayal and the loss of the baby she was looking forward to calling her own. Laura got the family lawyer involved in the investigation and search for the baby, David, and Gia. Laura and the lawyer eventually became closer because of the awful experience.

Stolen's cast included Nollywood big stars and U.S. independent film stars like Tony Umez, Robert Peters, Sana Kanu, Soleil Diva, Andy Koehler (*Tyler Perry's Medea Witness Protection* fame), Elechi Wordu, Divine Shaw, Sudana Showalter, Bridget John, Lady Dagashi, Greggory Erwin, and many others. Directed by Robert Peters, a U.S.-based Nollywood director, *Stolen* was released under Whitestone Studios in Atlanta and marketed in the African diaspora in America and the United Kingdom. The cast is very diverse, with Tony Umez being the only well-known Nollywood star in the movie. Andy Koehler was effective but appeared awkward in delivering his lines, which made him unconvincing in his role. The female characters brought the melodrama, which was a bit over the top. Several scenes were used to paint a picture of Gia as a self-absorbed, shallow human being with limited goals toward self-actualization. Some scenes were shot in her dark, ominous-looking bedroom, where her friends and family members openly discussed with her the fact that her life is on a downward spiral with limited options. She was a party girl. This gloomy unflattering portrayal portends what she would eventually do—steal the baby she was carrying as a surrogate as well as the father of the baby. In a classic binary picture of good versus bad, Laura on the other hand was presented as a very serious individual who was married (albeit without a child), obviously in a much higher socioeconomic bracket than Gia, took herself seriously, and acted responsibly. Her calm demeanor and sensible clothes are quickly contrasted with the tight and short clothes worn by Gia, and her spacious, bright, and welcoming spaces are contrasted with Gia's dark room with barely enough room for two people beyond the bed and mirror in the room. David, the husband, was portrayed as a reasonable, standard-issue, modern African husband. He wore a demeanor of the long-suffering but tolerant spouse in the early part of the movie. His attitude sparks of righteous indignation—after all, he was the one tolerating his wife's inability to carry babies to full term. The four main characters, together, did what they needed to do to bring the story to life. The storyline is tired and universal. The themes of childlessness, desperation for a child, and betrayal are well-seasoned themes in Nollywood movies. The cinematography was adequate but not mind-blowing. The production value appeared to be the lowest of the three movies evaluated. The sound was good but not great, and the picture quality was spotty. The movie was distributed and circulated mainly in the United States. There was no information available on how the movie was received by its intended audience and how much money the movie might have made.

Doctor Bello

In the film *Doctor Bello* (2012), Cancer specialist Dr. Michael Durant (Isaiah Washington) immerses himself in his work to avoid dealing with the traumatic loss of his ten-year-old daughter from cancer and the ensuing blame from his wife (Vivica Fox), who has taken to alcoholism to deal with her pain. He forms an unlikely bond with a sick but loving 11-year-old boy Sam, the son of a rich Jewish couple who are major contributors to the hospital cancer research fund. Unfortunately, Sam's health deteriorates drastically. With only a few days to live, Durant becomes desperate, willing to risk anything to save the child's life. A Nigerian nurse at the hospital convinces him to seek the help of Dr. Bello (Jimmy Jean Louis), an uncertified Nigerian immigrant doctor with an interesting past, but well known in the Brooklyn-African underground as a miracle worker. Bello was allowed into the hospital to secretly administer a strange African potion to Sam and miraculously, the child began to recover, and the cancer went into remission. In the ensuing interactions, Bello taught Durant to look at medicine in a new way. In investigating the miraculous recovery of Sam, the hospital board discovered that an uncertified doctor gave Sam a potion. This led to criminal proceedings against Bello, who was consequently imprisoned for medical malpractice. Because of his complicity in the crime, Durant was suspended from the hospital. In a series of twists, Bello becomes ill and it falls to Durant to save him by locating the secret elixir, which is found only in the "Garden of Life" on a mountain range in Nigeria. The rest of the movie at this point was shot in Nigeria. Durant gets to the town of Olumo in Nigeria and meets up with Dr. Olumide (Tony Abulu, the writer, director, and producer of the film), who tells him of another place where he should visit before he gets to his final destination. Genevieve Nnaji (a leading Nollywood actress whom Oprah Winfrey dubbed the Julia Roberts of Nigerian movies), the new assistant to Olumide and love interest to Durant, led him to his final destination—the climbing of the Olumo rock to get the potion. However, prior to the climbing, there is a ritual for Durant to strengthen him for the climbing of the rock. He gets to the top of the mountain, and there was Bello and Durant's dead daughter heading towards the light, but not before a few words, which led to a form of spiritual cleansing, love, forgiveness, and self-discovery in Durant.

This movie first premiered in 2012 at the John F. Kennedy Center for Performance Arts Washington DC. It later premiered in Nigeria as well.

It subsequently showed in some UK cinemas and about 20 AMC cinemas in major cities in the United States with large African immigrant populations. The reception of the movie was mixed among audiences in both Nigeria and the United States. The move was also a first product from the $200 million loan made available by the immediate past Nigerian president, Jonathan Goodluck.[7] It was obvious right from the start that this film had a point of view that included portraying both traditional and modern Africa as well as Africans, including the diaspora, in a positive manner. The characters were all portrayed with dignity, even when there appeared to be limited and constricted roles for the Nigerian cast. Isaiah Washington was good in his role as Dr. Durant. The leading cancer physician at a New York hospital is a Black man. But like all humans, he's also flawed. His marriage is in a rocky place because he has not learned how to deal with his pain and loss. But we are reassured that he is a good man because of his relationship with Sam, his patient with cancer, and with his nurse. Dr. Bello is the unorthodox doctor who knows more than the world gives him credit for and has knowledge beyond the Western concepts about healing. His potion heals a boy with cancer, and rather than receive praise and adulation from the people, he was imprisoned for practicing medicine without a license.

Dr. Bello is Africa—the downtrodden continent that no one believes in, and even when something spectacular comes out of it, it is not valued. The Western world undervalues that which it does not understand. So, Bello was thrown in jail. Imprisonment cuts him off from his root, so he gets sick and now he needs help from Durant. The irony is that Durant went to Africa in search of the potion to heal Bello, but instead, he found his own healing, forgiveness, cleansing, and freedom. The trip to Africa freed him from his own psychological prison of guilt. He was restored. Rather than find a potion for Bello, Durant found healing for his own soul. The storyline relied on metaphors and irony to tell a story with a purpose. The underlying message seem to be that Africa has value to offer to the world, but we have to be willing to search and sacrifice before we can receive the value. The themes of healing, love, self-sacrifice, forgiveness, and self-discovery were predominant in this movie. The movie used suspense and an unpredictable ending to keep the viewer interested. The viewer had to keep wondering if Durant was going to be able to do all he needs to do to get to the mountain top. Would he succumb to the ritual required before climbing the mountain? Would he get the potion? Would he get it in time to save Bello? These questions created suspense for the viewer. The unexpected ending also left more questions than answers. It turns out the journey was for self-discovery for Durant—more psychological than physical.

The film had great production value. The scenes shot in New York were excellent with great sound and picture quality. The film went a bit off the rails with the Nigerian scenes, which seemed unnecessarily prolonged, forced, and confusing. The end of the movie was unexpected, but not in a good way. The American cast was excellent except for Jimmy Jean Louis (Dr. Bello), who struggled with his Nigerian accent. The Nigerian cast was a parade of the big names in Nollywood such as Genevieve Nnaji, Stephanie Okereke, and Olumide Bakare, all well-known names in the industry. Unfortunately, the Nigerian cast was not able to flex their individual acting muscles, as their roles were muted and unchallenging. It appeared that it was more important to show the faces than showcase their acting prowess.

One Night in Vegas

Shot entirely in Northern Virginia and Las Vegas, United States, and using a multicultural cast, *One Night in Vegas* (2013) is the story of infidelity, trust, loss, and betrayal. At the end of a two-year court case with a mob that required them to be in the witness protection program, husband and wife James (John Dumelo) and Genie (Yvonne Nelson)—and Nick (Jimmy Jean Louis), their assigned bodyguard during the witness protection program—decided to head to Vegas for a much needed short vacation. Unknown to James, while Nick was teaching him self-defense strategies during the witness protection program, Nick was also lusting after Genie, James' wife. The marriage was on a rocky patch and the trip to Vegas was supposed to rejuvenate the relationship. The couple asked Nick along as a treat for being their bodyguard during the program. Once in Vegas, while James was out partying with his friends, Nick consummated his lust for Genie without using any protection. On his way back from the club, drunken James ran into Ashley (Sarodj Bertin), a complete stranger, they had a one-night stand, again, without any protection. Both Ashley and Genie got pregnant from the encounters. Later, Ashley returned to Vegas in search of James to share the pregnancy news, but James was long gone. She met Nick at the bar, had another unprotected sexual encounter, and later got married to Nick. James assumed he was the father of the unborn child Genie was carrying and Nick assumed the same of Ashley's pregnancy. Eventually, the truth was exposed and what happened in Vegas did not stay in Vegas, but rather followed them home.

Like *Doctor Bello*, the strength of *Vegas* was in its high-profile multicultural cast. The cast worked great. Yvonne Nelson and Sarodj Bertin were both fabulous, and Jimmy Jean Louis and John Dumelo also held their own. Bertin struggled a bit opposite the better thespian, Nelson. The film, handling a story that is improbable, made up for credibility through a remarkable production value that would rival any Hollywood production, with amazing picture quality and excellent sound.

Vegas was also a film that is obviously more interested in displaying a particular social status, a particular positioning of elite African immigrants, than telling a credible story. Every shot in the movie was focused on highlighting a mobile, urban, sophisticated lifestyle, starting from the opening shot of a modern highbrow brick home of James and Genie. The house is a signifier of the social economic class of the inhabitants. Equally glamorous is the trip to Las Vegas, upon which the movie was predicated. The Las Vegas scenes showcased James and his buddies as young, upwardly mobile individuals with a comfortable lifestyle, possibly all young professionals. The movie was peppered with glamor shots of the exteriors of Las Vegas hotels and streets, as well as shots of slots machines and roulette tables with people lounging at pools. These shots were used to indicate that the characters were at a resort, a place where people might be expected to lower their guards and relax, a place where people would be excited and therefore behave in less than morally appropriate manner. The shots were used to foreground a setting in which one might expect that anything goes. The setting was also used to tell a story where one would not expect a family. Individuals were walking about in professional and evening outfits or beach clothing. The message was clear: this setting is a place where adults go to have fun. The events that unfolded were therefore surprising to the viewers but not shocking. Unlike *Stolen*, the scenes were fluid and unselfconscious. The movie's official release in Ghana was reported to have had the largest turnout in the history of Silverbird Theater in Accra, Ghana. Nominated in about 12 categories, the movie won the 2013 Nollywood and African Film Critics Awards (NAFCA, also known as African Oscars) awards for Best Film in Diaspora, Best Cinematography, and Best Actor in a Supporting Role. There was no information on how much money the movie made, but it was well received by audiences in Africa and in the diaspora.

The three movies shared the themes of couples and the challenges, heartbreaks, triumphs, failures, and other intricacies of maintaining a married life. These are universal human themes. Nothing in these themes signify the particularity of race or ethnicity as a factor, except *Doctor Bello,* in an implicit manner. Most global cultures can relate to the challenges of living as a couple and the impact of cultural expectations on marriages as well as the frustrations, temptations, betrayals, regrets, faith, hope, reconciliations, and permanent fractures that attenuate human relationships. Therefore, as far as thematic focus is concerned, NollywoodUSA, based on these samples examined, is not breaking new grounds thematically. A new ground thematically would include, for example, addressing transsexuality as an African immigrant parent with strong ties to Africa. However, in dealing with its basic themes in classic Nollywood style, NollywoodUSA play to its strength in its effusive use of melodrama, emotional roller coaster, and didactics in these three movies. Nollywood is notorious for being message-driven, very similar to many Black films in the United States, particularly the Tyler Perry type. NollywoodUSA maintains this essentialism in the three movies selected for review. Faith and hope always win in the end is the message of *Stolen*. A disappointment can lead to blessing and what goes around comes around are some of the lessons in *Vegas*. The only one with an ideological theme and plot is *Doctor Bello*, which found the cure for cancer in the mountains of a Nigerian city. It was also the one with a storyline in which a disaffected, disillusioned, and sad African-American professional man found peace, reconciliation, healing, and love by making a seemingly selfless trip to an African city.

The filming locations played a huge part in telling the stories in these movies. *Stolen* uses the Atlanta skyline liberally in the shots, just as *Vegas* and *Doctor Bello* were very generous in the use of the New York, Nigeria, and the Las Vegas skylines respectively. All three movies have a diversity of cast, more so in *Doctor Bello* and *Stolen* than *Vegas*. All three movies used a cast of recognizable iconic characters from the continental Nollywood industry such as Tony Umez in *Stolen*, Genevieve Nnaji in *Doctor Bello*, and John Dumelo and Yvonne Nelson in *One Night In Vegas*. The use of these iconic continental Nollywood faces helped establish the movies as Nollywood products. All three also made copious use of actors and actresses who permanently reside in the United States, but have connections to Africa. These would include people like Robert Peters, who was the director in *Stolen*; Koby Maxwell, producer and one of the actors in Vegas; Tony Abulu, director/producer of *Doctor Bello*; and cast members such as Sarodj Bertin (*Vegas*), Haitian lawyer best known as a beauty pageant contestant, and her fellow countryman, Jimmy Jean Louis (Vegas and Dr. Bello). The sharing of talents between actors from several countries across the continent is not new. Particularly between actors from Nigeria, Ghana, and Kenya (who all share English as the national language), Nollywood has traditionally had such exchanges and cooperation of talents. Similarly, shooting a portion of the movie in the United States and another portion in an African country is not a unique feature of NollywoodUSA; it a fairly frequent practice in Nollywood as an industry. However, the combination of the use of transnational locations such as Nigeria and the United States, multiple locations within the United States, and use of internationally known African-American actors and actresses in lead roles such as in *Doctor Bello* are all unique to NollywoodUSA. There are also movies like *Stolen* that are shot entirely in the United States and are distributed exclusively in the African diaspora. There are also Nollywood movies that are shot entirely in Africa using African-American actors such as *93 Days*, which addresses the Ebola crisis and featured Danny Glover and Tim Reid in lead roles. The latter would be regarded as a 'New Nollywood' movie while this author would regard *Vegas* and *Doctor Bello* as falling into the subcategory of NollywoodUSA simply because of the distribution pattern. Distribution method would be a determining factor between movies that exhibit the high production values and globally appealing themes of 'New Nollywood' but are premiered in Africa and mostly oriented and distributed within the continent. Movies that are made with similar high production value and with global themes, but premiered in theaters and mainly distributed in the United States and Europe, signifying a particular targeted audience, would belong in the category of NollywoodUSA.

Theories of Being African in the World: Pan-Africanism/Afropolitanism

The need to bring people of African descent together under African nationalism was first floated by Edward Blyden in the 19th century. According to Mudimbe (1998), Blythe started out as a supporter of the Christian abolitionist agenda with the ultimate motivation of cleansing Africa of its paganism and mimicking Europeans as a way to advance the future of Africa. He later amended his view and came to the conclusion that the unity of Africa and the path for progress for Africa depended on avoiding mimicry of white people, and the pursuit of African solutions to African problems through education (Mudimbe, 1998, p. 115). His idea of African unity was dependent on race/Blackness and the use of racial purity as an identifier of the African people (Kebede, 2004, p. 166). At this stage of Black solidarity consciousness, the elevation and commendation of Black culture, identity, and dignity depended on people who are racially Black. Pan-Africanism later evolved to include people from the continental Africa including sub-Saharan Africa as well as the Maghreb.

This evolution of Black unity and consciousness drew strength from the shared experience of colonialism by Western hegemonies (Kasanda, 2016, p. 182). This era and the next era of Black unity and consciousness included the works of people like Booker T. Washington, Anna Julia Cooper, Marcus Garvey, W.E.B. Du Bois, Kwame Nkrumah, Jomo Kenyatta, etc. Through several decades and generations, African leaders, both on the continent and in the diaspora, gave a lot of thought to what it means to be African or be of African descent. What role should race play in the definition of an African? What should solidarity between people of African descent look like? Who should be able to participate in the resistance against Western hegemony, institutional racism, as well as the issue of identity construction on what makes one African, are all ongoing topics of contemplation and ideology. The reality of colonization and post-colonization, slavery and post-emancipation challenges, and the persistent social, economic, and political inequities of apartheid combined fueled a persistent, multigenerational, deepening need for an African identity and philosophy that is encompassing of what it means to be dehumanized, oppressed, and deprived. Different iterations of Pan-Africanism evolved throughout the different experiences of people of African descent as they struggle to find a unifying identity and philosophy to uplift the African experience and raise consciousness about the inequalities, and effect change. The use of race as a qualifier for being African soon proved inadequate. Then came the realization that the African identity and solidarity among Africans to fight injustice could not be defined solely by race because race is exclusive by nature (Kasanda, 2016, p. 190). As noted by Kasanda, given the fact that the rehabilitation of Black people with regard to the misdeeds of slavery and colonization was the constituting principle and the mobilizing ideal of Pan-Africanism, to the founding fathers of the theory, an African "refers spontaneously to someone who is not white" (Mbembe, 2005, p. 1). The 20th century was dominated in a major way by the paradigms of Pan-Africanism, which is no longer a relevant approach to African reality and debate. Mbembe noted that Pan-Africanism and other such theories "no longer make it possible to analyze transformations in process with the slightest bit of credibility" (2005, p. 1). As a consequence of the fact that Pan-Africanism became confined to racial and Afrocentric discourses, its limits and anachronisms were often decried (Appiah, 1992, pp. 175–180). The basic premise of Blackness and victimhood of slavery and colonization as the organizing principle for African solidarity discounted current configurations and interdependencies that shape Africa and African diasporas around the world (Kasanda, 2016, p. 190). The need to develop a new theory and a new approach to collate the meanings of all the different meanings of being in the world as an African or of African descent became apparent.

Afropolitanism and Cosmopolitanism

Afropolitanism (Mbembe, 2005; Selasi, 2005) and Cosmopolitanism (Appiah, 2007) both invoke the principle of the inwards and outwards flows of people and is cognizant of the diversity that shapes the African identity (Kasanda, 2016). This encompasses the view that Africa is a destination for people from all over the world and of different races, such as the Afrikaners of South Africa and the people of Indian origin dispersed all over southern Africa (Kasanda, 2016). The movements of people induce such people to contribute to the identity formation of their newfound land as well as reshape their own individual identity as they intermarry and reshape their identities over several generations in the newfound lands. Similarly, Africa is also a place of departure for people and cultures around the world (Kasanda, 2016, p. 191). Departures from Africa can be grouped based on their motivations. There is the forced departure caused by the slave trade, which was marked with pain, victimization, and humiliation, and necessitated the struggle for self-esteem and rehabilitation embarked upon by the fathers of Pan-Africanism (Kasanda, 2016, p. 191). The other form of departure from

Africa was motivated by other factors including foreign study, job offers from multinational corporations, exile, and other choices (Kasanda, 2016). These second groups of people departing from Africa do not have the same pain, humiliation, and victimization endured by the first group. They are therefore free to define all the complexes that make up their identity inclusive of their roots and multiculturalism. Afropolitanism, as a theory of being in the world, relies, to a large extent, on the definition of identity as a result of interdependencies between individual and collective history, local and global factors, us and others (Kasanda, 2016, p. 192). According to Mbembe (2005, p. 2 as translated by Kasanda, 2016), Afropolitanism is

> a way to be in the world that refuses by principle, any form of victimized identity (based on race or ethnicity)... it is also a political and cultural attitude with regard to the nation, race, and issue of difference in general.

This view rejects the Pan-African essentialism of Blackness as a condition for being African. What or whom it includes and excludes exemplifies the limitations of Afropolitanism. Musila (2015, p. 2) notes that Afropolitanism "paints a picture of connectivity, heterogeneous blends of cultures and an ethos of tolerance, the unasked question remains: what about those excluded from these circuits of consumption and access?" As for Pan-Africanism, continued criticisms abound of Pan-Africanism in which the dominant narratives of Africa are located within "an intellectual genealogy based on a territorialized identity and a racialized geography,"[8] in which African identity is defined in "difference" and "opposition to the world" and does not recognize the "thematics of sameness" that now describes Africa's modernity. While the search for a theoretical framework for being in the world that captures the varied experience of people of African descent is still ongoing, and the ideas of Pan-Africanism and Afropolitanism, vulnerable to criticisms, continue to encapsulate the sense of shared identity of being in the world as an African. This is especially true for Africans in diaspora all over the world, particularly in the Northern hemisphere for most of whom the experiences of discrimination, racism, exclusion, and being undervalued are all too familiar.

Nollywood and Being African in the World

Quoting Achille Mbembe (2005), Carmela Garritano (2014) argues that Nollywood could be understood "as an everyday practice through which Africans manage to recognize and maintain with the world an unprecedented familiarity."[9] This engagement with the world, with consciousness of being Black or being African in the United States, foregrounds the stories being told in the NollywoodUSA movies. While the topics of discrimination and socioeconomic inequalities were not specifically mentioned in most of the movies, a diasporan African or an African-American audience member, watching the movies, would appreciate seeing people of African descent living in the neighborhoods featured in *Vegas*. Such an audience member would also appreciate the fact that a leading cancer doctor in a New York hospital looks like Isaiah Washington. Having so many individuals who are obviously of African descent in many roles in which they are in control of their lives, and living financially independent lifestyles, is an affirmation of what is possible and a reimagined life for these audiences. This becomes pertinent when one considers that this is not the typical way African-Americans are portrayed in Hollywood movies when they are featured. Vivica Fox was alluding to this in the YouTube videos cited earlier when she encourages others (ostensibly African-American actors) to work with Nollywood because they would have the opportunity to act and be featured in roles that may not often be available to them in Hollywood. She also mentions that Africans love to see their own people (Fox on YouTube).[10] This would seem to be referencing audiences in Africa appreciating and responding to other people of African descents such as herself.

However, effusive showcasing of seemingly successful people of African descent in movies, while good for the morale of certain audiences, may not speak to specific societal inequities, systemic racism, and other such problems that immigrants and African-Americans contend with in Western societies, particularly in the United States. This obsessive focus on success, financial freedom, and a life characterized by leisure and physical manifestations of consumer culture is what Afropolitanism theory of being in world supports. The theory does not, much like movies like *Stolen* and *Vegas*, take into consideration the huge populations of people that are not included in that lifestyle. A movie like *Doctor Bello* tries to include this aspect of the life of an immigrant in the character of Dr. Bello. Bello appears to be struggling financially and is marginalized by society even with his wealth of medical knowledge. This is a more realistic outlook on the life of African immigrants, who, oftentimes with advanced degrees, are underemployed.

NollywoodUSA movies like *Stolen* and *One Night in Vegas* exemplified the essence of Afropolitanism as a theory—the aspirational theory of Africans and a world where Africans of all orientation, as well as people with little or tenuous relationship to Africa, regardless of the hue of their skin, are equally successful and have equal access to global financial capitals. The characters in these movies are all mostly successful people who are successfully pursuing upward mobility or are affluent to a certain degree, and for whom race or ethnicity is not an impediment to success. These movies are intended for the global audience and not exclusively to people of African descent. The themes and plots in these movies also follow the same patterns. The characters have problems that are global—marital infidelity, betrayal of trust, disappointments, and restoration. None of these themes have peculiarities with the characters' race or ethnicity. There was no castigation of any government or reference to systemic problems that disproportionately favor one group over another. NollywoodUSA movies, therefore, represent one way in which Nollywood 'gestures' and 'solicits' the world and 'pulls the world in' (Garritano, 2014, p. 46). Not in an apologetic or race-conscious way as many African-American films, but in a manner that is unbridled and insists on being included and reckoned with as a legitimate being in the world.

Conclusion

Given the cross-pollination, comingling, and collaboration ongoing between the continental Nollywood and NollywoodUSA, it is obvious that the goal of the industry is to enlarge the audience for the industry as a whole and expand the reach of Nollywood content beyond continental Africa, the diasporic Africans, and transnational Africans. It is also obvious that, to a majority of the professionals who work in the industry, the goal is not necessarily to change the content of Nollywood to respond to an assumed global audience; rather, it is to orient the global audience to Nollywood content (Adejunmobi, 2014). Through a cable channel called Africa Magic owned by MultiChoice Media Company in South Africa, Nollywood content is available throughout most of sub-Saharan Africa to not just people who can afford to pay the subscription fees for cable but also to the neighbors and friends of such people who may not have their own access to cable (Miller, 2016). From Uganda and Kenya, Ghana, and South Africa, covering most of southern, eastern, and western Africa, Nollywood content is available on TV or via cable service. For the transnational and diasporic audience, iROKO, an online streaming service, provides Nollywood content to anyone in the world online via their online service. Amazon Prime videos, Netflix, and VUDU both recently started streaming Nollywood content, and Nollywood DVDs are available for purchase from Alaba market in Nigeria to African-themed convenience or grocery stores all over the United States and Europe.

Despite these formal systems of distribution, individual filmmakers in the industry are financed mostly from informal networks, and recouping the cost of making the movies becomes very difficult given the extensiveness of piracy in the industry. However, theatrical releases and streaming allow producers to cut down a bit on the rampant piracy. High production values, global themes, and use of recognizable theatre and television faces provides a better chance for NollywoodUSA to have theatrical releases and big time streaming through Netflix, VUDU, and Amazon Prime. Profit is therefore a high consideration in the NollywoodUSA subgenre, and that is not necessarily a bad thing. However, Nollywoo-dUSA must also tell stories that resonate with African-Americans as well as other Blacks around the world. This can be done by focusing on shared themes that connect with the shared experiences of being Africans in the global sphere. Nollywood as an industry is capable of doing this right now because it already has a tier system, a segmentation, which allows it to tell both particularized stories of Africans as well as globalized stories of being Africans. This allows audiences all over the world to continue the conversations about the particularities and the commonalities of the experiences of being African in the world.

In an interview on SaharaTV with Fungail Maboreke, Tony Abulu, producer/director of *Doctor Bello*, says his motive in making the specific movie was his frustration with what appears to be a case of contemporary Africa trying to get away from traditional Africa in the current trends in Nollywood moviemaking (ChannelsTV 2013).[11] Abulu, an avowed Afrocentric, spoke of the need to tell the story of Africa about the depth and spirituality of Africa as one of his motivations for making the movie. Abulu conceded that the movie is targeted at Americans in general but specifically at African-Americans (SaharaTV 2013).[12] He also says having African-Americans play lead roles in African movies is a fantastic way to bring international attention to the Nollywood industry (SaharaTV 2013).[13] In other interviews about *Doctor Bello*, Abulu also expressed interest in becoming the Tyler Perry of African movies in America (Semple, 2013). At a showing of the movie at the Kennedy Center in the United States, Vivica Fox (Dr. Durant's wife in *Doctor Bello*), when asked about the difference in doing Nollywood movie and her usual Hollywood fare, said, "You will get to act and Nollywood is huge and you get the opportunity to travel. Hollywood doesn't really allow us African-Americans the roles we should be playing."[14] One can only speculate what she meant by the last phrase. Koby Maxwell, the producer of *Vegas*, in his articulation of why the need for NollywoodUSA, told the *Washington Post* reporter that there is need for Nollywood to improve visual and technical aspects of the industry content to compete in the global marketplace. He also noted that Nollywood USA provides the opportunity to combine African creativity with what he calls American technical chops (Brown, 2013).

It does seem like the concept of NollywoodUSA, and 'New Nollywood' in general, is an ideology. It is an ideology that is not and does not want to be apologetic about its content. It is also an ideology that believes that this content is consumable to the global audience if the technical aspects and general cinematography are improved. The NollywoodUSA movies in the caliber of *Stolen* and *One Night in Vegas* do not generally address systemic oppressive standards in American society that would naturally be appealing to historically oppressed groups like African-Americans. They also currently do not reflect the inequities and the legal challenges that immigrants contend with in the Western countries into which they emigrate. Rather, they are focused on the success of the individual characters and everyday problems of upwardly mobile successful people. This is very afropolitan in outlook. These types of movies will remain important and relevant to a group of transnational and diasporic Africans but may have limited acceptance into the Black film audience in the United States where audiences are used to Black films that often touch on the struggles of everyday African Americans vis-à-vis a system that does not always work for them but against them. Thematically, because Nollywood USA movies tend to remain internally focused on everyday universal societal issues, they tend to add very little to the conversation about the actual lived experiences of Africans in the diaspora, the immigrant experience, or the possible intersection with the global Black experience.

The *Doctor Bello* kind of NollywoodUSA movies, similar to the continental Nollywood movie such as the Steve Gukas' Ebola story in *93 Days* (2016), although completely shot in Nigeria, are more likely to be integrated into the Black movie cult and also have a more global appeal. These address more substantial issues that are cultural but with global implications. Their appeal does not repose just in the use of big name African-American actors and actresses, but also their exploration of themes that are both essential, humanistic, and cultural. There is very little available information on how *Doctor Bello* was received in the African-American community, but this information would have been valuable in evaluating the value of NollywoodUSA to the Black film experience in the United States. These latter group of movies support a notion of African identity that connects Africans in all its diasporas based on mutual respect, human dignity, shared struggles, and the universal achievement of human rights (Kasanda, 2016).

Having said this, there is room for mutual coexistence of both kinds of themes in NollywoodUSA. The current segmentation in the industry allows for both an Afropolitan outlook on being African in the world and a Pan-African outlook. Both outlooks serve to affirm the universality of being an African and the particularity of being an African in the world.

Notes

1 http://globalriskinsights.com/2015/01/nigerias-nollywood-putting-hollywood-shame/ (Last visited March 27, 2017).
2 Tori Arthur. (2016) The Reimagined Paradise: African Immigrants in the U.S., Nollywood Film, and the Digital Remediation of 'Home'. A doctoral dissertation completed in August 2016 for Bowling Green State University, p. 142, (citing "What's Nollywood ? Nollywood Week Film Festival).
3 https://qz.com/512699/nollywoods-runaway-success-has-inspired-a-new-nollywood-in-nigeria-and-beyond/ (Last visited March 1, 2017).

4 http://globalriskinsights.com/2015/01/nigerias-nollywood-putting-
hollywood-shame/ (Last visited March 27, 2017). See also www.pressreader.
com/canada/bloomberg-businessweek-north-america/20160222/282733
405926654 (Last visited March 27, 2017).
5 www.washingtonpost.com/lifestyle/magazine/nollywood-usa-african-
movie-makers-expand-filming-to-dc-area/2013/05/22/c132bae6-b107-
11e2-baf7-5bc2a9dc6f44_story.html?utm_term=.84326abaf71e (last visited
January 21, 2017).
6 https://vimeo.com/15235341
7 Jonathan Goodluck made available $200m grant from which artists, pro-
ducers, and directors can borrow to globalize the culture, arts, and entertainment industry in Nigeria. Tony Abulu's $250,000 for *Doctor Bello* was
one of the first loans to be made from the fund.
8 Achille Mbembe, "African Modes of Self-Writing," *Public Culture* 14, no. 1
(2002): 258. (As cited by Garritano, 2014).
9 Ibid., 257.
10 www.youtube.com/watch?v=bRGzKJeLREI @ 7:37–9:10. Accessed October
24, 2017.
11 www.youtube.com/watch?v=2mUWcQBdrz8
12 Fungail Maboreke, Sahara TV, (2013). Inside Look into Nollywood. www.
youtube.com/watch?v=2mUWcQBdrz8 @26:00.
13 Fungail Maboreke, Sahara TV, (2013). Inside Look into Nollywood. www.
youtube.com/watch?v=2mUWcQBdrz8
14 www.youtube.com/watch?v=bRGzKJeLREI @ 7:37–9:10. Accessed October
24, 2017.

References

Access Nollywood. (2016, February 22). *PressReader*. Retrieved from
www.pressreader.com/canada/bloomberg-businessweek-north-america/
20160222/28273340592665
Adejunmobi, M. (2014). Evolving Nollywood templates for minor transnational
film. *Black Camera*, 5(2), 74–94. Indiana University Press. Retrieved October
30, 2017, from Project MUSE database.
Appiah, Kwame Anthony. (2007). *Cosmopolitanism. Ethics in a World of
Strangers*. London: Penguin Book.
Appiah, Kwame Anthony. (1992). *In My Father's House: Africa in the Philoso-
phy of Culture*. New York: Oxford University Press.
Arthur, T. (2017). Glocal Nollywood: The Politics of Culture, Identity, and
Migration in African Films Set on American Shores. *Glocalism: Journal of
Culture, Politics and Innovation*, 2, 1–28.
Arthur, T. (2016). *The reimagined paradise: African immigrants in the U.S.,
Nollywood film, and the digital remediation of 'Home'*. A doctoral disserta-
tion completed in August 2016 for Bowling Green State University.
Barber, K. (1987). Popular arts in Africa. *African Studies Review*, 30(3), 1–78.
doi:10.2307/524538
Berry, C., & Farquhar, M. (2006). *China on screen: Cinema and nation*. New
York: Columbia Press.
Brown, D. (2013, May 23). Nollywood USA: African movie makers ex-
pand filming to D.C. area. *The Washington Post*. Retrieved from www.
washingtonpost.com/lifestyle/magazine/nollywood-usa-african-movie-

makers-expand-filming-to-dc-area/2013/05/22/c132bae6-b107-11e2-baf7-5bc2a9dc6f44_story.html?utm_term=.06677202d160

Burton, N. (2010, March 10). Celebrating 100 years of black cinema. *The Root*. Retrieved from www.theroot.com/celebrating-100-years-of-black-cinema-1790878492

Curry, R. (2016). Transnational and diasporic cinema. *obo*. Retrieved October 30, 2017, from www.oxfordbibliographies.com/view/document/obo-97801 99791286/obo-9780199791286-0243.xml

Enwezor, O. (2007), Coalition building: Black Audio Film Collective and Transnational Post-colonialism, In Kodwo Eshun & Anjalika Sagar (Eds.), *The Ghosts of Songs: the film art of the Black Audio Film Collective* (pp. 106–129). Liverpool: Liverpool University Press.

Garritano, C. (2014). Introduction: Nollywood—An archive of African worldliness. *Black Camera*, 5(2), 44–52. Indiana University Press. Retrieved October 26, 2017, from Project MUSE database.

Haynes, J. (2016). *Nollywood: The Creation of Nigerian Film Genres*. Chicago: University of Chicago Press.

Haynes, J. (2007), Nollywood: "What's in a name?, *Film International*, 5(4), 106–108.

Hoffmann, C. (2012), Made in America: Urban Immigrant Spaces in Transnational Nollywood Films, in M. Krings and O. Okome (eds.), *Global Nollywood: The Transnational Dimensions of an African Video Film Industry*, (pp. 121–138). Bloomington: Indiana University Press.

Iwabuchi, K. (2002). *Recentering globalization: Popular culture and Japanese transnationalism*. Durham, NC: Duke University Press.

Kasanda. (2016). "Exploring Pan-Africanism's theories: From race-based solidarity to political unity and beyond". *Journal of African cultural studies (1369–6815)*, 28(2) 179-195

Kebede, M. (2004). *Africa's quest for a philosophy of decolonization*. Amsterdam: Rodopi.

Lawrence, N. (2011) Black Exploitation Films of the 1970s, In John Downing (ed.), *Sage encyclopedia of social movement media*. Thousand Oaks, CA: Sage Publications, Inc.

Lipsitz, G. (1998). *The possessive investment in whiteness: How white people profit from identity politics*. Philadelphia, PA: Temple University Press.

Marks, Laura (2000). *The skin of the film: Intercultural cinema, embodiment, and the senses*. Durham and London: Duke University Press.

Mbembe, A. (2005). Afropolitanisme. Retrieved from www.africultures.com/php/?nav=article&no=4248

Miller, J. (2016). *Nollywood Central*. Basingstoke: Palgrave Macmillian.

Mudimbe, V. Y. (1998). *The invention of Africa. Gnosis, philosophy, and the order of knowledge*. Bloomington: Indiana University Press.

Musila, G. (2015). "Part-time Africans, Europolitans and 'Africa lite." *Journal of African Cultural Studies*, 28(1), 109–113. doi:10.1080/13696815.2015.1099424

Obenson, T. (2014). S&A 2013 Highlights: The 'Why Can't Black Filmmakers In The USA Adopt The Nollywood Model' Question... Indiewire.com. Retrieved October 20, 2017 from http://www.indiewire.com/2014/01/sa-2013-highlights-the-why-cant-black-filmmakers-in-the-usa-adopt-the-nollywood-model-question-162780/

Naficy, H. (2001). *An Accented Cinema: Exilic and Diasporic Filmmaking*, Princeton, NJ: Princeton University Press.

Ogunleye, F. (2003). Female Stereotypes in the Nigerian Video Film: A Case ofr Re-Socialization. *Humanities Review Journal*, 3(2) 1–14.

Okhai, V. (2008, June 22). Emerging Talents: Nollywood and the future of African Cinema. Nigerian.com. Retrieved March 15, 2017, from www.inigerian.com/emerging-talents-nollywood-and-the-future-of-african-cinema/

Quinn, E. (2013, July 1). Black talent and conglomerate hollywood: Will smith, tyler perry, and the continuing significance of race. *Popular Communication*, 11(3), 196–210.

Ryan, C. (2015). New Nollywood: A sketch of Nollywood's metropolitan new style. *African Studies Review*, 58(3), 55–76. doi:10.1017/asr.2015.75

Selasi, T. (2005). *Bye Babar*. Retrieved February 2016, from http://thelip.robertsharp.co.uk

Semple, K. (2013, February 21). Seeking a Hollywood audience for a Nollywood film. *The New York Times*. The New York Times. Web.

Tolchinsky, M. (2015, January 16). Nigeria's Nollywood is putting Hollywood to shame. *Global Risk Insights*. Retrieved from http://globalriskinsights.com/2015/01/nigerias-nollywood-putting-hollywood-shame/

Part IV

Audiences' Responses and Effects

8 Exploring African Female Immigrants' Perceptions of Their Portrayal in the U.S. Media

Gloria Nziba Pindi

African feminism[1] emerged as a movement to promote an African epistemological framework applicable to the lived experiences of African women in reaction to the theorization of their lived experiences by Western feminism. An important argument emerging from African feminist scholars is that "Western writings [representations] on Africa have been racist and ethnocentric, projecting Africans, among other things, as savage, subhuman, primitive, and hyper-sexed" (Oyewumi, 2003a, p. 27). Steady (2007) appears to agree with Oyewumi when she mentions that "the Western cameras tend to pick on the worst conditions, such as sick and starving children surrounded by flies, and tend to lack sensitivity and respect for the suffering and humanity of the victims" (p. 187). According to Oyewumi (2003b), such portrayal is the result of a long tradition ever since "Africa has been central in Western discourses of difference and degeneration" (p. 162) from colonial era up to date. She points out that during colonization, "because Africans were seen to be physically different from Europeans, who presented themselves as the norm, certain ideas and images were deployed to enunciate what Europeans perceived as the pathologies of difference" (pp. 162–163).

A long-term effect of such practice is that "this is the 21st century, but the image of the African Savage in one form or another still resonates with many Western consumers of the mass media" (Steady, 2007, p. 187). Moreover, in the contemporary context of globalization, with the power dynamics at stake characterizing countries as North verses South, there is an uneven distribution of flow of information between the North and the South. As a result, in many countries of the North, like the United States, there is "a tendency towards and ideology of a 'free press' that, when it comes to Africa, is really nothing short of the homogenization, stereotyping and caricaturing of African peoples and people of African descent with racial and sexist overtones" (Steady, 2007, p. 187). The African female immigrant is not exempt from this portrayal, which in turn automatically impacts the way she may be perceived in the host culture (U.S.).

The goal of this study is to examine how a group of female African immigrants living in the United States—particularly in a small, Midwestern town—perceive themselves in relationship to their portrayal in mainstream U.S. media and how such portrayal impacts their lives. This chapter is organized as follows. I first provide a brief overview of African women's lifestyle in the United States and develop an African feminist theoretical approach on the African woman's representation in Western culture. Then, I describe critical ethnography as a methodological framework guiding this research. Next, I present the thematic findings of the study and end with some concluding thoughts.

Discovering African Women's Lives in the United States

According to Osirim (2008), the current African diaspora in the United States "emerged with the significant increase in African (and Caribbean) migration from the 1980s to the present – a change from about 30,000 African immigrants arriving in the mid-late 1960s to over 350,000 in the decade of the 90s" (pp. 374–375). Anderson (2017) notes that the African immigrant population moved from 0.8 percent in 1970 to 4.8 percent in 2015. Despite this change, as of today, African people still constitute the smallest percentage of the overall number of immigrants who move to the United States each year. Based on the 2015 U.S. Census Bureau data, there were 2.1 million African immigrants, and particularly 1.7 million from Sub-Saharan Africa, out of the 43.3 million immigrants living in the United States (Zong & Batalova, 2017). However, it is important to note that the total number of Africans who enter the country may exceed these approximate statistics, because they exclude undocumented immigrants and encompass only those who enter from such categories as: refugees, relatives of U.S. citizens/permanent residents, international students, and those receiving visas through diversity programs (Osirim, 2008). The largest number of African-born populations in the United States comes from West Africa, followed by East Africa, and finally North Africa (Anderson, 2017; Zong & Batalova, 2017).

African women constitute an important part of the overall diasporic African population who have immigrated to the United States since the 1970s (Osirim, 2008). Their move is often dictated by a number of political and socioeconomic conditions that have made their lives precarious on the African continent, among which are the current phase of globalization, political instability and corruption, wars, civil unrest, natural disasters, education, poverty, search for asylum, etc. (Crawford, 2004; Gatua, 2009; Ojo, 2009; Osirim, 2008). Therefore, for many women, the United States becomes "the land of freedom and opportunity" where they can achieve their goals and improve their living conditions. For instance, they seek for various educational and job opportunities to ensure their future, improve their economic status, and support their families economically in their home countries (Osirim, 2008).

Moreover, throughout their exile, African women constantly face "the need for a construction and reconstruction of self" (Ojo, 2009, p. 75). Nnaemeka (2005) argues that in the actual context of globalization, they "do not have the luxury of contending with a distinct outside and grappling with a clear-cut inside" (p. 31) in their process of identity negotiation, since "the internal and the external are evolving, always contaminated and contested, mutually creating and recreating each other" (p. 31). Thus, these women are expected to embrace hybridity, which "carries notions of melding, mixing, and multiple origins" (Okome, 2001, p. 2) as they constantly construct their identity at the borderlands of cultural worldviews from their home culture and their host culture.

African women's identity negotiation process is often marked by numerous challenges including "adjustment to new academic cultures, limited social support, discrimination and racial prejudice, alienation and isolation, financial constraint, invisibility and loneliness, and cultural fragmentation" (Ojo, 2009, p. 75). To cope with these various issues, African women have learned to show "resilience in the face of adversity, to gather courage and strength through collective use of social support, and to have faith in the Creator of the universe" (Ojo, 2009, pp. 76–77). In the same vein, as transnational subjects, maintaining ties with their home countries while simultaneously celebrating their African cultural legacy and a shared collective memory is an important coping strategy used to foster their national pride in their host culture (Crawford, 2004; Osirim, 2008).

African Feminism and African Women's Representation in Western Culture

Various scholars have attempted to theorize an "African feminist framework." To name a number of alternative African approaches to feminism: womanism (Kolawole, 1997; Ogunyemi, 1985, 1996), motherism (Acholonu, 1995), stiwanism—"Stiwa" is an acronym for Social Transformation Including Women in Africa—(Ogundipe-Leslie, 1994), and nego-feminism (Nnaemeka, 2003). Nnaemeka (2005) argues that "the differences and conflicts among Africans notwithstanding, there exist common features and shared beliefs that undergird their work" (p. 32). For example, a common goal emerging from all these movements is to resist an imposed version of Western feminism that does not see beyond Western societies and hence ignores or marginalizes the specific problems of African women (Arndt, 2000, 2002). These J130
scholars aim to define an African feminism emanating from African culture and exclusively applicable to African women's lives.

African feminism operates as a form of social activism that brings up for scrutiny women's everyday living conditions in order to transform their social reality in the context of oppression (Mama, 2010). African feminism argues that feminism existed in Africa *in practice* prior to its theorization in contemporary society (Mama, 2010; Nnaemeka, 1998, 2003, 2005; Ogundipe-Leslie, 1994; Steady, 1981, 1987). From this perspective, it valorizes the historical legacy of African women performing advocacy, activism, and consciousness-raising within and outside the academy in various areas including education, literature, performance, cinema, teaching, politics, involvement in NGOs, and so forth (Nnaemeka, 2003). Unfortunately, claims Mama (2010), many African women remain historically unknown because the significant events and activities that happened outside of a Western cultural context were not documented or validated. As argued by Mama (2010), African feminism cannot historically be situated as a movement because it emerged as an ad hoc form of activism and advocacy whenever women gathered to fight for a common cause at diverse places all around the African continent.

An important commitment of African feminism is the insistence on the uniqueness of African women's lived experiences (Nnaemeka, 2003). More specifically, African feminism refutes the overgeneralization as well as theorization of African women's experiences in the world by Western feminism. Arnfred (2002) refers to this phenomenon as ethnocentricity saying it "is produced when third world legal, economic, religious and familial structures are treated as phenomena to be judged by Western standards only" (p. 9). For example, some African scholars complained about Western feminists' misinterpretation of a same-sex marriage practice in Nigerian culture as a form of lesbianism (Amadiume, 1987). Similarly, other scholars have advocated for the use of the term "female circumcision" and rejected the label "female genital mutilation," which, according to them, is often used by Western scholars to portray this practice as voyeuristic and barbaric (Arndt, 2000; Oyewumi, 2003a, 2003b). From this perspective, African feminism stands against various stereotypes attached to African women that impede their ability to find emancipatory practices in today's society. This is why African feminism questions the ways that African women's lived experiences are portrayed, particularly in relation to the colonizing Western gaze.

Oyewumi (2003a, 2003b) discusses three strategies through which a negative portrayal of Africa, and the African woman in particular, is pervasive in Western discourse about Africa: othering, villagization, and exceptionalizing. First, the process of othering operates through a binary opposition of the West vs. the Rest that positions Africa as the ultimate Other (Oyewumi, 2003a, 2003b). Oyewumi (2003b) argues that "for centuries, Europeans have envisioned and written about Africa mainly in terms of Otherness, a vehicle for articulating what the West is not" (pp. 162–163). For example, using Western filmmakers as an illustration, Nnaemeka (2003) claims that "the only image they represent of Africa is the impoverished one they've been taught–the worldview of others" (p. 14). Second, "the villagization of Africa" refers to "the assertion of the powerful myth that Africa is a homogenous, unitary state of primitivism in words and deeds" (Oyewumi, 2003b, p. 166). As noted by Steady (2007), "most of the coverage of Africa deals with violence, wars, insensitive coverage of HIV/AIDS, and so forth" (p. 187). Consequently, a "negative image of the African woman is partially created and promoted by Western media" (Nnaemeka, 1998, p. 14). For example, describing media portrayal of the African woman, Aidoo (1992) writes:

> She is breeding too many children she cannot take care of, and for whom she should not expect other people to pick up the tab. She is hungry, and so are her children. In fact, it has become the cliché of Western photojournalism that the African woman is old beyond of years; she is half-naked; her drooped and withered breasts are well exposed; there are flies buzzing around the faces of her children; and she has a permanent begging bowl in her hand.
>
> (p. 319)

Third, "exceptionalizing" is used by cultural outsiders to reproduce the "exotic" Africa and/or African woman. Oyewumi (2003b) argues that, "used positively or negatively, once the observer [cultural outsider] has made up [his] her mind about a person, a practice, a group or phenomenon, nothing else changes the perception" to the extent that "all contrary evidence is made into the exception that proves the invented rule" (p. 168). For example, "both AIDS and female circumcision, then serve as convenient vehicles for articulating centuries-old European stereotypes about Africa" (Oyewumi, 2003b, p. 166). Referring to female circumcision, Arndt (2000) denounces how some Western scholars, who might not necessarily be familiar with such cultural practice, often talk about it with so much exoticism that they end up objectifying the African woman. In her study on *Reading Alice Walker on African and Screening the Color "Black*," Oyewumi (2003b) decries how U.S. African-American scholar Walker portrays female circumcision voyeuristically:

> It is my contention that Walker's claim of consanguinity with Africans notwithstanding, she is best read within the context of Western imperialism in relation to Africa and the narcissism of navel-gazing of contemporary American life. (p. 160) ...These portrayals are not informed by African realities; instead, they reflect the mind of the writer and the Western culture of which she is a part.
>
> (p. 161)

According to Acholonu (1995), all these negative representations are perpetrated in Western culture to confirm existing stereotypes people hold about Africa in the West. Consequently, Steady (2007) mentions that "with regard to the United States, essentializing through stereotypes has

been a staple of the media and an important element in maintaining racist policies and practices since the days of the trans-Atlantic Slave Trade"
(p. 188). As a result, "the picture of Black women [African woman] as
universally deprived only reinforces racism" (Amadiume, 1987, p. 5).

In reaction to this imperialistic view, African feminism calls for a
critical theory that deconstructs the Euro-American and/or Western-
ization cooptation and validation of all forms of African knowledge
(Nnaemeka, 2003; Okome, 2001; Oyewumi, 2002). African feminism
argues that African women's experiences remain contextual to the peculiarities of African culture, shaped by specific cultural issues—such as
female circumcision, marriage conventions (e.g., polygamy and institution of the bride price), widowhood practices, inheritance laws, and so
forth (Amadiume, 1997; Arndt, 2000, 2002; Namemeka, 1998, 2005;
Okome, 2001; Oyewumi, 2002; Steady, 1981, 1987)—that should not
be analyzed through a Western lens. Instead, as argued by Oyewumi
(2002), analysis and interpretations of African women's experiences
"should derive from social organization and relations paying close attention to specific cultural and local contexts" of African culture (p. 8).
In other words, African feminists reclaim the ability to (re)define their
experiences in African terms by advocating for a feminism based on
African philosophy/epistemology that can best engage the lived experiences of African women. By doing so, they validate African ways of
knowing and recommend "the location of African women as knowledge producers and as subjects/objects for knowledge production"
(Nnaemeka, 2003, p. 366).

Purpose of the Study

In accordance with the previous African feminist argument, this study
strives to explore African women's perception of their representation in
the U.S. culture. More specifically, the purpose of this study is to examine and compare the ways in which female African immigrants define
themselves and the ways in which they are represented in the U.S. media.
By doing so, this study strives to answer to the following questions: how
do African female immigrants define *themselves* as "African"? What
are different discourses emerging from U.S. media about their representations? What are their reactions to these representations and how do
these representations impact them in everyday life?

Methodology

Madison (2012) claims that "critical ethnography begins with an ethical responsibility to address processes of unfairness or injustice within
a particular domain" (p. 5). This ethnographic genre focuses on social
differences, based on gender, race, class, age, sexual orientation, and

other identity attributes alike, as a structural cause of social conflict to divulge the darker and oppressive side of social life that often remains unknown (Fiske, 1990). Critical ethnography posits that social inequalities result from culture, which is always and already laced with the politics of conflicting ideologies (Rosaldo, 1993). This study used critical ethnography to deconstruct U.S. media portrayal's impact on African female immigrants' lived experiences and thereby promote social justice by providing participants the opportunity to define themselves in their own terms.

I selected my participants through snowball sampling. Lindlof and Taylor (2011) argue that this strategy is appropriate for studying people who have certain attributes in common, and more specifically people belonging to a subculture. Similarly, I made sure that my participants shared a number of common characteristics including, but not limited to: Black, female, immigrant, over 21, African, fluency in English, moved to the United States at least three years ago, and living in the Midwestern town. I recruited my participants through my personal networking and via local African organizations of the town's community. I ended up working with ten participants from nine countries. For reasons of confidentiality, participants are referred to by pseudonyms: Chad (Aida), Ivory Coast (Fatouma), Benin (Angelina), Burundi (Feza), Ghana (Amina and Fifi), Cameroon (Maimouna), Congo (Ngalula), Nigeria (Ifeoma), and Kenya (Aisha). Despite their common characteristics, participants differed from each other in terms of their demographics (e.g. age, education, religion, status, profession, etc.). For example, participants' ages ranged from 25 to 35 years old and included single women and married women with and without children. Similarly, while all participants attended school in Africa before moving to the United States, their level of education varied from undergraduate to graduate in a variety of fields including engineering, computer sciences, history, social work, communication/media studies, business administration, and education. Participants' occupations varied from being students to being in the workforce, as well as stay-at-home wives and mothers. Indeed, participants were in majority Christian—either Baptist or Catholic—and some identified as Muslim. Finally, participants were fluent both in English and their respective local languages.

As an African female immigrant living in the United States for almost ten years, I entered the field as a Critical Complete-Member-Ethnographer (CCME). Toyosaki (2011) defines Critical Complete-Member-Ethnographers (CCME) as those researchers who are full members of a culture/community they are interpreting/working with and who share with their participants a series of characteristics, roles, experiences, socialization, cultural system of codes, symbols, and meanings. Obviously, such positionality impacted this study, and I was always aware of the significance of my own cultural proximity within this community of female diasporic immigrants. I saw myself in how these women may experience this process of identity negotiation as well as how they make meaning of it in their lives. Consequently, CCME allowed me to negotiate this "epistemological intimacy" (Toyosaki, 2011, p. 66), by embracing an "insider-looking-in-and-out critical approach" (Toyosaki, 2011, p. 66) through self-reflexivity by questioning how my own positionality impacted my participants and vice versa, and thereby reach a level of intersubjectivity with participants (Madison, 2012).

I collected data through qualitative interviewing. Lindlof and Taylor (2011) assert that interview methods are particularly suited for understanding the social actor's experience, knowledge, and worldviews through stories, accounts, or explanations. By using qualitative interviewing, I aimed to engage into an interactive practice with participants by privileging a certain level of flexibility to allow them openly share their personal stories (Holstein & Gubrium, 2002). This methodology helped me produce data, by getting out of the way to let them provide the information that they think is important (Bernard & Ryan, 2010). More precisely, I relied on personal narrative interviews by asking open-ended questions to allow participants to create a dynamic interplay between self and others by sharing their stories as immigrants in relationship to cultural discourses such as race, class, and gender (Lindlof & Taylor, 2011). All interviews were conducted in English and lasted each from 60 to 90 minutes. They were recorded and then transcribed verbatim for further analysis.

I examined my data by applying a thematic analysis. Thematic approach interrogates "what" is spoken in the content of the narratives (Riessman, 2008). I strove to see what my participants shared through the narrative to detect recurrent patterns related to the topic of study. In other words, I examined the narratives by looking for plots connected to the topic of study. Emerson, Fretz, and Shaw (1995) state that thematic narrative "requires selecting only some small portion of the total set of field notes and then linking them into a coherent text representing some aspects or slice of the world studied" (p. 170). Similarly, relying on an open coding and in vivo coding (Lindlof & Taylor, 2011), I was able to identify the major themes emerging from interviews transcripts, which were in turn interpreted in light of the theoretical framework.

Findings

Themes that emerged from interview data revealed a gap between participants' conceptualization of their selfhood and the ways in which they are represented in the U.S. media as well as perceived in the U.S. culture. In this section, I present participants' responses via three themes: Self-Perception as "African," A Stereotyped Media Portrayal of Africa, and Social Perception as the "Other."

Self-Perception as "African"

In response to the question "how do African female immigrants define themselves as 'African'?" themes emerging from interview data revealed that participants hold a positive image of themselves. Consistent with African feminism's commitment of challenging oppressive structures characterizing African women's everyday living conditions to promote social change (Mama, 2010; Nnaemeka, 1998; Ogundipe-Leslie, 1994; Steady, 1987), participants utilized the various positionalities as well as roles they embody and/or occupy in their lives to break negative images of the African woman and thereby define themselves in positive terms. For instance, as a married woman and mother of two kids, Aisha from Kenya said: "I see myself as a beautiful and strong African woman. I am educated. I am a spouse, a mother, and a teacher." Similarly, as a graduate student pursuing her degree in computer sciences, Maimouna from Cameroon stated: "I am smart and hardworking. I am not some stupid savage coming from the jungle like people think it in this country. I am not ashamed of being African, I am proud to be African." Likewise, as Ph. D. student from Ghana, Fifi mentioned: "I see myself as culturally unique because as a woman from Africa I have a lot to offer to this country. Africa is so beautiful and culturally diverse. I'm proud to be African."

Additionally, in contrast to their lived experiences in Africa, participants claimed that being Black in the United States does not determine one's origin. Thus, unless they open their mouths and their accents betray them or they disclose their African ethnic identity, participants' Black bodies are often misread as African-American. For instance, Ngalula from Congo said:

> Quite frankly no one can easily tell that I am from Africa from my skin color. All the customers at work always think that I am an African-American. The moment I open my mouth, they ask me where are you from?

For some participants, such perception is a proof of the complexity of their Blackness, rooted in Africa, the "land of ancestors" for all Black people around the globe, yet perceived differently depending on geographical and/or cultural context. For instance, in reaction to being perceived as African-American, Ifeoma from Nigeria shared the following statement:

> I think that many African-Americans identify me with their ancestors because of my African origin. I meet many of them and when I tell them that I am from Africa, they start asking so many questions because they want to know so much about Africa, what they call "the land of our ancestors."

Although there is often confusion between participants and African-American women, they believe that there are major differences in their Black identity. Thus, many of them expressed the need to emphasize how their "Blackness" as "African" differed from "African-American Blackness." Participants relied on a variety of strategies to highlight "the uniqueness" of their "Blackness." Some participants claimed that performing cultural and traditional African values is a distinct marker of their African identity. For example, as a married woman and mother of two kids, Aida mentioned that traditional gender roles are a core value of her African heritage: "I think that I'm different because my African culture has taught me to take care of my household chores (cooking especially African food and cleaning), and of my family (my husband and children)." Similarly, as a mother of one child, Fatouma from Ivory Coast shared the following statement:

> I always tell any African woman who moves to this country to be aware of her African roots. We have to preserve our African culture it is what makes us unique as African. For instance, most women in this country don't respect their men. They yell at them. This is not allowed in African culture. That is why it is crucial for us as African women to transmit this cultural legacy and all those cultural values to our children.

While the aforementioned values are more internalized and invisible, another group of participants claimed to perform consciously or not a number of practices to enhance their physical appearance as a way to communicate their African identity. For instance, as a Muslim woman, Aisha believes that her attire is a great asset to enhance her African identity:

> I am African not only from my skin color, but also from my dressing style. As a Muslim woman from Africa, wearing a scarf is an important aspect of my African identity...I use different types of scarves, and particularly those made of African fabrics such as *kente* and I style them in an African way.

Aisha believes that doing so demarcates herself from Muslims of other parts of the world. In the same way, as a married woman and a Christian, Aida mentioned that what distinguishes her as an African woman is also the way she carries her body:

> I don't shave my body. I wear African braids. I dress up in African fabrics. And as a Christian, a mother, and a married woman, I make sure I dress up decently. I don't wear anything too tight or sexy. I don't show my body. I'm surprised that even married women wear those kinds of clothes in this country.

Ojo (2009) claims that it is important for female African immigrants to remain culturally aware of their origins in their host culture to fight against the negative stereotypes associated with their African identity. In a resonating vein, participants' prior stories demonstrate that by positioning themselves as custodians of African culture and legacy in the diaspora (Gatua, 2009), participants are culturally aware of their African values and use them in a variety of ways to communicate a positive image that they hold of themselves in their host culture.

A Stereotyped Media Portrayal

In response to the question, "what are different discourses emerging from U.S. media about African women," this study revealed a pervasive negative image of Africa and the African woman in particular. Exemplifying Oyewumi's (2003b) denunciation of "the villagization of Africa," participants unanimously decried a stereotyped media portrayal of Africa in a stage of constant primitiveness, suffering, and poverty. For instance, Aisha said: "In the U.S. media, Africa is nothing, but this homogenous jungle…no diversity of cultures is emphasized at all… no wonder Americans think of it as a country rather than a continent." Similarly, as a student majoring in media studies, Fifi complained that U.S. media always pick on the negative side of Africa: "Look at Eddie Murphy's movie *Coming to America* with all these negative stereotypes about Africa as a jungle…and it is the same thing with media coverage: disease, poverty, etc." Subsequently, as claimed by participants, the African woman is portrayed as "the savage" and "uncivilized." For example, Fifi shared her frustrations as follows: "Mainstream U.S. media portray us Africans as poor, savages, uneducated, uncivilized." Along the same lines, Feza from Burundi said: "everything you see about Africa on TV is war, starving and weak children, diseases, dirty and poor people, and bare breast women and all other kinds of bad things as if that's what Africa is all about."

Additionally, participants' lived experiences revealed further alignment with African feminism's criticism of "exceptionalizing" (Oyewumi, 2003b) in reproducing a negative image of the African woman through exoticism. Participants complained about being a target of "cultural markings" associated to this series of mediated negative images, which in turn result in stereotyping. For example, Maimouna said: "American people ask me stupid questions like: How did you get here? Do you live in trees? Do you pet lions? Do you see giraffes crossing the street while driving? This is very embarrassing." In the same way, Angelina from Benin complained about being stereotyped on campus:

> It's not easy to be respected in this country because usually people look at us as "savages" coming from a jungle. We are stereotyped

every time and in so many ways just because of the negative way Africa is represented in the media.

Moreover, some participants complained about being sexually objectified due to U.S. negative media portrayal of female circumcision. For instance, as a Muslim woman from Benin, where female circumcision is practiced, Angelica said: "American people ask me stupid questions about whether or not I experienced female circumcision just because they saw on TV that women get circumcised in West Africa, and particularly in Muslim countries." Similarly, despite being a Christian woman from the Congo, a country where there is no female circumcision, Ngalula complained about being a target of sexual objectification. She shared the following story:

Female genital circumcision is not practiced in my country, yet I've been sexually stereotyped to have no clitoris. I once met this African-American guy who asked me out. During our date, he shared that he likes dating women from other countries to learn more about other cultures. He said he had dated women from Latin America and Asia, but none from Africa yet. I was shocked when he told me that, watching all these documentaries on TV and the net about "female genital mutilation" in Africa made him curious about trying sex with an African who doesn't have a clitoris.

Other participants criticized mainstream Western media portrayals of female circumcision for culturally exoticizing the African woman. For instance, as a Muslim woman from Kenya, where female circumcision is practiced, Aisha believes that such media portrayal is simply biased:

I've watched some of those documentaries and reports. It is always the same scenario of some western movie maker, scholar, or researcher on a trip in those remoted areas of Africa and speaking only negatively about female circumcision. None of them strives to explore the cultural meaning embedded in this practice. All they care about is to exocitize these poor women. Yet, we Africans we don't make movies about Western women relying on plastic surgery to tighten up their vaginas.

Speaking of the sexual objectification of the African woman, Oyewumi (2003b) mentions that "it must be remarked that though Saartje [Venus Hottentot] was displayed for European consumption because her parts were hyper-sexual from a Western perspective, the African woman today is displayed for the hypo-sexuality of her presumed missing parts" (pp. 160–161). Likewise, as demonstrated in participants' earlier statements, U.S. media's portrayal of female circumcision reinforces a negative portrayal of the African woman as "hypo-sexual." While

African women are not the only ones subject to othering, Oyewumi (2003b) specifies that through such depiction, "African women in particular, however, appear to represent the ultimate Other, combining in one category as racial and sexual Otherness with a special role as the 'Other's Other'" (pp. 162–163). This argument speaks specifically to Ngalula's experience positioned as the other's other vis-à-vis other women of color, particularly Latinas and Asians in this case. She got stereotyped not only as the racial other (Black woman), but most importantly the "exotic sexual other" from Africa with no clitoris.

The negative images associated with participants' lived experiences as demonstrated in the prior comments are not innocent, nor can they be taken for granted. Instead, they point to the widespread issue of "exoticism" African women are subject to as people belonging to "a dark continent" often portrayed in U.S. media via "villagization" and "exceptionalizing" (Oyewumi 2003a, 2003b) and living now in "the land of civilization" or "paradise on Earth," the United States of America. Denouncing such exoticism, some participants called attention on how the African woman remains a constant target of "cultural marking" as opposed to the white woman. Pursuing her comments, Aisha stated: "Isn't it ironical that African women get criticized and exoticized for undergoing female circumcision whereas U.S. women get praised for tightening up their vaginas." Such a depiction demonstrates that "the labeling of African women as primitive, and therefore more sexually intensive, [is] antithetical to the portrayal of the European woman as sexually passive" (Oyewumi, 2003a, p. 37).

Embracing African feminism's allegiance of deconstructing Western media's inaccurate representations of Africa (Steady, 2007), participants called out Americans on their lack of knowledge about African culture. They expected American people to be more educated about African culture just the way they are about theirs. Unfortunately, this is not the case. Participants unanimously decried such lack of knowledge as "ignorance." As an illustration, Aida made the following comments:

> American people are not well-informed about our culture because they are ignorant. All they think is: Africa is a country, we are all the same, we are coming from the same place, we all look the same, and we all speak the same language. For instance, I met a woman who asked me to teach her an African language. I didn't even know what to say. I don't mind teaching an African language to someone here, but which one? We have so many languages (laughs). Come on, they can improve this by trying to educate themselves even a little bit about Africa.

Situating themselves as agents of knowledge production about Africa (Nnaemeka, 2003), some participants deal with this "ignorance" with patience by taking on the responsibility to educate Americans about their culture. For instance, as a minority instructor in her department, Aisha is constantly using education as a vehicle for disseminating her African culture. She expressed her feelings as follows:

> I think that people should educate themselves a little bit more instead of relying on media as the only source of information, especially when we all know that American's portrayal of African culture is so biased. I used a documentary from my class to clean their mind about Africa. There were so many reactions in the class among which: Oh, this is really Africa? It looks clean. So people also wear these kinds of clothes and you can see cars, buildings, etc.

However, for other participants, it is important to distinguish between ignorance and choosing to be ignorant. In other words, some participants claimed that while a lack of knowledge can be forgiven, choosing ignorance over an invitation to become educated reinforces only prejudice. As an illustration, Feza said "I believe that most Americans choose to remain ignorant about the rest of the world, and particularly Africa, instead of striving to educate themselves. And this is only reinforcing the stereotyping instead of stopping it."

Social Perception as the "Other"

In accordance with African feminism's criticism of Western media's representations of Africans in terms of "Otherness" (Nnaemeka, 2003; Oyewumi, 2003b; Steady, 2007), participants' lived experiences show that they are not only portrayed as the "other" in mainstream U.S. media, but also perceived as the "cultural exotic other" in the U.S. society. More specifically, in response to the question, "what is your reaction to U.S. mediated representations of the African woman and how do these representations impact your everyday life," themes from interview data revealed that this process of othering operate at three levels: racism, linguistic discrimination, and social rejection.

Racism

Participants complained about facing challenges of racism due to the negative stereotypes attached to their portrayal as "the Other" in mainstream U.S. media. For instance, Fatouma complained about being labeled "monkey" because of her ethnic identity: "when I was in highschool, so many White kids used to bully me by comparing me to a monkey just because I am African. They said that all they see about Africa on national geographic are monkeys and safari." Ngalula faced a similar situation:

I once met this White woman who asked me where I was from and I told her I was from Congo and she replied "oh, you are from the monkeys' land?" That's so offensive! She said that is all she sees on TV about Africa.

Additionally, participants believe that their skin color influences the way Americans, and more specifically, White people, treat them in public settings. For instance, as the only Black woman from Africa working at a predominantly White environment, Fatouma complained about being subject to potential attacks. She shared the following tale:

One day, I made a mistake by letting someone, who supposedly was a "stranger," get in the daycare. My boss yelled at me in public and I felt very uncomfortable. She is a White middle-class woman. Although I misbehaved, I wonder if she would have treated me in the same way if I was White.

Osirim (2008) argues that African immigrants "often experience the intersection of gender, race and class in their lives, which affects their life chances and is likely to have an impact on the development of their communities" (p. 374). Decrying Black women's struggle with racism, Ogunyemi argues that "African women experience the racial discrimination, socio-economic oppression and imperialism of White Western societies and that the political, cultural and socio-economic experiences of Black/African women – as a social group– differ from those of White women" (as cited by Arndt, 2002, p. 41). Similarly, the previous stories reveal that participants are subject to potential challenges of discrimination by White Americans as Black women in the United States as a result a negative portrayal of their selfhood in U.S. media.

Language

Participants complained about being victims of linguistic discrimination. For instance, most participants from non-native English speaking countries mentioned that not being able to speak English fluently made them subject to mockery. Fatouma from Ivory Coast who attended high school in the United States shared the following tale:

Although I am able to interact quite fluently with American people in English today, this took me a while. I arrived in the U.S. in August 2006 and I had to start school in September, just a month after my arrival. I didn't have a chance to prepare myself with this challenge. I didn't have a chance to learn English back home prior my move to the U.S. I mean, what I knew was just the basics of what we all learn, I believe across the country, things such how to say hi, to apologize, and so on. This was really tough. Whenever I tried to say something, everyone made fun of me in class. That completely shut me down. I ended up just sitting there in the classroom without saying anything.

The struggle with English is not only an issue of fluency, but it also about accentuation.

Amina, an English-speaker from Ghana, told the following story:

It's not only about English, but it's also about your accent. For example, I had just moved to a new apartment and I called to get the power fixed home. I don't know if the woman on the line had a hard time understanding me or if only she assumed that she could not understand what I was saying. I just heard "I don't understand what you say." She did not even give me time to explain the situation; she just decided to transfer me to a Spanish service. I was shocked because I'm not Spanish and I don't speak Spanish.

In response to the previous frustrations, some participants constantly strive to imitate the American accent. This coping strategy seems efficient for some like Angelina, a French-speaking student from Benin, for passing as African-American:

I do have an accent, but it's weird sometimes people identify me as African-American. Many people, just like my teacher, think that I'm from Chicago. I think that I picked up the American, and more specifically African-American accent, pretty quickly. Sometimes, I take advantage of this if I want to talk like an African-American girl. I went to a meeting and while introducing people, the presenter said: "I'm glad that we also have around this table people from other countries such as Benin." People were surprised looking at each other wondering who she was referring to since I was not the only Black person in the room. Then, when she said my name, I had all eyes on me.

In contrast, other participants rejected the idea of imitating the American accent because they consider it as another form of colonization. For instance, Aisha said:

We all know that neither French nor English are our original languages. We inherited them from colonization. As an historian, I feel like expecting people to speak like "Americans" is telling them to speak like their "colonizers" because what is emphasized here is speaking like "White Americans." To me, this is another type of colonization. As Africans, we have to strive to decolonize our minds from colonization instead of getting colonized again.

As demonstrated in participants' stories, unlike the "European accent," which get romanticized in the United States because it is Western, there is a negative perception of the "African accent," which get "otherized." However, Okome (2001) argues that speaking like an "American" is an expectation on the African woman's integration in the U.S. culture. Ultimately, due to the inability and/or refusal of speaking English like "Americans," participants are often perceived as the "culturally incompetent other" in the host culture, which in turn results into discrimination.

Social Rejection/Isolation

This study revealed that participants suffer from social isolation as a result of their social perception as "the cultural exotic other." For instance, Aisha shared how her Muslim identity makes her a subject of threat: "when I walk down the streets with my scarf, people give me all sorts of looks. On campus, they don't talk to me. They probably think of me as a terrorist, a threat to this country." This, in turn, results in a lack of connection and integration into society. For instance, Feza said:

> I feel very lonely in this country. It's not that easy to make friends. People avoid you. They don't talk to you. They don't communicate with you just because you are different. May be because you can't speak English fluently like them or because of your accent. In Africa, people live in community. They enjoy things together and everything. It is warm. We are all brothers and sisters.

To overcome this isolation, participants seek social support from African associations and groups. As a member of an African Christian association, Aida shared her personal experience as follows:

> This group provides me the unique opportunity to pray and celebrate African culture with my sisters. I can interact with women about our specific issues. In fact, we have various meetings with other women on how to encourage each other in difficult time, how to take care of our house and kids. I would say that my relationships with these women are good in general. To me, they are more than friends or sisters in Christ. They are people I can really count or rely on any time.

Indeed, participants use the African community as a space for the celebration of African culture. In the tale that follows, Angelina describes her experience as a member of an African Campus organization:

> For me, it is a space to educate people about our African culture. It's not just about performing African culture, but also showing

differences between countries. For example, I performed Benin dance; I made Benin food; and, I had worn Benin outfit for the African cultural show.

Eventually, these associations become favorable spaces for African identity performance through commemoration of collective practices, cultural events, etc. Similarly, Aida described her Christian community as a site of African Identity performed as follows:

> We do it in many ways: food, praying, partying, games, etc. For example, there is what we call Mission Sunday at the church. It's a big celebration during which different people sing songs from their cultures and countries. We dress up in African clothes and then we sing in African songs in local languages. It's interesting. This means that this group also gives me a chance to practice my African languages. For example, I have friends with who I can speak in Swahili besides French.

Ojo (2009) asserts that many diasporic Black women come from environments where individual development depends heavily on social interaction and their personal identity is intricately connected to their community identity. In a resonating vein, Osirim (2008) reminds us that diasporic identities are produced and reproduced through the collective memory of a group of people. Similarly, the prior narratives demonstrate that participants' identities are intersubjectively constructed through group membership as they rely on different African organizations and associations to fulfill their needs of networking and socialization.

Discussion and Concluding Thoughts

This critical ethnographic study examined how a group of female African immigrants living in a small Midwestern town perceive themselves in relationship to their portrayal in mainstream U.S. media and how such portrayal impacts their lives. The findings revealed a gap between participants' conceptualization of their selfhood and the ways in which they are represented in the U.S. media as well as perceived in their host culture. While participants hold a positive image of themselves as African—such as strong, beautiful, hardworking, smart, clean, and proud—there is a pervasive negative image of the African woman depicted in mainstream U.S. media as "savage/uncivilized." Indeed, participants are socially perceived as the "cultural exotic other," which in turn makes them subjects to racism and linguistic discrimination. Ultimately, such negative portrayal and social perception result in a lack of social interaction in their host culture. In light of these findings, this study calls for a more systematic and critical reading of African women's representations of the self in Western culture.

In contrast to the pervasive negative image of the African woman in mainstream U.S. media, participants in this study hold a positive image of themselves. Commenting on the positive image of the African woman of her generation in her novel *Efuru*, literary writer Flora Nwapa states:

> They were solid and superior women who held their own in society. They were not only wives and mothers but successful traders who took care of their children and their husbands as well. They were very much aware of their leadership roles in their families as well as in the churches and local government.
>
> (as cited by Nnaemeka, 1998, p. 13)

Pointing to the contrasting negative representation of the African woman in Western culture, Nnaemeka (1998) invites us to reflect on what generated a denigrating image of today's African woman. She writes:

> If strong, powerful, activist, independent, and socially relevant women populate African history and traditional cultures, how does one explain the contemporary pathetic, despondent, hungry, helpless and dependent women enshrined in photojournalism? Whose creations are they? How does one explain the current image of the African woman as dilemma?
>
> (p. 13)

Answering these questions inherently calls for the deconstruction of Euro-American rationalization of knowledge production as advocated by African feminism (Oyewumi, 2002). Decrying the colonizing process of knowledge production, African feminism invites us to question the intellectual, political, and ethical questions of knowledge production: "the question of provenance (where is the theory coming from?); the question of subjectivity (who authorizes?); the question of positionality (which specific locations and standing [social, political, and intellectual] does it legitimize?)" (Nnaemeka, 2003, p. 362). All these issues are crucial to deconstruct cultural misrepresentations—such as those of the African woman—as a hegemonic aesthetic of Western supremacy intended to reproduce the colonizing project of "othering," which results in the objectification of the nonwhite population, and particularly third-world women (Chavez, 2009).

In response to the previous questions, this study calls upon advocacy for the rebranding of Africa. As argued by Steady (2007), important initiatives must be taken by Western media industries to take action against the 'branding' of Africa for 'the re-branding of Africa' in mainstream Western media by stressing the need to portray the joys, creativities, and values such as human compassion, family life, reciprocity, and redistribution. For instance, it is imperative to promote the visibility of African women, and by extension Africans, by positioning them as subjects and creators of their own cultural realities, rather than objects of creation for Western knowledge production. And to reach such a goal, "the inclusion of voices from the African continent should be seen as a question of relevance and necessity...Such voices are crucial not only in debates about Africa but also in discussions of global issues" (Nnaemeka, 1998, p. 79). Doing so would "lead to redefinitions and critical examinations of concepts, perspectives, and methodologies used in research [knowledge] and inspire vital changes that will render research activity [knowledge production] as a basic human right and a process of liberation for oppressed groups" (Steady, 1987, p. 4).

In light of the previous argument, an important contribution of this study is positioning African women as subjects and creators of their own realities by providing them a space to deconstruct the "negative branding" of the African woman in mainstream U.S. media and to construct a "positive re-branding" of the African woman by defining themselves in their own terms. Nevertheless, the study has limitations that need to be pointed out and extended for future research. This study focused only on educated African women, which positions them as privileged subjects vis-à-vis non-educated women. Thus, their status as educated women might explain their level of knowledge about the topic of this study. From this perspective, I think that it is important for future research to include the voices of non-educated African women to get other perspectives on the phenomenon studied. Indeed, whereas this study focused primarily on the experiences of African women as the population of interest, future research could expand on the experiences of African male immigrants to investigate this identity negotiation as a two-way process.

Note

1 I do acknowledge that Africa is culturally diverse in terms of countries and cultures. Nonetheless, with respect to these cultural differences, there are also common/shared features, beliefs, and practices that characterize Black African countries in the geographical area of the continent that lies south of the Sahara (see Nnaemeka, 2005). Thus, the term "African feminism" is used in this study not to dismiss these cultural differences, rather to emphasize the commonalities characterizing the lived experiences of participants as diasporic Black subjects from Africa living in the United States and identifying with the African culture of this area.

References

Acholonu, C. O. (1995). *Motherism: The Afrocentric alternative to feminism.* London: Afa Publications.

Aidoo, A. A. (Summer, 1992). The African woman today. *Dissent, 39,* 319–325.

Amadiume, I. (1987). *Male daughters, female husbands: Gender and sex in an African society*. London: Zed.

Amadiume, I. (1997). *Re-inventing Africa: Matriarchy, religion, and culture*. New York, NY: St. Martin's Press.

Anderson, M. (February, 2017). *African immigrant population in U.S. steadily climbs*. Retrieved from www.pewresearch.org/fact-tank/2017/02/14/african-immigrant-population-in-u-s-steadily-climbs/

Arndt, S. (2000). African gender trouble and African womanism: An interview with Chikwenye Ogunyemi and Wanjira Muthoni. *Signs: Journal of Women in Culture and Society, 25*(3), 709–726.

Arndt, S. (2002). *Dynamics of African feminism: Defining and classifying African-feminist literatures*. Trenton, NJ: Africa World Press.

Arnfred, S. (2002). Simone de Beauvoir in Africa: "Woman = the second sex?" issues of African feminist thought. *A Journal of Culture and African Women's Studies, 2*, 1–20.

Bernard, R. H., & Ryan, G. W. (2010). *Analyzing qualitative data: Systematic approaches*. Thousand Oaks, CA: Sage.

Chavez, K. C. (2009). Postcolonial feminism. In S. W. Littlejohn & K. A. Foss (Eds.), *Encyclopedia of communication theory* (pp. 766–767). Thousand Oaks, CA: Sage.

Crawford, C. (2004). African-Caribbean women, diaspora and transnationality. *Canadian Woman Studies/Les Cahiers de la Femme, 23*(2), 97–103.

Emerson, R. M., Fretz, R. I., & Shaw, L. L. (1995). *Writing ethnographic fieldnotes*. Chicago, IL: The University of Chicago Press.

Fiske, J. (1990). Talking American: Cultural discourses on Donahue, by Donal Carbaugh. *Quarterly Journal of Speech, 76*, 450–451.

Gatua, M. W. (2009). Overcoming the odds: Challenges and successes of Sub-Saharan African women seeking higher education in the United States. *Adult Learning, 20*, 16–19.

Holstein, J. A., & Gubrium, J. F. (2002). Active interviewing. In D. Weinberg (Ed.), *Qualitative research methods* (pp. 112–132). Malden, MA: Blackwell.

Kolawole, M. E. (1997). *Womanism and African consciousness*. Trenton, NJ: Africa World Press.

Lindlof, T. R., & Taylor, B. C. (2011). *Qualitative communication research methods*. (3rd ed.). Los Angeles, CA: Sage Publications.

Madison, D. S. (2012). *Critical ethnography: Methods, ethics, and performance* (2nd ed.). Thousand Oaks, CA: Sage.

Mama, S. (2010). *The woman in me: The struggles for an African woman to discover her identity and authority*. Bloomington, IN: Authorhouse.

Nnaemeka, O. (1998). Introduction: Reading the rainbow. In O. Nnaemeka (Ed.), *Sisterhood, feminism, and power: From Africa to the diaspora* (pp. 1–35). Trenton, NJ: Africa World Press.

Nnaemeka, O. (2003). Nego-feminism: Theorizing, practicing, and pruning Africa's way. *Signs, 29*(2), 357–383.

Nnaemeka, O. (2005). Mapping African feminisms, adapted version of Introduction: Reading the rainbow, from Sisterhood, feminisms, and power: From Africa to diaspora. In A. Cornwal (Ed.), *Readings in gender in Africa* (pp. 31–41). Bloomington, IN: Indiana University Press.

Ogundipe-Leslie, M. (1994). *Re-creating ourselves: African women and critical transformations*. Trenton, NJ: Africa World Press.

Ogunyemi, C. O. (1985). Womanism: The dynamics of the cotemporary Black female novel in English. *Signs, 11*(1), 63–80.

Ogunyemi, C. O. (1996). *Africa wo/man palava: The Nigerian novel by women*. Chicago, IL: The University of Chicago Press.

Ojo, E. D. (2009). Support systems and women of the diaspora. *New Directions for Adult and Continuing Education, 122,* 73–82.

Okome, M. O. (2001). African women and power: Reflections on the perils of unwarranted cosmopolitanism. *A Journal of Culture and African Women's Studies, 1,* 1–18.

Osirim, M. J. (2008). African women in the new diaspora: Transnationalism and the (re) creation of home. *African and Asian Studies, 7,* 367–394.

Oyewumi, O. (2002). Conceptualizing gender: The Eurocentric foundations of feminist concepts and the challenge of African epistemologies. *A Journal of Culture and African Women's Studies, 2,* 1–9.

Oyewumi, O. (2003a). The White woman's burden: African women in Western feminist discourse. In O. Oyewumi (Ed.), *African women and feminism: Reflecting on the politics of sisterhood* (pp. 25–43). Trenton, NJ: Africa World Press.

Oyewumi, O. (2003b). Alice in motherland: Reading Alice Walker on Africa and screening the color "Black." In O. Oyewumi (Ed.), *African women and feminism: Reflecting on the politics of sisterhood* (pp. 159–185). Trenton, NJ: Africa World Press.

Riessman, C. K. (2008). *Narrative methods for the human science*. Thousand Oaks, CA: Sage.

Rosaldo, R. (1993). *Culture and truth: The remaking of social analysis*. Boston, MA: Beacon Press.

Steady, C. F. (1981). The Black woman cross-culturally: An overview. In C. F. Steady (Ed.), *The Black woman cross-culturally* (pp. 1–41). Cambridge, MA: Schenkman Publishing Company.

Steady, C. F. (1987). African feminism: A worldwide perspective. In R. Terborg-Penn, S. Harley, A. B. Rushing (Eds.), *Women in Africa and the African diaspora* (pp. 3–24). Washington, DC: Howard University Press.

Steady, C. F. (2007). The Black Woman and the essentializing imperatives: Implications for theory and praxis in the 21st century. *Race, Gender, & Class, 14,* 178–195.

Toyosaki, S. (2011). Critical complete-member ethnography: Theorizing dialectics of consensus and conflict in intracultural communication. *Journal of International and Intercultural Communication, 4*(1), 62–80.

Zong, J., & Batalova, J. (May, 2017). *Sub-Saharan immigrants in the United States*. Retrieved from www.migrationpolicy.org/article/sub-saharan-african-immigrants-united-states#Immigration_Pathways_and_Naturalization

9 Hardly Ever, I Don't See It

Black Youth Speak about Positive Media Images of Black Men

Valerie N. Adams-Bass and Erin Joann Henrici

A longstanding critique of visual media content, specifically television, addresses the frequency of harsh representations of Black people that reinforce negative stereotypes and influence people's actual perceptions of Black people (Allen, 1998; Allen & Bielby, 1979; Allen & Thornton, 1992; Berry, 1998, 2000; Browne Graves, 1982; Spurlock, Berry, & Mitchell-Kernan, 1982). For many viewers, the stereotypes about Black people presented on TV impact day-to-day interactions. For example, depictions of urban Black males on shows, such as *Power*, offer characters that are aggressive, criminal, violent, and predatory. These storylines, while meant to provide a view of life in urban communities, often fail to include or critique the systems that have a significant impact on the lives and choices of the characters. These portrayals serve to reinforce racial stereotypes about Black men that link back to the historical legacy of slavery (Jackson, 2006). The images instill fear into viewers, who have little to no interactions with Black people (Holt, 2013; Hurley, Jensen, Weaver, & Dixon, 2015). For example, Hurley et al. (2015) found that after viewing a 30-minute segment on crime, participants were more likely to label the Black character personally culpable than the White character.

When viewers watch U.S.-produced television and movie content that feature Black males, these representations are interpreted as actual examples of Black men. This is problematic because of the large number of images that present Black men as criminal, lazy, violent, hypersexual, or unintelligent (Bogle, 2016). Exposure to images of Black men as angry and violent translate to actual fear when people have real or "live" encounters with Black males (Steele, 2010). Recently, encounters with police and other law enforcement officials have been documented and shared via social media. While these types of encounters are not new, affordable access to cameras via smartphones and social media has led to mainstream exposure of these incidents. Media-influenced biases also create tension and strain relationships among Black Americans, Caribbean, and Latino people of African descent. While this chapter focuses on stereotypes of Black Americans, we note that stereotypes of Africans exist globally and reinforce racial stereotypes that preserve the social inequalities that keep Africans at the lower end of the global social spectrum.

Black Media Images

Scholars have consistently criticized stereotypical Black images and hypothesized that exposure to these images influences the self-esteem and behavior of Black youth (Gorham, 1999; Milkie, 1999; Tynes & Ward, 2009; Watkins, 2005). In 1973, Bogle released the robust text *Toms, Coons, Mulattoes, Mammies and Bucks*, in which he organized and criticized media content for its representation of African-Americans as: (1) Toms—Black men who were subservient to whites and unwilling to stand up for Black rights and social justice; (2) Coons—uneducated Blacks who were prone to repetitive erroneous behavior; (3) Mulattoes— Black people of mixed race, who were tragically trapped in a light-skinned body affording them privilege among white people, yet created anguish among darker-hued Black Americans; (4) Mammies—larger-framed subservient Black women whose primary concern and responsibility was to the children and family of her White employers, often at the expense of her own family; and (5) Bucks—physically-imposing Black men who could manage hard labor and harbored sexual desires for white women (Bogle, 1973). Later editions included a sixth caricature—the sidekick. Sidekicks are desexualized characters that are cast in contrast or support of lead characters (Bogle, 2001b).

Black Media Images and Youth

Black youth have the highest television viewing hours per day of all of their peers (Park & Villar, 2015; Tynes & Ward, 2009) and a prefer- ence for viewing content that features Black characters or personal- ities (Adams, 2011). A limited number of studies have examined the relationship between media exposure, racial identity, and self-esteem (Gordon, 2008; Ward, 2004). Balaji (2009) argues that representations of Black music artists, including youth, are easier to market using pre- existing archetypes rather than risk packaging using images not ordi- narily associated with Black artists. Ward's (2004) study of televised content suggests exposure to media stereotypes has an unexpected in- fluence on Black youth. While there are some Black characters that rep- resent positive stereotypes about Black people, these images are limited (Bogle, 2016); as such, much of the research with Black youth examines exposure to negative media content.

We know that Black youth prefer Black media content (Abrams, 2008; Botta, 2000; Poindexter & Stroman, 1981), watch high levels of TV

(Tynes & Ward, 2009), and that images of Black people are most often negative (Berry, 1998, 2000; Bogle, 2016; Gorham, 1999). The images become problematic due to the wide distribution of U.S.-produced media content. Many media outlets are now owned by large conglomerates, whose main concern is financial gain, and therefore most companies do not take risks or support the production of images that offer positive and/or nuanced perspectives of Black artists (Balaji, 2009).

In this chapter, we suggest that Black youth are able to identify and distinguish between negative and positive media images, critique the absence of positive images of Black men, and offer a rationale for the exclusion of these types of images. While some laymen and even some scholars would argue that contemporary Black characters are new and refreshing, we suggest that the archetypes of Black characters, such as those presented in Bogle's seminal work (1973), still exist and that contemporary terminologies, such as "ratchet" and "thug," are extensions of these characterizations. Rarely are Black male characters represented beyond the common stereotypical archetypes of Buck, Sambo, Uncle Tom, or the Sidekick. Black men are presented as shiftless, violent, unintelligent, and aggressive, or as criminals or "Bucks" (Bogle, 2016; Hazell & Clarke, 2008; Jackson, 2006; Tynes & Ward, 2009).

Theories of Socialization

While many studies measure the relationship between media socialization and implicit/explicit racial bias, little is known about how Black youth are socialized to interpret negative media messages about Black people. Our concern is how the exposure of negative Black images impacts the development of Black youth. We offer racial-ethnic socialization (R/E Socialization) as a lens through which Black American youth view and interpret media, and critical media literacy (CML) as a paradigm for critiquing and understanding the messages that are communicated through visual media.

Racial Socialization

For decades, researchers have been trying to understand how Black parents prepare their children to understand the racial politics and barriers that may impact them while growing up. Racial socialization has become a term that has been primarily associated with African-Americans, given the deeply entrenched systems of racism that exist with the United States' culture (Hughes et al., 2006).

Racial socialization is defined as the processes by which children acquire behaviors, perceptions, values, and attitudes through direct or indirect messages and modeling from the important people around them as well as from societal cues (Bentley et al., 2009). It includes the process that Black parents employ for raising healthy youth with a solid sense of self while preparing them for living in a society where they are likely to encounter negative racial experiences (Stevenson, 1994). Proactive racial socialization involves acknowledging inequitable treatment of African-Americans, providing youth with pragmatic examples and instructions about how to manage racial encounters, sharing the historical and cultural legacy of African-Americans, and validating ethnic standards of beauty and attractiveness (Stevenson, 1994; Stevenson, McNeil, Herrero-Taylor, & Davis, 2005).

For African-American youth, racial/ethnic socialization helps to strengthen their level of resiliency and coping; it is an essential value-added component of identity development that shapes their self-image and identity (Hughes et al., 2006; Spencer, 1990; Stevenson, 1995; Swanson & Spencer, 1999). For example, an African-American youth who has experienced racial socialization that includes bias preparation messages will be able to identify media content that projects negative messages about Black people and reject these messages as unrealistic (Adams & Stevenson, 2012).

Critical Media Literacy

Rapid developments in technology have increased the influence that media and broadcasting have on the spread of information and values in modern society. Education has now expanded from not only books and texts, but to multimodal sources within and outside the classroom (Kellner & Share, 2007a). A combination of information from all these sources has the power to create a public pedagogy, especially when producing messages about gender, race, and class (Giroux, 1999; Luke, 1997). Despite the pervasiveness of media culture, many K-12 schools fail to acknowledge or address the influence of media on their student's development.

Accordingly, educators have called for a reconstruction of the term literacy to include learning from multiple sources, as well as the use of critical approaches to deconstruct, analyze, and evaluate the messages provided by multimedia. Kellner and Share (2007a) define literacy as the process of "gaining the skills and knowledge to read, interpret, produce texts and artifacts, and to gain the intellectual tools and capacities to fully participate in one's culture and society" (p. 5). These authors also argue that literacy is socially constructed within a world of social institutions, rules, and norms.

Media education has taken many forms and approaches within educational contexts. Many authors are critical of the limited scope of media arts education approaches due to the complexity of media influence. As a standard, media literacy is defined as the ability to access, analyze, evaluate, and communicate messages in a wide variety of forms

(Aufderheide & Firestone, 1993). According to the definition of media literacy provided by National Association of Media Literacy Education (NAMLE), this analysis "is seen to consist of a series of communication competencies, including the ability to access, analyze, evaluate and communicate." Ferguson (1998) critiques this "tip of the iceberg" approach for only focusing on the superficial messages of media, while neglecting the economic, political, and social ideologies that define relationships of power and subordination within media.

As a result, CML adds to the traditional definition of media literacy in order to address this limitation. It includes the politics of representation of gender, race, class, and sexuality, as well as a critical understanding of ideology, power, and domination. Orlowski (2006) suggests that media and the public education system are the two main sources of information in our society. For that reason, advocates of CML stress the importance of using this methodology within classrooms. Educators have the opportunity to provide a space that allows for counter-narratives against the traditionally White hegemonic mainstream media (Orlowski, 2006). For some, CML is entrenched within values of radical democracy and civic participation (Kellner & Share, 2007b).

Through education, this form of media literacy helps teachers and students understand how power and media are linked through the lenses of message deconstruction and alternative media production (Kellner & Share, 2007a). This approach also integrates ideas from multicultural, intersectional, feminist, and postmodern theories (Kellner & Share, 2007b). Alvermann and Hagood (2000) also posit that the concepts of audience and popular culture are core when it comes to definitions of critical media literacy. Both audiences and media content must be situated within a social-historical framework in order to understand the content and impact of messages within certain populations and cultures.

Although CML includes race as a dimension of critique, it often neglects the systemic hierarchies that influence racialized media content in its discussion and analysis. In this chapter, we use the CML model to explore Black television content. Our exploration considers how Black youth interpret media images of Black people and how globally distributed American media influences perspectives and interactions with Black people.

Media Socialization

While media can influence viewers of all ages, the established definitions of media socialization primarily focus on children and youth (Adams & Stevenson, 2012). Media socialization lays the foundation for how youth come to acquire stereotypic and static self-and-other representations. The definition of media has evolved with the introduction of constantly emerging and evolving technologies; as a result, media includes every broadcasting and narrowcasting media, such as newspapers, magazines, TV, radio, billboards, direct mail, telephone, fax, and internet. Along with inclusivity, it has also come to be accepted as a socializing agent (Arnett, 1995).

However, there is no consensus on a definition of media socialization. McQuail (2005) defines media socialization as the process of teaching norms and values by way of symbolic reward and punishment for different kinds of behavior as represented in the media, or a learning process whereby people learn how to behave in certain situations and the expectations which coincide with a given role or status in society. Heide (1995) defines media socialization as "the manner in which we establish a relationship to social reality through media representation" (p. 135). It has also been defined as the internalization of attentional cues via a "thorough initiation into the terrain of television's forms and conventions." Attentional cues are described as formal features of active viewing that guide an individual's cognitive processing (Biocca, 1988, p. 61). Adams and Stevenson (2012) define media socialization "as the exposure to mass communication (television, radio, internet, newspapers) messages, which teach people socially accepted behaviors that have: (a) a direct influence on cognitive ability and behavioral functioning, and (b) a mediating or facilitative indirect influence on learning" (p 30).

Although media is a prominent and influential tool, R/E socialization and CML skills are tools for interpreting media content that feature Black people. Media socialization is premised on repeated exposure to messages via media content. What are the messages associated with Black characters? In the next section, we present insightful findings from a content analysis of mainstream television shows featuring Black characters to provide a perspective on the content.

Mainstream Black Televised Content

Nama (2003) analyzed mainstream dramas in order to address three research questions: (1) To what degree are African-American characters present in dramatic television programming? (2) How are African-American characters present in dramatic television programming? (3) To what degree are African-American characters participating in dramatic television programming? Fifty-three episodes of 33 one-hour prime-time dramatic series on ABC, CBS, NBC, Fox, UPN, and WB were analyzed for five weeks between October 17, 1999, and December 4, 1999. Tabulations were based on the quantity of African-American television portrayals and their social characteristics. Content was not analyzed based on negative or positive representation.

Four categories of representation of African-American characters were measured: (a) the number of African-American characters appearing in the sampled programming; (b) the social characteristics of the roles (for example, age, occupation, education, gender, etc.); (c) the functions of the characters in the narrative stories (for example, hero, villain, etc.); and (d) the prominence of the African-American characters in the overall series (for example, series regular, guest star, etc.). The presence of African-American characters was measured according to physical characteristics and direct references to a character's race. Characters were coded as "male" or "female" on the basis of physical characteristics (Nama, 2003).

How African-American characters were presented in dramatic television programs was operationalized between two categories, casting position and narrative position. Of the 3,341 character appearances on dramatic television programming, African-American characters appeared 405 times (12 percent) across the various episodes. The percentage of Blacks on TV correlates with the percentage of Blacks in America according to the U.S. census. Of the 33 shows analyzed, nearly one half (49 percent) had no Black series regular. Moreover, shows that did not have Black series regulars were primarily family, friend, and lifestyle-oriented dramas. In contrast to this pattern, among dramatic television programs that had at least one Black series regular, ten (56 percent) of these shows were fundamentally law-enforcement-oriented shows such as legal, police, and detective dramas (Nama, 2003).

Although dramatic television series with African-American characters as series regulars or guest stars present the opportunity for African-American characters to play a significant part in the narrative, they do not guarantee it. Only 12 out of 33 dramas with African-American leads gave them over ten minutes of airtime. Less screen time means less time to participate in the narrative. Of the 405 appearances, 373 out of 405 (92 percent) had appearances shorter than ten minutes. Nama (2003) documented that while there has been an increase in Black actors being cast in mainstream TV Shows,[1] their on-screen time is less than their White costars.

Given the projection of TV characters as real-life representations, the scarcity of appearances symbolizes African-American marginality in the television narrative and their value in society (Nama, 2003). Severely limited screen time operates to reduce African-American characters to backdrop ambiance and generic objects: "these characters are not subjects of the narrative they are merely objects in the narrative" (Nama, 2003, p. 33). The lack of African-American characters series regulars on half of network dramatic series expresses an implicit ideology of the creators: primarily that White audiences will fail to identify with African-American characters (Nama, 2003).

We argue that the overrepresentation of Blacks in law enforcement shows and limited airtime in general serve to reinforce stereotypes about Black people. While network television programming may have added more African-Americans on the screen, the results of this study suggest that these representations are more symbolic than substantive in providing a meaningful space for African-American representation to take place. Considering that the genre of dramatic television is reality-centered, "this takes on a more ominous tone because in the final analysis these images are considered to be true-to-life, acceptable, believable and in the end, valid" (Nama, 2003, p. 36). In spite of the dearth of diversity among Black media images, some Black youth are able to identify stereotypical messages that are projected about Black people through televised content. In the next section, we present a selection of findings about images of Black men from a larger study of Black media images and adolescents.

"Hardly Ever, I Don't See It." Positive Media Images of Black Men

Seven focus groups were used to gather information about adolescent perceptions of Black media images, centering on the question *What are the dominant messages represented by images of Blacks in the media?* Three focus groups were coed and four were unisex, with one of those being an all-male focus group. Four focus groups were held with high school students; two of these were held with participants in all-male and all-female after-school leadership and mentoring programs at an inner-city public school. One session was held with suburban students enrolled in a district-wide after-school technology program. The last of these groups was held with high school students who live in a college town located in the middle of a northeastern state and were enrolled in an affinity program. The remaining three focus groups were held with college students who attended a Historically Black College or University (HBCU). A total of 63 youth, ages 14–21 years old participated in the focus groups: 20 males and 43 females.

During the focus groups, youth were shown images of Black men ranging from rapper 50 Cent to abolitionist Frederick Douglas and asked to share their interpretation of the images. During the first segment of the focus group a total of eight freestanding images were shown; three of them were images of Black men; two were images of Black women; and three were coed print advertisements to which participants were asked to respond and interpret the associated message(s). In the second segment of the focus group, participants were asked to respond to 25 images that were a part of a quantitative media measure pilot. With the exception of an image of President elect Barrack Obama and his wife Michelle, and an image of LeBron James and Gisele Bündchen, there were six individual images of Black males include in this measure. The findings from the analysis of the focus group data revealed differences in interpretation between images of artists and athletes and/or politicians and social justice figures. Youth tended to interpret the messages associated with politicians or athletes as positive compared to images of artists, whether actors, comedians, or musicians. They identified images as representing both positive and negative messages, but virtually all of the youth reported "hardly ever" or "rarely" viewing positive images on television.

Response to images of LeBron James and Frederick Douglas elicited positive remarks. Some comments about basketball star LeBron James in an ad were, "You have to play a sport to be successful," "I made it," "Determination," and "Champion." When asked, "How about how he's standing?" One youth offered:

> Humble picture. Seems like he want to unleash himself. Like he got a lot of titles around the world but instead of being that person they try to make him seem to be, he just stays LeBron James and who he is as a basketball player on the court and don't let anybody get to him. Just stays humble—like he's tied up by all the critics, wants to unleash but staying humble by being very calm.

When asked about frequency of viewing similar images on TV participants responded, "Hardly ever," "Every now and again," and "If it has something to do with sports or around Black history." A female participant's comment about the Frederick Douglass image was "Strong Black man. Mental and emotional strength." When asked about the frequency of exposure to similar images, she replied, "Hardly ever...except maybe President Obama, but other males, I don't see it. You may see physical strength but not mental and emotional strength."

In each focus group an image of President Barack Obama and First Lady Michelle Obama initiated discussions about "Black Love." Both male and female participants shared remarks about how nice it was to see images of a successful Black married couple on television. One female participant stated "not only is it nice to see, but this is a real couple!"

While appreciative of the positive images of Black males, discussions about the frequency of viewing these images often shifted the energy in the room from joyous and animated to forlorn. One youth offered "Not that every Black man has to be a thug. He can wear a suit also." And another youth contributed to the discussion by adding the statement "A leader, courage and conqueror."

Thoughtful discourse among the youth about why positive images of Black men were rarely seen on TV revealed their critical analysis of media messages and the dearth of positive images of Black men. When asked "Why?" why aren't there more positive images of Black males, one youth stated, "I think people are scared. They don't show the good part of Black men because they have a lot to contribute."

Unsurprisingly, youth easily identified negative images of Black males and reported viewing these types of images at a higher frequency on television then they reported viewing positive images. In fact, youth expected to see negative stereotype characters (Adams, 2011). Although, one youth responded to an image of J. J from *Good Times* by stating, "You can make it and still be yourself...you can be successful and not be stuck-up." Over all, images of J. J, Martin Lawrence, and Flava-Flav were most frequently interpreted as it is a joke to be a Black man as noted in the following quote, "A joke to be Black. Yes, it is original, but it is a joke, that is what people see." Characters that portray Black men in this fashion predate television (Jackson, 2006) and are defined as *coons*: uneducated Blacks who were prone to repetitive erroneous behavior (Bogle, 1973). When asked about frequency of viewing negative stereotype images, youth responded "often." In this chapter, we focus on youth's interpretation of media images that represent positive stereotypes about Black people because of how thoughtfully youth engaged in a critical discussion of the limited presence of these types of images and the implications for their lived experiences.

Global Eyes

With the growth of media as a globalizing mechanism and the pervasiveness of negative stereotype depictions of Black people, consumers, particularly Black consumers, are concerned about the implications of this exposure. When stereotypical Black media content is viewed outside the United States, viewers have limited experience with the American context and rely on media for realistic depictions (Havens, 2013). Thus, perspectives about Black people by other racial/ethnic groups are based largely on these scripted images. As American content is circulated in global media outlets, it has the potential to influence the script development of non-American content. We caution those who use American-produced media content as a reference for scripting Black characters because these representations are often stereotypical depictions that reinforce negative perceptions of Black men (Orbe, 1998; Dixon & Maddox, 2005) (and women) (Coltrane & Messineo, 2000; Horace & Smith, 2012)and too often serve as justification for racist behaviors, attitudes, and social practices. CML calls for critical consumption of media and teaching consumers how to identify racialized messages, as protective racial/ethnic socialization experience is an important skill set for filtering these messages, particularly for Black viewers.

Mainstream Messaging

According to Gerbner's cultivation theory (1998), televised messages become mainstream. Gerbner describes cultivation as the "individual contributions television viewing makes to viewer conceptions of virtual reality" (p. 180). Cultivation depends on a person's relation with mainstream media in terms of group membership, lifestyle, and cultural values (Gerbner, 1998). The extent to which these mainstream messages are pervasive depends upon audience vulnerability and viewing behaviors. Media is heavily influenced by social, political, and historical contexts. Viewers, without skills of critical media literacy or protective r/e socialization experiences, appear to accept what is viewed on television as mainstream and realistic. Consider the case of Trayvon Martin, an ordinary teenager who was followed home and murdered. Throughout the case, Trayvon was described in the media as brooding and menacing. We must pause, and ask how much did media depictions reinforce George Zimmerman's fear of this young Black male?

Conclusion: Black Americans, Critical Media Consumers

Chitiga's (2003) study of televised Black media content demonstrates that Black American viewers "appreciate the positive portrayal of the various types of strength among different characters, who successfully and even humorously negotiate the adverse conditions that the majority of ordinary African-Americans confront in their daily lives (p 55)." Contrarily, participants detested unrealistically happy representations of Black families and those sitcoms that portray Black families as totally dysfunctional, negative, and perpetually fighting, arguing that reinforcing such negative stereotypes about African-Americans is detrimental (Chitiga, 2003). Black Americans, including Black youth, have this critical perspective because their social experiences are generally shaped in significantly similar ways, by "their group's status in the power hierarchy of the United States" (Chitiga, 2003, p 48) and is thus shaped by their r/e socialization experiences. Globally, international viewers of American media content are limited to televised representations of Black American culture and experience.

Black adolescent consumers prefer to see images of Black people in the shows they elect to watch (Adams, 2011; Brown & Pardun, 2004), but much like adult Black viewers, they are critical of both the character portrayals and the messages that are scripted for Black artists (Adams, 2011; Adams-Bass, Bentley-Edwards, & Stevenson, 2014; Berry, 1998; Chitiga, 2003; Punyanunt-Carter, 2008; Horace & Smith, 2012; Muhammad & McArthur, 2015). For example, in a class discussion about the movie *Get Out*, many of the youth found it remarkable that the Black male character, Chris, did not die within the first 15 minutes of the film, although the introductory music was described as "eerie" and foreshadowing. Their comments suggest prior exposure to similar cues and schema led them to believe Chris would die. One participant remarked, "I can't believe he made it to the end of the movie," to which many of the other Black youth responded with head nodding, and some even clapped. While discussing *Get Out*, Black youth described feelings of affirmation derived from seeing a lead Black male character in a movie who was not portraying a criminal, rap star, or athlete. One participant remarked, "I just like that he was not thugged out." In this discourse, the student is addressing the Buck stereotype of Black males that is entrenched in American television and movies. The percentage of storylines that present negative stereotype messages about Black people is higher than those that present positive stereotype messages (Adams & Stevenson, 2012; Adams-Bass et al., 2014).

For Black American consumers who are familiar with the racial hierarchy and context of American media, filtering the message of Black media images through the lens of racial socialization is almost reflexive. Youth use the r/e socialization experiences they have been exposed to and internalized about Black people to filter and interpret the messages presented (Adams & Stevenson, 2012; Adams-Bass et al., 2014). This ability is an aspect of resilience that affords them the opportunity to develop counter-narratives, which may serve as protective factors for their individual and group identities. However, the ability, willingness, or skills to critically engage or question media images is low for non-Black consumers who have no or limited encounters with Black people.

Note

1 United States of America TV shows. (Watkins, 2005)

References

Abrams, J. R. (2008). African-Americans' television activity: Is it related to perceptions of outgroup vitality? *Howard Journal of Communications, 19*(1), 1–17. doi:10.1080/10646170701801961

Adams, V. N. (2011). *Messages in the medium: The relationships among black media images, racial identity, body image, and the racial socialization of black youth*. PhD dissertation, University of Pennsylvania, Philadelphia, PA.

Adams, V. N., & Stevenson, H. (2012). Media socialization, black media images and black adolescent identity. In D. Slaughter-Defoe (Ed.), *Racial stereotyping and child development contributions to human development* (vol. 25, pp. 28–46). Basel: Karger.

Adams-Bass, V. N., Bentley-Edwards, K. L., & Stevenson, H. C. (2014). That's not me I see on TV: African-American youth interpret images of Black females. *Women, Gender and Families of Color, 2*, 79–100. Allen, R. L., (1998). The media, group identity, and self esteem among African Americans: A program of research. *African American Research Perspectives, 4*: 61–67.

Allen, R. L., & Bielby, W. T. (1979). Blacks' attitudes and behaviors toward television. *Communication Research, 6*(4), 437–462. doi:10.1177/009365027900600403

Allen, R. L., & Thornton, M. C. (1992). Social structural factors, black media and stereotypical self-characterizations among African-Americans. *National Journal of Sociology, 6*(1), 41–75.

Alvermann, D. E., & Hagood, M. C. (2000). Critical media literacy: Research, theory, and practice in "New Times." *Journal of Educational Research, 93,* 193–205.

Arnett, J. J. (1995). Adolescents' uses of media for self-socialization. *Journal of Youth & Adolescence, 24*(5).

Aufderheide, P. & Firestone, C. (1993). *Media literacy: A report of the national leadership conference on media literacy.* Queenstown, MD: Aspen Institute.

Balaji, M. (2009). Why do good girls have to be bad? The cultural industry's production of the other and the complexities of agency. *Popular Communication: The International Journal of Media and Culture, 7*(4), 225–236.

Bentley, K., Adams, V. N., & Stevenson, H. (2009). Racial socialization: Roots processes and outcomes. In H. Neville, B. Tynes, & S. Utsey (Eds.), *Handbook of African-American psychology* (pp. 255–267). Sage Publications.

Berry, G. L. (1998). Black family life on television and the socialization of the African-American child: Images of marginality. *Journal of Comparative Family Studies, 29*(233–242).

Berry, G. L. (2000). Multicultural media portrayals and the changing demographic landscape: The psychosocial impact of television representations on the adolescent of color. *Journal of Adolescent Health, 27S,* 57–60.

Biocca, F. A. (1998). Opposing conceptions of the audience: The active and passive hemispheres of mass communication theory. In J. A. Andersonm (Ed.), Communication Yearbook (Vol. 11, pp. 51–80). Beverly Hills: Sage Publications In.

Bogle, D. (1973). *Toms, Coons, Mulattoes, Mammies & Bucks: An Interpretive History of Blacks in American Films.* New York, NY: Bantam Books.

Bogle, D. (2001a). *Primetime blues: African-Americans on network television.* New York: Fararr, Straus & Giroux.

Bogle, D. (2001b). *Toms, coons, mulattoes, mammies & bucks: An interpretive history of blacks in American films* (4th ed.). New York: Continuum International Publishing Group.

Bogle, D. (2016). *Toms, coons, mulattoes, mammies & bucks: An interpretive history of blacks in American films* (5th ed.). New York: Continuum International Publishing Group.

Botta, R. A. (2000). The mirror of television: A comparison of Black and White adolescents' body image. *Journal of Communication, 50*(3), 144–159. doi:10.1111/j.1460-2466.2000.tb02857.x

Brown, J. D., & Pardun, C. J. (2004). Little in common: Racial and gender differences in adolescents' television diets. *Journal of Broadcasting & Electronic Media, 48*(2), 266–278.

Browne Graves, S. (1982). The impact of television on the cognitive and affective development of minority children. In G. L. Berry & C. Mitchell-Kernan (Eds.), *Television and the socialization of the minority child* (pp. 42–67). New York: Academic Press.

Chitiga, M. M. (2003). Black sitcoms: A black perspective. *Cercles, 8,* 46–58.

Coltrane, S., & Messineo, M. (2000). The perpetuation of subtle prejudice: Race and gender imagery in 1990s television advertising. *Sex Roles, 42*(5), 363–389.

Dixon, T. L., & Maddox, K. B. (2005). Skin tone, crime news, and social reality judgments: Priming the stereotype of the dark and dangerous black criminal. *Journal of Applied Social Psychology, 35*(8), 1555–1570.

Ferguson, R. (1998). *Representing 'race': Ideology, identity and the media.* New York: Oxford University Press.

Gerbner, G. (1998). Cultivation analysis: An overview. *Mass Communication and Society, 1*(3), 175–194.

Gerbner, G., & Gross, L. (1976). Living with television: The violence profile. *Journal of Communication, 26,* 172–199.

Giroux, H. (1999). *The mouse that roared: Disney and the end of innocence.* Boulder, CO: Rowman & Littlefield.

Gordon, M. K. (2008). Media contributions to African-American girls' focus on beauty and appearance: Exploring the consequences of sexual objectification. *Psychology of Women Quarterly, 32,* 245–256.

Gorham, B. W. (1999). Stereotypes in the media: So what? *The Harvard Journal of Communications, 10,* 229–247.

Greenberg, B. S. (1988). Some uncommon television images and the Drench hypothesis. In S. Oskamp (Ed.), *Applied Social Psychology Annual: Television as a Social Issue* (pp. 88–102). Newbury Park, CA: Sage Publications.

Havens, T. (2013). *Black television travels: African-American media around the globe.* New York: New York University press.

Hazell, V., & Clarke, J. (2008). Race and gender in the media: A Content analysis of advertisements in two mainstream Black magazines. Journal of Black Studies, 39, 5–21.

Heide, M. J. (1995). Television culture and women's lives: Thirty something and the contradictions of gender. Philadelphia: University of Pennsylvania Press.

Holt, L. F. (2013). Writing the wrong can counter-stereotypes offset negative media messages about African Americans? *Journalism & Mass Communication Quarterly, 90*(1), 108–125.

Horace, R. H., & Smith, E. L. (2012). "This Is Not Reality ... It's Only TV": African American girls respond to media (mis)representations. *The New Educator, 8,* 222–242.

Hughes, D., Rodriguez, J., Smith, E. P., Johnson, D. J., Stevenson, H. C., & Spicer, P. (2006). Parents' Ethnic-Racial Socialization Practices: A Review of Research and Directions for Future Study. *Developmental Psychology, 42*(5), 747–770.

Hurley, R. J., Jensen, J. J., Weaver, A., & Dixon, T. (2015). Viewer ethnicity matters: Black crime in TV News and its impact on decisions regarding public policy. *Journal of Social Issues, 71*(1), 155–170.

Jackson, R. L. (2006). *Scripting the black masculine body identity, discourse, and racial politics in popular media.* Albany, NY: State University of New York Press.

Kellner, D., & Share, J. (2007a). Critical media literacy, democracy, and the reconstruction of education. In D. Macedo & S. R. Steinberg (Eds.), *Media literacy: A reader* (pp. 3–23). New York: Peter Lang Publishing.

Kellner, D., & Share, J. (2007b). Critical media literacy is not an option. *Learning Inquiry, 1*(1), 59–69.

Luke, C. (1997). Media literacy and cultural studies. In S. Muspratt, A. Luke, & P. Freebody (Eds.), *Constructing critical literacies: Teaching & learning textual practice* (pp. 19–49).

McQuail, D. (2005). McQuail's mass communication theory (5 ed.). London: Sage Publications, Inc.

Milkie, M. A. (1999). Social comparisons, reflected appraisals, and mass media: The impact of pervasive beauty images on Black and White girls' self-concepts. *Social Psychology Quarterly, 62*, 190–210. doi:10.2307/26958

Muhammad, G. E., & McArthur, S. A. (2015). "Styled by Their Perceptions": Black adolescent girls interpret representations of black females in popular culture. *Multicultural Perspectives, 17*, 133–140.

Nama, A. (2003). More symbol than substance: African-American representation in network television dramas. *Race and Society, 6*, 21–28.

Orbe, M. P. (1998). Constructions of reality on MTV's "the real world": An analysis of the restrictive coding of black masculinity. *Southern Journal of Communication, 64*(1), 32–47.

Orlowski, P. (2006). Educating in an era of Orwellian spin: Critical media literacy in the classroom. *Canadian Journal of Education/Revue canadienne de l'éducation*, 176–198.

Park, D. J., & Villar, M. E. (2015). Comparing frequency of TV and internet use among African-American students and their effects on material values and sociability. *Online Journal of Communication and Media Technologies, 5*(1), 21-40.

Poindexter, P. M., & Stroman, C. A. (1981). Blacks and television: A review of the research literature. *Journal of Broadcasting, 25*(2), 103–122. doi:10.1080/08838158109386436

Punyanunt-Carter, N. M. (2008). The perceived realism of African-American portrayals on television. *The Howard Journal of Communications, 19*, 241–257. doi:10.1080/10646170802218263

Spencer, M. B. (Ed.). (1990). *Black Families Interdisciplinary Perspectives*. New Brunswick: Transaction.

Spurlock, J. (1982). Television, ethnic minorities, and mental health: An overview. In G. Berry, C. Mitchell-Kernan, (Eds.), Television and the Socialization of the Minority Child (pp. 71–80), Los Angeles, CA: Academic Press.

Steele, C. M. (2010). *Whistling Vivaldi and other clues to how stereotypes affect us*. New York: W.W. Norton & Company.

Stevenson, H. C. (1994). Racial socialization in African American families: The art of balancing intolerance and survival. *Family Journal, 2*(3), 190–198.

Stevenson, H. C. (1995). Relationship of adolescent perceptions of racial socialization to racial identity. *Journal of Black Psychology, 21*(1), 49–70.

Stevenson, H. C., McNeil, J. D., Herrero-Taylor, T., & Davis, G. (2005). Influence of perceived neighborhood diversity and racism experience on the racial socialization of black youth. *Journal of Black Psychology, 31*(3), 273–290.

Swanson, D. P., & Spencer, M. B. (1999). Developmental and cultural context considerations for research on African American adolescents. In H. Fitzgerald, B. M. Lester & B. Zuckerman (Eds.), *Children of color: Research, health and public policy issues* (pp. 53–72). New York: Garland Publishing Inc.

Tynes, B. M., & Ward, L. M. (2009). The Role of Media Use and Portrayals in African Americans' Psychosocial Development. In H. A. Neville, B. M. Tynes &

S. O. Utsey (Eds.), *Handbook of African American Psychology* (pp. 143–158). Thousand Oaks: Sage Publications.

Ward, L. M. (2004). Wading through the stereotypes: Positive and negative associations between media use and black adolescents' conceptions of self. *Developmental Psychology, 40*, 284–294.

Watkins, S. C. (2005). *Black youth and mass media: Current research and emerging questions.* www.rcgd.isr.umich.edu/prba/perspectives/winter2000/cwatkins.pdf

10 For Us Only? Examining the Effect of Viewing Context on Black Audiences' Perceived Influence of Black Entertainment

Omotayo O. Banjo

Entertainment media help to construct our social world by assigning meaning through images and character portrayals. Symbolic interactionism explains that individuals learn about their social world through cultural engagement, and scholars contend that viewers learn about other actors (i.e. people) in their social world by engaging with symbols in the media. Chidester (2008) further argued that media not only inform our understanding of our social world though what is seen, but through symbolic annihilation—that is the exclusion of social groups.

African-Americans have historically been among minority groups who have been ignored in media. In addition, Blacks were portrayed negatively in the media landscape, and these portrayals have been found to significantly impact Whites' stereotypes and attitudes toward Blacks (Entman & Rojecki, 2001; Oliver, Jackson, Moses, & Dangerfield, 2004; Tan, Fujioka, & Tan, 2000; Valentino, 1999). While much scholarly attention has focused primarily on mainstream media, lesser attention has been given to contemporary Black entertainment in which similar representations are just as evident (Ford, 1997; Means Coleman, 2000; Watkins, 2002). For example, popular Black films such as *Menace II Society*, *Set it Off*, and *Boyz in the Hood* often displayed Blacks as violent, of low socioeconomic status, and involved with drugs and gang activity (Guerrero, 1993). Arguably, such films exacerbate stereotypes of Blacks, which seem to justify Whites' fear-motivated violence against Black teens. As was highlighted in the Trayvon Martin case, the stigmatization and threat to Black American men also work to damage group vitality, and thus self-concept, further engendering fear of misperceptions among the Black community. Regardless of potential social effects, these films seem to resonate with Black audiences yielding box office successes

However, Blacks' responses to Black representations have been ambiguous and cannot be easily generalized (Matabane, 1988; Means Coleman, 2000). On one hand, Blacks have been outspoken about their discomfort with negative representations of Black identity. On the other hand, some findings have shown that while Blacks recognize poor portrayals of Black culture, they often dismiss the negatives for the sake of enjoyment

(Brigham & Giesbrecht, 1976; Watts & Orbe, 2002). Even programming featuring more positive representations of Blacks has engendered criticism (Bodroghkozy, 1992). For example, some audience segments rejected the Cosby Show expressing concern that it masked the real hardships of the Black community (Inniss & Feagin, 1995; Jhally & Lewis, 1993).

After Spike Lee released *School Daze*, a film about the dissensions between Blacks in the Black community, the director received much flak from Black audiences contesting that the director was publicly "airing the Black community's dirty laundry" (McDowell, 1989; Russell, Wilson, & Hall, 1992). Cartoonist Aaron McGruder received similar feedback with the introduction of his comic strip "Boondocks," which features majority Black characters and situates urban youth in White suburbia (Cornwell & Orbe, 2002). Some judged McGruder's liberal use of the N-word as problematic (Kyles, 2005; Rushing, 2004). Although the pejorative term appears acceptable among many Blacks within their community (Motley & Craig-Henderson, 2007), the recognition of the N-word as an offense appears to become most salient when a racial out-group member is a factor, like being in the audience for example.

Perhaps the reason for the backlash is that Black audiences are especially sensitive to their portrayal before mainstream audiences. Sigelman and Tuch (1997) have argued that the proliferation of poor images of Blacks in the media lead Blacks to believe that Whites endorsed negative stereotypes, even among those who were more likely to engage with Whites. Therefore, one might question whether Black audiences would have responded similarly if the media product were exclusive to Blacks.

Whereas symbolic interactionism describes how media influence individuals' social perceptions, other theories specifically address individuals' perceptions of media influence. Integrating hostile media and third-person perception, this study examines how the context in which Black audiences view Black-oriented films influences Blacks' evaluations of the film and their overall enjoyment experience.

Audience Perceptions and Perceived Influence

There are perhaps two explanations for the ambivalence of Black audiences' responses to Black-oriented content. Both hostile media and third-person perception assert that media consumers overestimate media's impact on a mass audience. Hostile media perception specifically argues that partisan viewers will judge neutral content as misrepresenting their views and negatively persuading out-group members, while third-person perceptions describe the tendency for individuals to believe that out-group members compared to themselves are more gravely impacted by media content. Each is described as follows in more detail.

The premise of hostile media research is that groups perceive media framing of an issue particular to a group as unfairly biased. As Tsfati

(2007) notes "perceiving that media cover our group negatively, and furthermore, perceiving that this coverage is influential, may indicate to us that society at large thinks negatively of our group" (p. 632). For Blacks specifically, when considering representations of Blacks *in* Black movies, the issues of *source and perceived reach* are of special consideration. Newer developments propose that individuals are more likely to evaluate mediated messages as biased when forced to *consider* the effect of media content on a presumably vulnerable audience (Gunther & Schmitt, 2004), referred to as the *audience effect*.

Ethnic group membership has been shown to specifically influence perceptions of bias. For example, a study on the media coverage of the *Beirut Massacre* revealed that pro-Arab groups viewed a neutral brief as favoring Israelis. However, Israelis perceived the same coverage as favoring Arabs (Vallone, Ross, & Lepper, 1985). Such findings have relevant implications for the role of hostile media perceptions between two racial groups in which a history of conflict exists. This study posits that social groups with violent social histories tend to be concerned with the effect negative representations may have on out-group members. Considering the racial tension between Blacks and Whites in America, it is probable that Blacks are more likely to question the accuracy of portrayals of Black culture in films directed by Blacks, especially when *considering* a White audience.

The main thesis of third-person perception is that individuals are more likely to believe that other people are more affected by media messages than themselves (Davison, 1983). For example, in a classic study, Gunther (1995) found that respondents believed they were less negatively influenced by pornography than other people. Scholars generally agree that there are at least two components of third-person, the perceptual and behavioral. To the extent an individual's beliefs or opinions are influenced, this is referred to as a third-person perception, whereas beliefs that turn into behavior is referred to as an effect. Although the concept of "the other" in third-person research has always been described as the general population, Scharrer (2002) clarifies the otherwise nebulous 'other' by arguing that variables such as gender, class, and race are integral to the study of perceived influence of groups in third-person research.

Furthermore, scholars maintain that people are generally more likely to believe that others who are at a greater social distance are more susceptible to media messages. For example, Lambe and McLeod (2005) found that parents/adults reported that individuals, aged 18–24, would be more affected by various types of communication than 40–50-year-olds. The authors suggested third-person perception was greater among the older respondents because parents/adults view 18–24-year-olds as out-group members. Most related to the present study, Choi, Leshner, and Choi (2008) found that women were more likely to perceive that their male friends were more impacted by images of women in advertisements than were their female friends or themselves. These studies emphasize the operations of third-person perceptions when individuals think about media impact on socially or psychologically distant others, also known as comparison groups. Consequently, people are more likely to believe that individuals similar to themselves—socially proximate individuals—are less likely to be negatively influenced by the media (Scharrer, 2002).

Self-categorization seems to be the most fitting explanation for empirical investigations of racialized cultural products (or ethnic media) specifically (Johnson, 2010). Perloff (2009) explains that viewers form evaluations of media content by "determin[ing] the fit among themselves, a group of third persons, and the [media] message" (p. 258). After establishing distinctions between themselves and people like them (the in-group) and people who are different from them (the out-group), viewers are likely to overestimate the potential impact of the message on out-group members. Blacks may view the stereotypical representations of Black culture as a threat to their need to maintain a positive image, thereby yielding a third-person effect perception (Tal-Or, Tsfati, & Gunther, 2009).

Based on previous scholarship, the following conclusions can be made. First, while Black audiences' responses to Black-oriented films are ambivalent (Squires, 2009), we know that Blacks generally express more favorable responses to Black characters (Appiah, 2002; Lind, 1996) and are at the same time concerned about their public image. Second, individuals generally perceive that mediated messages can misrepresent their group and thus influence others' opinions about the group. Moreover, perceptions of bias are most likely to occur when an individual is forced to think about out-group members (Gunther & Schmitt, 2004). Last, in-group members desire to maintain a positive group image and are thus more likely to express concern that socially distant others will be negatively impacted by media representations of the in-group (Perloff, 2009; Scharrer, 2002). Given these suppositions, it is likely that

$H1_a$: Black viewers will report more favorable attitudes toward Black films when viewing with an All-Black audience than when with a Mixed group.

$H1_b$: Black viewers will report greater perceived bias against Blacks in Black films when viewing with a Mixed group than when viewing with an All Black audience.

$H2_a$: Blacks who view with a Mixed group are more likely to perceive that Whites' attitudes compared to self and Other Blacks, will be more negatively affected by images in Black films than Blacks who view with an All Black audience.

$H2_b$: Blacks who view with a Mixed group are more likely to perceive that Whites compared to self and Other Blacks, will be less likely to interact with Blacks than Blacks who view with an All Black audience.

Method

Research Design

The present research employs a randomized experiment that examines the impact of viewing condition on Black viewers' enjoyment, hostile media, and third-person perception. In this study, the main independent variable is the co-viewing condition and has two levels, All Black and Mixed. Enjoyment, hostile media, and third-person perception are the dependent variables. For additional analyses, this study also includes two films (discussed as follows) yielding a 2 (Condition: All Black, Mixed) × 2 (Films: *ATL*, *Diary*) factorial design.

Participants

The present study took place at a university in the northeastern United States where Black representation is limited. Therefore, recruitment strategies for Black and non-Black participants differed. Non-Black participants were recruited from communication courses to participate in a media study entitled "Trends in Entertainment" for extra credit. Black participants were recruited from listservs populated by predominantly African-Americans (e.g. Gospel choirs, Black caucus, Black graduate student groups, etc.) as well as by posted flyers in on-campus multicultural centers. Black participants were invited to participate in a study entitled "Trends in Black Entertainment." Flyers clearly stated the eligibility criterion for participation in the study, namely participants must be African-American, 18 years or older, and students or employees of the university. Extramural funding was sought and obtained to encourage Blacks' participation. The project was funded by a university grant that enabled the researcher to provide a $10 incentive for willing Black participants.

Each condition was allotted specific time slots and availabilities on a given day to allow for up to eight participants per session. Black participants were given sign-up options with four time slots for some sessions (allotted for the Mixed condition) and eight time slots for other sessions (allotted for the All Black condition), while non-Black participants were given sign-up options allowing only four people to sign up for a session (for the Mixed condition). Volunteers were randomly assigned to one of the two conditions. For the All Black condition, each session consisted of an average of six participants. For the Mixed condition, each session consisted of an average of five Black participants viewing with a maximum of three non-Black students.

At the time of the study, participants were asked to identify their primary racial ethnicity and given the option to check all categories that applied. Although the non-Black participants completed the debriefing questionnaires, data from these participants were not analyzed for purposes of this study. Analyses were conducted on individuals who self-identified as Black since this was the population of interest.

The total sample included 66 Blacks. Of the 66 Black participants, 53 percent were male ($N = 35$) and 47 percent were female ($N = 31$). A majority of the sample was composed of undergraduate students (87.3 percent) with the remaining (12.6 percent) categorized as graduate students. About half of the 66 Black participants were assigned to one of the two experimental conditions, viewing one of two Black films. There were 31 subjects in the All Black condition (*Diary*, $N = 20$; *ATL* $N = 11$) and 35 subjects in the Mixed condition (*Diary*, $N = 16$; *ATL* $N = 19$). There were seven viewing groups of Blacks in the All Black condition and 13 viewing groups of Blacks in the Mixed condition. Session group size was controlled for in the analysis and revealed no effect.

Stimulus

Because the definition of Black movies is ambiguous (Squires, 2009), the researcher relied on Reid's (2005) definition to identify films that met the following criteria: directed by Blacks, written by Blacks, starring majority Blacks, and including themes central to Blacks. Films that were released within the past ten years were given special consideration because it was important that the films were not so old that participants would feel disconnected and recent enough that participants would recognize the film and/or its actors. Popular or mainstream Black films were preferred to independent films in order to simulate the access that White audiences have to the films as well as to establish a sense of familiarity among the Black participants. After establishing criteria for "Black movies," the researcher operationalized popularity with mass audiences by box-office ranking. Using boxofficemojo.com, the researcher reviewed all of the top films across the designated ten-year span and identified films that met the criteria. Forty-one films were extracted from this list.

Although the list met the stipulative definition as guided by Reid (2005), it was also important that Black audience members identified these films as representative of their culture given the discrepancy among Black viewers about the definition of a Black film. Therefore, prior to the actual experiment, a small convenience sample of Black volunteers were solicited to complete a survey on whether or not they would categorize the movies in the list as Black films. The survey listed all of the films extracted from boxofficemojo.com and asked respondents to check 'Yes' or 'No' to indicate whether or not the movie could be categorized as a Black film. Respondents were also given an opportunity to suggest films that were not on the list. Fifty percent of the respondents returned and completed the survey. Of these responses, films that were (1) most consistently identified as Black films, (2) most recent, and (3) consisted of popular stereotypes of Blacks were identified as possible stimuli. Of this list, films that varied in genre were selected to control for genre effects. The two selected films were Tyler Perry's *Diary of a Mad Black Woman* (2005) (referred to hereafter as *Diary*), a comedy, and Chris Robinsons' *ATL* (2006), a drama.

Ten-minute clips were extracted from each film intended to provide enough dialogue to engage audience members into the plot. Most important, each clip depicted Black stereotypes as informed by established literature: low socioeconomic status, the Black matriarch, the use of Black English and profanity (including the N-word), and dress that might otherwise be perceived as *urban*. For example, in the extracted clip from *Diary*, Helen, who has been betrayed by her husband, seeks refuge in her gangster grandmother, Madea, an overweight and obnoxious woman played by director Tyler Perry. Madea takes Helen to retrieve her clothes from her husband's house. When the husband's new girlfriend challenges them, Madea threatens her with violence while using urban slang. For example, when the girlfriend screeches at Madea destroying her Vera Wang dress, Madea responds, "Who that is? I need to get my nails did." As another example, in response to the young woman calling the police, Madea replies, "Call the po-po, whoe! Call the po, whoe!" She later destroys Helen's ex-husband's furniture after discovering he threatened Helen.

In the extracted clip from *ATL*, Black youth of an Atlanta neighborhood dance and skate to hip-hop music at a skating rink, Cascades. The main character, Rashad, narrates and introduces the audience to the variety of cliques in Cascades (e.g. the Fly girls and the Get Money Crew). Rashad discusses an upcoming skating competition while hanging with three male friends at a gas station where one of his friends, Brooklyn, is working. In response to being fired from his job as a gas attendant, Brooklyn aggressively confronts his Indian boss who continues to mock Brooklyn's slang by saying, "Keep it moving son." Meanwhile, Ant, Rashad's younger brother, flirts with a much older woman by making remarks about the size of her buttocks. After being rejected by the woman, Ant calls her a derogatory name. A friend later suggests that Ant work for a drug dealer to acquire status and money. The clip ends with a mother dropping off her twin daughters at Cascades. The girls complain because the AC is broken and because the car door is broken, so they have to crawl out the back of the car.

Addressing universal issues, such as a broken relationship and sacred friendships, both films embed Black cultural themes and exaggerate African-American stereotypes. The preceding portrayals reiterate stereotypes of African-Americans' social position, language, aggression, and hypersexuality. In both clips, characters are referred to as 'ghetto.' In addition, the character Madea in *Diary* is a reiteration of the cross-dressing stereotype of the Mamie and Jezebel blend often perpetuated by Black male comedians. In congruence with the underlying hostile media phenomenon, both films illustrate present realities (e.g. domestic abuse and drug dealing), which occur across cultures, but by which Blacks are mostly stigmatized.

Measurement

Enjoyment

A seven-point Likert enjoyment scale was adapted from Oliver, Weaver, and Sargent (2000) to assess audience favorable attitudes toward of the film clip. The summated scale described the enjoyment experience using adjectives like *enjoyable, entertaining, humorous, involving, boring, creative, unpleasant,* and yielded strong reliability (α = 0.93).

In order to assess enjoyment of different characteristics of the Black-oriented films (Appiah, 2002), using a seven-point scale, participants were asked to rate the extent to which they enjoyed aspects of the film including characters, language, message, and content. In addition to these questions, participants were asked about the likelihood they would watch the movie after watching the short clip, the likelihood they would recommend the film to their friends, and the frequency with which they watch Black films.

Hostile Media Perception

Gunther and Schmitt's (2004) hostile media perception scale was adapted to measure perceptions of bias. Using an 11-point Likert scale (–5 to +5), the measure included five items with questions like "Overall, do you think the portrayal of Black culture in this film is consistent or inconsistent with your personal beliefs about the subject matter?" Anchors were tailored to match the nature of each question (See Appendix A). When analyzing the data, value points were recoded into one (against) and 11 (in favor) with six as the neutral point. The five items were loaded on a singular factor and were computed into a single variable labeled Black Portrayals (α = 0.79).

Third-Person Perception

The second hypotheses posit that individuals will perceive greater media influence on a socially distant other compared to self. Therefore, questions were created to assess differences in perception for each corresponding target. Using an 11-point scale (–5 to + 5), participants responded to items asking them to consider the influence of the films on the attitude and interaction likelihood for the following targets: self, other Blacks, and Whites. After being instructed to *consider* or think about the influence of the clip on their (other Blacks' and Whites') opinions, participants were asked the following questions like "Overall, how do you think this movie would affect [your, other Blacks' or Whites'] attitudes toward Blacks?" and "Overall, how do you think that movies such as these would affect [your, other Blacks' or Whites'] interactions with African-Americans?" For analysis, the value points were recoded into 1–11 with six as the neutral point. Higher numbers were more positive, whereas lower number reflected more negative responses. Anchors were tailored to match the particular item (See Appendix A).

Experimental Procedure

Participants were randomly assigned to one of two viewing conditions— All Black or Mixed audience—and one of two film instantiations—*Diary* or *ATL*. Each All Black session was led by a Black proctor, whereas the Mixed sessions were led by a White proctor who viewed with the group in order to enhance the salience of White out-group presence. Participants in both conditions were told that the nature of the study involved identifying trends in Black entertainment and were encouraged to give input regarding this topic. After reading and signing an informed consent form, participants were instructed to read a short film description provided for them. The purpose of the description was to help participants locate the scene within a larger plot. Further, reading narratives has been shown to assist in the transportation process of media enjoyment (Green, Kaufman, & Brock, 2004; Oliver, 1993). Summaries for each of the films were taken from a review on imdb.com.

After reading the brief film description individually, participants collectively viewed the ten-minute clip on a common television screen set in the middle of the room. Once the clip ended, participants were instructed to log onto an online questionnaire made ready at the computer station where they were seated. Participants were instructed to log into the questionnaire using a six-digit ID number, which had been placed at their corresponding computer station. The six-digit ID number was assigned by the researcher and signified the condition, film, and session of the group. For example, the first digit was either a '1' signifying the All Black condition or '2' signifying the Mixed condition. The second digit was either a '1' for *Diary* or '2' for *ATL*. The next two numbers signified the session number. The last two numbers of the ID were participants' number. So, two participants in the same co-viewing and film condition would be 110101 and 110102. After completing the questionnaire, participants signed their names for the agreed upon compensation. Upon completing the study, participants were emailed and informed of the purpose of the study.

Results

First, descriptive analyses were computed to assess participants' overall responses to Black films in general and to the films independently. Overall, participants in the sample reported watching Black movies relatively

Table 10.1 Enjoyment Characteristics across Two Films

Enjoyment Characteristics	Diary	ATL
	M (SD)	M (SD)
Likelihood to watch film	5.89 (1.67)	5.30 (1.89)
Likelihood to recommend	5.50 (1.87)*	4.23 (1.91)
Enjoy content	5.56 (1.52)*	4.27 (1.76)
Enjoy language	5.33 (1.69)*	3.67 (1.78)
Enjoy message	5.67 (1.53)**	3.83 (1.87)

$*p < 0.05$, $**p < 0.001$.

often ($M = 5.97$, SD = 1.19). Black participants also reported relatively high means for enjoyment ($M = 5.39$, SD = 1.02), likelihood to watch the films ($M = 5.67$, SD = 1.72), and enjoyment of the characters ($M = 5.57$, SD = 1.72) for both films collectively. When examining the films separately, participants rated *Diary* higher for their likelihood to watch ($M = 5.89$, SD = 1.67) and for their likelihood to recommend to others ($M = 5.50$, SD = 1.87) than *ATL* ($M = 5.30$, SD = 1.89; $M = 4.23$, SD = 1.90). There was a significant difference between the films on the recommend item $F(1, 64)=7.36$, $p < 0.05$. Participants reported higher scores on enjoyment of content ($M = 5.51$, SD = 1.52), language ($M = 5.29$, SD = 1.69), and message ($M = 5.63$, SD = 1.53) for *Diary* than for *ATL* (See Table 10.1). Participants in this sample seemed to prefer the comedy to the drama.

Enjoyment & Co-Viewing Conditions

Hypothesis one (H1$_a$) predicted that Blacks in the All Black condition would report greater enjoyment of Black films than those in the Mixed condition. A one-way ANOVA revealed there was no main effect of co-viewer race on enjoyment ($F(1, 61) = 0.33$, $p > 0.05$). When including films into the analysis, a univariate ANOVA revealed a significant main effect of film $F(1, 62) = 5.05$, $p < 0.05$. Those who viewed *Diary* reported more enjoyment ($M = 5.52$, SD = 1.15) than those who viewed *ATL* ($M = 4.79$, SD = 1.35). There was no interaction between co-viewing condition and film $F(2, 62) = 0.195$, $p > 0.05$. Because it was expected that Black viewers would report more enjoyment when viewing with Black in-group members than when viewing with a mixed group, H1$_a$ was not supported.

Hostile Media Perception & Co-Viewing

As informed by the audience effect component of hostile media perception, it was also argued that Black viewers will report greater perceived bias against Blacks in Black films when viewing with a mixed group than when viewing with an All Black audience. For this scale, higher numbers

Table 10.2 Hypotheses One Dependent Measures for Each Condition

Dependent Measures	All Black	Mixed
	M (SD)	M (SD)
Enjoyment	**5.35(1.06)**	5.02 (1.46)
Diary	5.62 (1.08)	5.40 (1.27)
ATL	4.87 (.866)	4.70 (1.57)
Hostile Media Perception	**6.27(1.81)**	6.17 (1.99)
Diary	6.67 (1.83)	6.40(1.97)
ATL	5.45 (1.60)	5.98 (2.03)

Note
   Means in bold are the overall total scores for the dependent measures.

were more positive and lower numbers indicate more negative valence. An independent sample t-test revealed no significant differences in perceptions of bias against Blacks among participants in the mixed and all Black condition, $t(64) = 0.199$, $p > 0.05$. Both groups reported neutral ratings for the portrayals of Blacks in Black films. There were also no significant main effects of film or interactions between co-viewing condition and film on perceptions of bias against Blacks (see Table 10.2). Since results did not go in the anticipated direction, $H1_b$ was not supported.

Third Person Perception and Co-Viewing

It was also posited that Blacks would perceive greater third-person perceptions when considering White audiences. Moreover, those with White co-viewers will report greater third-person perceptions than those who viewed with Black in-group members. Third-person items were divided by influence of Black-oriented content on attitudes toward Blacks and likelihood to interact with Blacks for the following targets: self, other Blacks and Whites. Lower numbers for attitudes and interaction likelihood reflected responses with a negative valence, while higher numbers reflected responses with a more positive valence. Each third-person perception measure was treated as a within-subjects variable in the analysis to account for the measurement of the same characteristic under varying conditions—self, Other Blacks, and Whites. Each level of the factor included the self, Other Blacks, and Whites.

Attitude. For the attitude measure, a 2(Viewing Condition: All Black, Mixed) × 3 (Target: Self, Other Blacks, White) mixed model ANOVA revealed a significant main effect of target $F(2, 128) = 82.36$, $p < 0.01$, $n^2 = 0.56$. As shown in Table 10.3, Bonferroni post hoc means comparisons showed that reports for effects on Whites ($M = 3.90$, $SD = 2.15$) were significantly ($p < 0.05$) lower (more negative) than for Self ($M = 5.83$, $SD = 1.90$) and Other Blacks ($M = 6.14$, $SD = 1.86$). Consistent with $H2_a$, the target × condition interaction was significant, $F(2,128) = 5.79$,

$p < 0.05$, $n^2 = 0.15$). Figure 10.1 shows the plotted means for this inter-action. Independent samples t-tests were conducted to assist in the delin-eation of this effect by testing the effect of co-viewing condition for each of the targets. These analyses revealed a marginally significant effect of condition for the White target only, $t(64) = 1.68$, $p < 0.10$, with a more negative perception of Blacks occurring when the film was viewed in a mixed context. Thus, the general tendency for the effect on the White target to be more negative than for Self or other Blacks was intensified in the mixed viewing condition.

Interaction Likelihood

A 2(Viewing Condition: All Black, Mixed) × 3 (Target: Self, Other Blacks, White) mixed model ANOVA was conducted for the interaction likelihood measure and revealed a significant main effect of target $F(2, 128) = 59.67$, $p < 0.01$, $n^2 = 0.48$. Bonferroni post hoc means comparisons showed that reports for effects on Whites ($M = 4.03$, SD = 1.90) were significantly ($p < 0.01$) lower than for Self ($M = 6.63$, SD = 1.32) and Other Blacks ($M = 6.52$, SD = 1.38). Because there was a significant interaction between

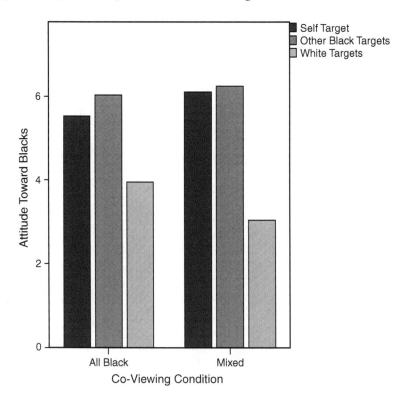

Figure 10.1 Co-viewing condition and attitude measures, $p < 0.05$.

Table 10.3 Means for Third Person Perception Measures Reported for Each Condition

Third Person Measures	All Black	Mixed
	M (SD)	M (SD)
Attitude		
Self	5.52[a] (2.01)	6.11[a] (1.78)
Other Blacks	6.03[a] (1.85)	6.23[a] (1.90)
Whites	3.94[b] (1.99)	3.06[b] (2.22)
Interaction Likelihood		
Self	5.71[a] (1.04)	6.37[a] (1.48)
Other Blacks	6.35[a] (.950)	6.74[a] (1.67)
Whites	4.35[b] (1.80)	3.77[b] (1.96)

Note
  Means with no subscript in common differ at the $p < 0.05$ level using Bonferonni pairwise comparisons.

the target and viewing condition $F(2, 128) = 3.70, p < 0.05, n^2 = 0.05$, H2$_b$ was supported. Shown in Figure 10.2 are the plotted means for this interaction. Independent samples t-tests were conducted to determine the effect of co-viewing condition for each of the targets. The analyses revealed a significant effect of condition only for the Self target $t(64) = -2.08, p < 0.05$, for which a lower interest to interact with Blacks occurred when the film was viewed in the All Black condition compared to the Mixed condition. As with the attitude measure, opinions about Whites' likelihood to interact with Blacks were more negative in the Mixed condition, but the difference was not significant $t(64) = 1.26, p = 0.21$.

Secondary Analysis

To more directly test the third-person hypothesis with the films, a 3(Target: Self, Other Blacks, and Whites) × 2(Viewing Condition: All Black and Mixed) × 2(Film: *Diary* and *ATL*) mixed model ANOVA was conducted for the attitude and interaction likelihood measure. There were no significant interactions between co-viewing condition, film, and attitude $F(2, 124) = 0.565, p > 0.05$, partial $n^2 = 01$. However, there was a significant two-way interaction between condition film and the interaction likelihood measure $F(2, 124) = 4.31, p < 0.05$, partial $n^2 = 0.06$, with a marginally significant main effect of film $F(1, 62) = 3.33, p < 0.10, n^2 = 0.05$. A univariate analysis of variance revealed a significant interaction between condition and film $F(1, 62) = 5.41, p < 0.05$ and determined that participants reported lower (more negative) effects on Whites when viewing *ATL* (drama) with All Blacks ($M = 3.36$, SD = 1.43) than when viewing with a mixed group ($M = 4.05$, SD = 2.04), $F(3, 62) = 2.56, p < 0.10$. However, there was no statistically significant difference between the means. Participants also

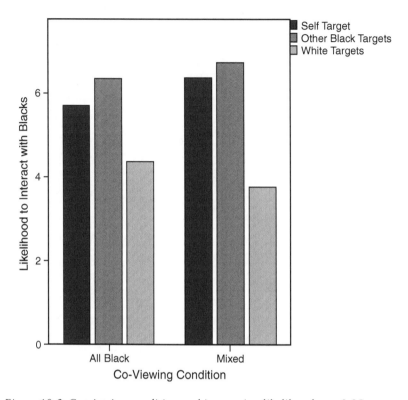

Figure 10.2 Co-viewing condition and interaction likelihood, $p < 0.05$.

reported the effects on Whites were lower (more negative) for those who viewed *Diary* (comedy with a mixed group ($M = 3.44$, SD = 1.86) than for those who viewed with all Blacks ($M = 4.90$, SD = 1.77). However, Bonferroni adjustments did not reveal significant differences between the means.

Correlations between Dependent Measures

Last, correlational analysis was conducted to identify any meaningful associations between the dependent measures. Bivariate analysis revealed a significant positive relationship between enjoyment and perceived bias ($r = 0.524$, $p < 0.01$), suggesting the more participants experienced enjoyment, the less likely they were to perceive the bias in the films. Put another way, perceptions of bias in the films could impact participants' overall enjoyment. Enjoyment was also significantly correlated with Whites' attitudes ($r = 0.338$, $p < 0.01$) and interaction likelihood ($r = 0.314$, $p < 0.05$). There were also significant relationships between perceived bias and Whites' attitudes toward Blacks ($r = 0.446$, $p < 0.01$) and Whites' likelihood to interact with Blacks ($r = 0.397$,

$p < 0.01$), suggesting that the more participants enjoyed and evaluated the representations favorably, the more likely they were to judge the film as having a positive, rather than negative, impact on White viewers' social judgments. Analysis also revealed a significant positive relationship between perceived influence on attitudes and interaction likelihood for White targets ($r = 0.721$, $p < 0.01$), suggesting that more positive attitudes toward Blacks could lead to more interest in interacting with African-Americans for White targets. There were no significant associations between hostile media perception or enjoyment and the target variables.

Discussion

The purpose of this study was to examine Black audiences' ambivalence toward stereotypical portrayals in Black films. Integrating hostile media's audience effect and third-person perception, it was argued that the context in which these portrayals are viewed would impact audiences' enjoyment, perceived bias, and third-person perceptions of the media content. Although the first set of hypotheses were not supported, there was support for the third-person hypotheses. Based on previous third-person research (Davison, 1983; Lamb & McLeod, 2005), it was suggested that because of concern with their public image, Black audiences would express concern that White audiences would be negatively influenced by images similar to what they viewed in the study. Third-person perception was analyzed on two factors—attitude toward Blacks and interest in interacting with Black people. Consonant with previous scholarship, findings revealed that Blacks reported greater negative effects for socially distant others compared to self. Blacks were concerned that films such as those viewed in the study would negatively impact Whites' attitudes toward African-Americans and would also decrease the likelihood that Whites would want to interact with Blacks. Specific to the hypothesis, findings also revealed significant interactions between the target variables and the co-viewing situation. Those who viewed with a majority White group compared to those who viewed with an all-Black group seemed more concerned.

An effect of co-viewing condition on the Self target was unexpected, but interesting nonetheless. Participants in the All Black condition reported more negative interest in interacting with Blacks, while those in the Mixed condition reported more neutral or positive interest. It is possible that Black participants were hypersensitized to their Black social identity and expressed a disinterest in interacting beyond the current viewing context. Put another way, *Black* participants viewing *Black* films with *other Blacks* may have felt burdened by the homogeneity of the film and viewing context and thus felt a need to distinguish themselves from the social group. On the other hand, Black participants viewing with a mixed group were not as sensitive to the exclusive nature

178 Omotayo O. Banjo

of the film context and thus were generally indifferent about interacting with other Blacks.

Although it was hypothesized that Black audiences would report less enjoyment of Black films when viewing with majority Whites than when viewing with all Blacks, results indicated that the viewing context did not significantly influence their enjoyment. Consistent with a host of research on Black audiences (Appiah, 2002; Brigham & Giesbrecht, 1976), participants in this study reported high levels of enjoyment of Black-oriented media, regardless of the race of their co-viewer. Based on Gunther and Schmitt's (2004) audience effect hypothesis, it was also argued that Black audiences would report greater perceptions of bias against Blacks while watching with majority Whites than when watching with all Blacks; however, the data yielded no support for this supposition. Overall, Blacks judged the representations as neutral and did not seem to question the authenticity of the representations of Blacks in the films regardless of the race of the co-viewer. However, correlational analysis showed that enjoyment was positively correlated with hostile media perception suggesting that representation may impact Black viewers' evaluations of the film.

The summary of the findings suggests then that Black audiences are still able to appreciate Black entertainment even when in the presence of a racially mixed crowd. However, even though they may judge the representations in a Black cultural product as neutral, they are still concerned about the perceived influence Black films could have on a racially distant other, specifically a White person. Furthermore, their concerns might be heightened when they are viewing Black culturally relevant media content *with* a White individual. Although they are able to form their independent judgments about the content, Black audiences have little trust in White individuals to share in their enjoyment of Black cultural media.

Implications

The burden of race and racial discrimination continues to be a problem in the United States, and these problems have seemed to increase even after the election of the first Black president. As Goldberg (2009) contends, there are conflicts between the ideology of postracialism and the present hostile racial and political climate, which is demonstrated by the fact that Obama has received significantly more threats than his White predecessor. In the aftermath of discriminatory voting policies and the controversial Paula Deen and Trayvon Martin cases, the issues of systemic and private racism have worked together in alarming Black community leaders and bringing the country's attitudes about Black identity to the forefront of our cultural consciousness. Perhaps now more than before, many African-Americans are sensitive to unfair social judgments by which they continue to be stigmatized. Even more alarming is the potential for stereotype threat—that is, the fear that social perceptions may hurt Blacks' self-image and in-turn motivate negative stereotypical behavior.

As symbolic interaction theory suggests, films are significant tools through which culture is defined, identities are shaped, and values are learned. Media assign value to everything from products to people groups and, as such, convey messages about the worth of individuals in certain categories. Research has shown that media representations negatively impact individuals in the absence of having a personal experience. Participants' apprehension regarding the impact of Black films on Whites might point to a belief that Whites have a limited personal and genuine experience with African-Americans. Therefore, Black audiences may be concerned that films with Black-oriented themes that are accessible to majority groups in major theatres may do more harm than good if it is the only encounter that Whites have experienced with African-Americans.

Exposure to Black culturally relevant media content is more pervasive than before with an increase in media ownership by Blacks and the growth of films with Black cultural themes. With the influx of racial humor in mainstream programming and the coverage of issues pertinent to Black communities in the news, it is not atypical for Blacks to view culturally relevant content with a racially mixed group. This may occur at social gatherings with friends (e.g., a get together) or in more public domains with strangers (e.g., airport). The findings of this study suggest that Black viewers are likely to be aware of the race of their co-viewer and may be thinking about how White viewers are evaluating the message.

Although Black participants in this sample judged the portrayals in the films as neutral, there continues to be popular discourse surrounding representations of Blacks by Black directors or other Black figureheads. For example, directors Tyler Perry and Spike Lee have engaged in hostile public debates on the topic of Perry's representations of Black culture in his films and television shows (Izrael, 2011). The secondary analyses yielded a two-way interaction of condition and film revealing that participants reported less interaction likelihood for Whites when viewing Tyler Perry's *Diary* compared to the drama. Perhaps participants' reports reflected Lee's and other's perspectives regarding Mr. Perry's work. It is possible that while Black media creators both employ and exploit Black stereotypes, Black audiences perceive themselves to be immune to stereotypical portrayals of Blacks, but believe that Whites are susceptible to it. As was seen in the case of CNN anchor Don Lemmon after admonishing the Black community (Emdin, 2013), Black audiences are increasingly resistant to public critique and especially in the eyes of White out-group members.

Black audiences' alarm might be warranted as studies have indicated that Whites tend to show negative responses to welfare, crime, and single motherhood, associating such descriptions with Black culture (Neundorf & Atkin, 2000). Furthermore, less than 20 percent of White respondents indicated beliefs that Blacks are smart, hardworking, independent, and nonviolent individuals (Carlson & Chamberlain, 2004). In reference to entertainment, polls have indicated that Whites do not find Black gospel comedies or plays appealing (Johnson, 2005). Still today, all aspects of White American culture are often the standard by which other social groups are compared. Given these prior findings, Black Americans' fear of White Americans' perception of their culture may be justified and were revealed in the present study.

This study also bridges cultural studies and media effects approaches to audience research, providing empirical evidence for cultural theories about how minorities evaluate and interpret media messages. For example, providing a sociocultural explanation for these findings, hooks' (1996) oppositional gaze suggests that though Black viewers may experience enjoyment of poor self-representation, they are still able to identify reinforcements of whiteness and recognize its potential effects. This implies some level of dual processing when minorities engage with such entertainment.

In sum, the question is not whether or not Blacks deeply reflect on cultural portrayals, but perhaps the more pressing question for Blacks is *who* is seeing and what might *they* think. Perhaps considering the differences between these questions might shed insight into the current debates over representation, help Black audiences and organizations better understand their critiques of Black cultural productions, and possibly challenge Black cultural producers to think creatively about their portrayals of Black culture. Understanding Black audiences' concern could also help in developing media literacy strategies for consuming and decoding culturally oriented media products across all racial groups in the United States. In the same way mass media has been blamed for societal fractures, culturally oriented media could also entertain, enlighten, and educate out-group members.

Limitations and Future Research

This study is not without its limitations and thus leaves much room for theoretical and experimental exploration. Although it appears obvious that individuals would be aware of the presence of others, future research should confirm participants' awareness of the racial composition of co-viewers. Further, the ratio of Black to White audience members were not always even across each session, as number of participants present depended on whether or not participants showed up. Provided number of participants per session was more strictly controlled, this might yield different effects.

Participants in this sample judged the portrayals of Blacks in this film as neutral. Although there is a case to be made that the content of the films is known to be stereotypical, future studies should also include measures that empirically test the extent to which experimental subjects judge the content to be stereotypical and/or negative. Findings may have been different if participants identified portrayals of Blacks as significantly poor. It is also likely that participants could both perceive bias and seek confirmation from the same media content. Even more, future research should consider positive aspects of Black-oriented films and its potential positive effects on Black and non-Black audiences.

It is possible that the effects found in this study are due to the presence of others without regard to race. Future research should include a viewing alone condition to control for pure audience effects. Although session leaders were instructed to notate any outburst or negative reactions of out-group members, it was difficult to account for the influence of co-viewer reactions on participants' viewing experience. Future studies may consider training confederates as co-viewers to control for others' reactions. Because of the limitations of self-report measures, this study was not able to adequately attain psychological discomfort while viewing with out-group members. Future research should employ psychophysiological measures to gauge Blacks' discomfort with viewing stereotypical entertainment in a mixed race co-viewing situation.

Participants in this study also seemed to be less interested to interact with Blacks while watching Black films with in-group members, whereas those watching Black films with out-group members felt slightly more interested. Future research should entertain the impact of Black-oriented movies on the Black target and their attitudes toward their own group. This study focuses on Blacks specifically, but future research should consider how majority groups (i.e. Whites) evaluate racial stereotypes in films when in different viewing conditions. How do racial stereotypes of minority and majority groups impact Whites' self-concept? Moreover, research should examine whether Whites' responses vary, not only across viewing conditions, but also across video contexts. In other words, how do Whites respond when watching stereotypical images in Black-oriented media compared to White-oriented films when they are watching with all Whites and Blacks?

Last, future research should also examine Blacks' selective exposure to Black entertainment when in the presence of White viewers who are not strangers. Bryant and Davies (2006) argued that an examination of sociological influences on viewing responses is missing in media effects research. Specifically, the authors suggest that our knowledge of "how the presence of others influences individual media-use decisions" (p. 28) is in need of more exploration. More in-depth research on social psychological effects of viewing responses may have some implications for Blacks' selection of film when with a mixed group of friends or even when in the presence of an out-group member.

Though Black audiences were the population of interest for this study, the research question is applicable to all minority or low-power groups across race, sexual orientation, and religion. Enjoyment of in-group targeted entertainment is worthy of exploration because it is indicative of implicit social attitudes. The dearth of popular ethnic media makes it challenging to do a comparative analysis across various culturally-oriented media, but it could shed light on minority audiences' sense of status and power in relation to their mediated status and power. Furthermore, the ongoing tensions between minority ethnic groups and majority groups may have critical implications for understanding the potential social and psychological impact of ethnic entertainment and the overall consumption of racialized messages in the media landscape.

Appendix A

Measurement Appendix

Perceived Bias—Hostile Media Effect (Gunther & Schmitt, 2004)
   Cronbach's alpha = 0.85–0.87
   The next part of this questionnaire specifically regards your evaluations of the characters.

Black Portrayal

Would you say the depictions of the main characters in this clip were strictly neutral or were they biased in favor or against African-Americans?

–5	–4	–3	–2	–1	0	1	2	3	4	5
Strongly Biased Against					Neutral			Strongly	In favor	Biased

Overall, do you think the portrayal of Black culture in this clip is consistent with or inconsistent with your personal beliefs about the subject matter?

–5	–4	–3	–2	–1	0	1	2	3	4	5
Very Inconsistent					Neutral				Very Consistent	

How accurately do you feel the Black characters were portrayed?

–5	–4	–3	–2	–1	0	1	2	3	4	5
Not Accurately At All					Neutral				Very Accurately	

How positively or negatively do you feel the Black characters were portrayed?

–5		–4	–3	–2	–1	0		1	2	3	4		5
Very Negatively						Neutral					Very Positively		

Would you say that the producers and writers of this clip were strictly neutral or were they biased in favor or against African-Americans?

–5		–4	–3	–2	–1		0	1	2	3		4		5
Strongly Biased Against							Neutral			Strongly		In favor	Biased	

Perceived Effect on Others—Third-Person Perception
The following questions regard your overall evaluation of audiences of Black Movies.

Attitudes
(–5 to +5 scale, "Make More Negative" to "Make More Positive")
   Think about the influence of this clip on your own opinions
   Overall how do you think your attitudes toward Blacks could be affected, if at all?
   Think about the influence of this clip on typical Black viewers' opinions
   Overall how do you think typical Black viewers' attitudes toward Blacks could be affected, if at all?
   Think about the influence of this film on Whites' opinions
   Overall how do you think typical Whites' attitudes toward Blacks could be affected, if at all?

Interaction Likelihood
(–5 to +5 scale, "Make Interactions Less Likely" to "Make Interactions More Likely")
   Think about the influence of this clip on your own opinions
   How likely do you feel watching movies such as these can interest you to interact with African-Americans?
   Think about the influence of this clip on typical Black viewers' opinions
   How likely do you feel clips such as these can encourage African-Americans to interact with other African-Americans?
   Think about the influence of this film on Whites' opinions
   How likely do you feel clips such as these can encourage Whites to interact with African-Americans?

Appendix B

Diary of Mad Black Woman Description

Helen McCarter has everything a woman wants: a nice house and rich husband. However after her husband Charles throws her out of the house after admitting to an affair a distraught Helen turns to her mother, grandmother Madea and cousin Brian who take her in and turn her back to God. Helen learns for the first time in her life to stand up on her two feet and is ready to remove herself from her relationship with Charles and move on with Orlando, her new love. But when her husband is almost killed by a vengeful client, Helen wonders if she has the heart to forgive him despite everything she's endured.

ATL Description

For a kid growing up on the south side of Atlanta, the Cascade roller-skating rink is the place to be seen, and it's the place where the orphaned high school senior Rashad and his little brother Ant go every weekend to forget their financial troubles, hang with their friends and get their groove on. But outside the rink, the brothers have problems they can't avoid: Ant is being recruited into the posse of a charismatic drug dealer. Meanwhile, Rashad's three best friends are pulling him in different directions, and his new girlfriend New-New may not be as "street" as she seems. As Rashad tries to hold on to Ant, he realizes that he's going to have to step out of his skates and into the real world.

References

Appiah, O. (2002). Black and White viewer's perception and recall of occupational characters on television. *Journal of Communication*, 52(4), 776–793. doi:10.1111/j.1460-2466.2002.tb02573.x

Bodroghkozy, A. (1992). Is this what you mean by color TV? Race, gender and contested meanings in NBC's Julia. In L. Spigel (Ed.), *Private screenings: Television and the female consumer* (pp. 143–167). Minneapolis: University of Minnesota Press. Retrieved from http://profheitnerracemediaculture.files.wordpress.com/2009/08/is-this-what-you-mean-by-color-tv-julia.pdf

Brigham, J. C., & Giesbrecht, L. W. (1976). "All in the Family": Racial attitudes. *Journal of Communication*, 26(4), 69–74. doi:10.1111/j.1460-2466.1976.tb01938.x

Bryant, J., & Davies, J. (2006). Selective exposure process. In B. Jennings & P. Vorderer (Eds.) *Psychology of entertainment* (pp. 19–33). Mahwah, NJ: Erlbaum.

Carlson, E. D., & Chamberlain, R. M. (2004). The Black–White perception gap and health disparities research. *Public Health Nursing*, 21(4), 372–379. doi:10.1111/j.0737-1209.2004.21411.x

Chidester, P. (2008). May the circle stay unbroken: Friends, the presence of absence, and the rhetorical reinforcement of whiteness. *Critical Studies in Media Communication, 25*(2), 157–174. doi:10.1080/15295030802031772

Choi, Y., Leshner, G., & Choi, J. (2008). Third-person effects of idealized body image in magazine advertisements. *The American Behavioral Scientist (Beverly Hills), 52*(2), 147–164.

Cornwell, N. C., & Orbe, M. (2002). Keepin' it real" and/or "sellin' out to the man": African American responses to Aaron McGruder's The Boondock. In R. Means Coleman (Ed.), *Say it loud!: Black audiences, media, and identity* (pp. 27–43). New York: Routledge.

Davison, W. P. (1983). The third-person effect in communication. *The Public Opinion Quarterly, 47*(1), 1–15. doi:10.2307/2748702

Emdin, C. (2013, July 30). On Black culture, Don Lemon's got it all wrong. *Huffington Post.* Retrieved from www.huffingtonpost.com/christopher-emdin/don-lemon_b_3682561.html

Entman, R. M., & Rojecki, A. (2001). *The black image in the white mind.* Chicago, IL: University of Chicago Press.

Ford, T. E. (1997). Effects of stereotypical television portrayals of African Americans on person perception. *Social Psychology Quarterly, 60*(3), 266–275. doi:10.2307/2787086

Goldberg, D. T. (2009). *The threat of race: Reflections on racial neoliberalism.* Maiden, MA: Blackwell Publishing.

Green, M. C., Kaufman, G. F., & Brock, T. C. (2004). Understanding media enjoyment: The role of transportation into narrative worlds. *Communication Theory, 14*(4), 311–327. doi:10.1111/j.1468-2885.2004.tb00317.x

Guerrero, E. (1993). *Framing blackness: The African American image in film.* Philadelphia, PA: Temple University Press.

Gunther, A. C. (1995). Overrating the X-rating: the third-person perception and support for censorship of pornography. *Journal of Communication, 45*(1), 27–38. doi:0.1111/j.1460-2466.1995.tb00712.x

Gunther, A. C., & Schmitt, K. (2004). Mapping boundaries of the hostile media effect. *Journal of Communication, 54*(1), 55–70. doi:10.1111/j.1460-2466.2004.tb02613.x

hooks, bell. (1996). *Reel to real: Race, sex and class at the movies.* New York: Routledge.

Inniss, L. B., & Feagin, J. R. (1995). "The Cosby Show": The view from the black middle class. *Journal of Black Studies, 25*(6), 692–711. doi:10.1177/002193479502500604

Izrael, J. (2011, April 11). Tyler Perry Vs. Spike Lee: A debate over class and "coonery." *Tell Me More.* Retrieved from www.npr.org/blogs/tellmemore/2011/04/22/135630682/tyler-perry-vs-spike-lee-a-debate-over-class-and-coonery

Jhally, S., & Lewis, J. M. (1993). *Enlightened racism: The cosby show, audiences, and the myth of the American dream.* Boulder, CO: Westview Press.

Johnson, J. A. (2005, April 1). Wholesome film's themes resonate with black viewers. *The Columbus Dispatch,* p. 02.E.

Johnson, M. A. (2010). Incorporating self-categorization concepts into ethnic media research. *Communication Theory, 20*(1), 106–125. doi:10.1111/j.1468-2885.2009.01356.x

Kyles, K. (2005, November 4). Toxic toon ; "Boondocks" heads to cartoon network with its irreverence intact. *Chicago Tribune*, p. 47.

Lambe, J. L., & McLeod, D. M. (2005). Understanding third-person perception processes: Predicting perceived impact on self and others for multiple expressive contexts. *Journal of Communication*, 55(2), 277–291.

Lind, R. A. (1996). Race and viewer evaluations of ethically controversial TV news stories. *Journal of Mass Media Ethics*, 11(1), 40–52. doi:10.1207/s15327728jmme1101_5

Matabane, P. W. (1988). Television and the black audience: Cultivating moderate perspectives on racial integration. *Journal of Communication*, 38(4), 21–31. doi:10.1111/j.1460-2466.1988.tb02067.x

McDowell, J. (1989, July 17). He's got to have it his way. *Time*. Retrieved from www.time.com/time/magazine/article/0,9171,958165,00.html

Means Coleman, R. R. (2000). *African American viewers and the black situation comedy: Situating racial humor*. New York: Routledge.

Motley, C. M., & Craig-Henderson, K. M. (2007). Epithet or endearment?: Examining reactions among those of the African diaspora to an ethnic epithet. *Journal of Black Studies*, 37(6), 944–963. doi:10.2307/40034963

Neundorf, K. A., & Atkin, D. (2000). Explorations of the Simpson trial "Racial Divide." *The Howard Journal of Communications*, 11(4), 247–266. doi:10.1080/10646170050204545

Oliver, M. B. (1993). Exploring the paradox of the enjoyment of sad films. *Human Communication Research*, 19(3), 315–342. doi:10.1111/j.1468-2958.1993.tb00304.x

Oliver, M. B., Jackson, R. L., Moses, N. N., & Dangerfield, C. L. (2004). The face of crime: viewers' memory of race-related facial features of individuals pictured in the news. *Journal of Communication*, 54(1), 88–104. doi:10.1111/j.1460-2466.2004.tb02615.x

Oliver, M. B., Weaver, J. B., & Sargent, S. L. (2000). An examination of factors related to sex differences in enjoyment of sad films. *Journal of Broadcasting & Electronic Media*, 44(2), 282–300. doi:10.1207/s15506878jobem4402_8

Perloff, R. M. (2009). Mass media, social perception, and the third-person effect. In J. Bryant & M. B. Oliver (Eds.), *Media effects: Advances in theory and research* (3rd ed., pp. 252–268). New York: Routledge.

Perry, T. (2005). *Diary of a Mad Black Woman*. comedy.

Reid, M. A. (2005). *Black lenses, black voices: African American film now*. New York: Rowman & Littlefield.

Rushing, K. (2004). Racy "Boondocks" comics expose Black culture rift. Retrieved from www.africanamerica.org/topic/racy-boondocks-comics-expose-black-culture-rift

Russell, K., Wilson, M., & Hall, R. E. (1992). *The color complex: The politics of skin color among Blacks*. New York: Anchor.

Scharrer, E. (2002). Third-person perception and television violence: The role of out-group stereotyping in perceptions of susceptibility to effects. *Communication Research*, 29(6), 681–704. doi:10.1177/009365002237832

Sigelman, L., & Tuch, S. A. (1997). Metastereotypes: Blacks' perceptions of Whites' stereotypes of Blacks. *The Public Opinion Quarterly*, 61(1), 87–101. doi:10.2307/2749513

Squires, C. (2009). *African Americans and the media*. Maiden, MA: Polity.

Tal-Or, N., Tsfati, Y., & Gunther, A. C. (2009). The influence of presumed media influence: Origins and implications of the third-person perception. In R. L. Nabi & M. B. Oliver, (Eds.), *The Sage handbook of media processes and effects* (pp. 99–112). Los Angeles, CA: Sage.

Tan, A., Fujioka, Y., & Tan, G. (2000). Television use, stereotypes of African Americans and opinions on affirmative action: An affective model of policy reasoning. *Communication Monographs,* 67(4), 362–371. doi:10.1080/03637750009376517

Tsfati, Y. (2007). Hostile media perceptions, presumed media influence, and minority alienation: The case of Arabs in Israel. *Journal of Communication,* 57(4), 632–651. doi:10.1111/j.1460-2466.2007.00361.x

Valentino, N. A. (1999). Crime news and the priming of racial attitudes during evaluations of the president. *The Public Opinion Quarterly,* 63(3), 293–320. doi:10.2307/2991710

Vallone, R. P., Ross, L., & Lepper, M. R. (1985). The hostile media phenomenon: Biased perception and perceptions of media bias in coverage of the Beirut massacre. *Journal of Personality and Social Psychology,* 49(3), 577–585. doi:10.1037/0022-3514.49.3.577

Watkins, M. (2002). *African American humor: The best Black comedy from slavery to today.* Chicago, IL: Lawrence Hill.

Watts, E. K., & Orbe, M. (2002). The spectacular consumption of "true" African American culture: "Whassup" with the Budweiser guys? *Critical Studies in Media Communication,* 19(1), 1–20. doi:10.1080/07393180216554

Part V
Digital Diaspora

11   Social Media and Social Justice Movements after the Diminution of Black-Owned Media in the United States

Jeffrey Layne Blevins

Freedom begins the moment you realize someone else has been writing your story, and it's time you took the pen from his hand and started writing it yourself.
— Bill Moyers keynote address to the National Conference for Media Reform in Memphis, TN (2007)

Today, everyone can be a storyteller as social media and mobile streaming applications have flattened the communicative landscape. Moreover, social media platforms have the potential to change the relationship between news media and the public in significant ways, as virtually everyone now has the ability to document and live-stream events to a global audience. To say the least, social media has become a primary venue for public commentary about current events, disrupting the gate-keeping power once held by national news outlets and talk radio.

The most poignant examples of this restructuring of communicative power can be seen in social justice movements and the instant release of imagery and commentary in the wake of multiple shootings of Black men by police officers across the U.S. in recent years. For instance, Diamond Reynolds live-streamed the moments following the shooting of her fiancé, Philando Castille, when they were pulled over by police for a broken taillight in Falcon Heights, a suburb of the St. Paul and Minneapolis twin cities in Minnesota. Videos were posted online when police in Baton Rouge, Louisiana shot Alton Sterling, prompting an investigation from the U.S. Justice Department. Civil unrest followed the shooting of Michael Brown, an unarmed Black teenager in the St. Louis suburb of Ferguson, Missouri in the summer of 2014. As the hashtag #Ferguson trended on Twitter, national and international news outlets followed social media activity in covering the protests, looting, and militarized police response. And in Cincinnati, Ohio during the summer of 2015, Sam DuBose, an unarmed Black motorist, was shot and killed during a traffic stop by Ray Tensing, a University of Cincinnati police officer. Afterwards, local community groups led by @BlackLivesCincy and @theIRATE8 quickly mobilized on social media to decry the incident and confront competing narratives that it was justified.

A primary goal of this chapter is to understand how social justice groups and the public use social media to provide a more diverse array of commentary about the meaning and implications of civic activity, and it will show how historically marginalized groups have exercised their First Amendment rights in ways that have disrupted the gatekeeping power once held by national news outlets and networks. For Black social justice advocates, this is a significant moment, especially after Roberts Broadcasting (an African-American owned media company) announced the sale of its few television stations, as African-Americans owned the same number of full-power U.S. broadcast television stations in 2014 as they did in 1974—none (see Torres & Turner, 2013). Passage of the Telecommunications Act has hastened the diminution of minority-owned broadcast stations in the U.S. as 40 percent of minority-owned television stations were sold to nonminority entities between 1998 and 2007 (Blevins & Martinez, 2010, p. 225). As such, social media has become a vital platform for free expression for Blacks in the United States, especially on matters of social justice.

This chapter will discern specific lessons about the power and utility that social media can play in civil discourse about social justice. Understanding the impact that social media channels have on the power of voices can improve the informational, communicational, and relational livelihood of social justice movements. In today's media-saturated world, social justice efforts are necessarily linked to media access, and social media in particular, especially as ownership and control of legacy media outlets has become increasingly concentrated under neoliberal economic policy in the United States.

Additionally, this chapter applies a political economic perspective to the significance of social media platforms in social justice movements in the face of dwindling ownership of television and radio outlets by Blacks and the growth of hate speech in talk radio programing. The political economy of communication focuses on social relations organized around power and forms of control in the production, distribution, and consumption of media activities, including the use of "social networking sites to resist the concentration of power in business and government" (Mosco, 2009, p. 24). As McChesney (2016, p. ix) noted, "media and communication have significant power and influence in society, and the systems are the result of government policies." One of the primary endeavors of political economic studies of U.S. media since the late 20th century has been to understand the ways in which media systems may help advance the principles of a democratic society or reflect the more narrow interests of big business and government elites (see Herman & Chomsky, 1988; McChesney, 2008; Mosco, 2009). This analysis will show that Internet-based communication and social media have provided an important opportunity to counterbalance the lack of Black voices and influence in traditional media outlets, while also recognizing how telecommunication providers and social media mobs may temper some of this newfound success, and urge social justice movements to include media reform as part of their cause.

The Media Blackout: Minority Ownership Diminution and Hate Radio

The Federal Communication Commission's (FCC) media ownership report in November 2012 revealed a lack of diversity and demonstrated an ongoing dismal state of affairs for minority owners over the past 60 years (see FCC, 2012). Media ownership consolidation, which has been justified by the popularity of neoliberal economic philosophy, has been the most formidable factor in the diminution of minority ownership of broadcast television and radio properties, as well as the decline of diversity in media.

Neoliberal media policy emerged most notably in a famous law review article by former FCC Chairperson Mark Fowler and his chief legal advisor when they argued that the mechanisms of the marketplace would best determine the public interest, rather than any definition of the public interest created by the FCC (see Fowler & Brenner, 1982). For over three decades, neoliberal thinking has not only been prominent in media policy, but has become a dominant ideology among policymakers in Washington, DC. In general, neoliberal economic philosophy sees government rules as the problem and the marketplace as the solution, and its three primary goals include privatization of institutions, liberalization of markets, and deregulation of businesses. This kind of thinking has been evident in the FCC's review of media ownership rules, as the agency tends to reduce its knowledge base about media to matters that are primarily economic in nature, thus privileging the economic interests of commercial broadcasters over other principles, such as diversity and the concerns of racial minorities and women (Blevins & Brown, 2010).

The diversity principle is also one of the most complex, as it may involve several areas of media policy, including minority ownership and representation, consumer choice, content regulation, and ownership regulation. The Telecommunications Act of 1996 (TCA) significantly relaxed media ownership and required a biennial (now quadrennial) review of ownership rules under Title II, Section 202(h) to determine "whether any such rules are necessary in the public interest as a result of competition." The presumption of the 1996 law seemed to be that limits on broadcast ownership are no longer necessary to serve the public interest. However, the TCA did not address the impact of deregulation on diversity, or even the need for diversity.

After commencing its 2002 biennial review of media ownership rules, the FCC voted in 2003 to remove the ban on owning a television station and newspaper in the same market, as well as limitations on how many television stations a single entity could own in a given market, and raised the cap on the proportion of television households that could be reached via the owned-and-operated stations of a single entity. The rule changes were challenged and remanded back to the FCC in Prometheus Radio Project v. FCC (2004). In Prometheus Radio Project v. FCC (2011), a federal court dismissed the proposed newspaper/broadcast cross-ownership rule and challenged the FCC to consider the impact of its proposed rule changes on minorities and women.

As part of its 2010 quadrennial review, the FCC addressed the state of media ownership for minorities and women. The FCC's (2012) report showed that women collectively or individually hold a majority of the voting interests in only 6.8 percent of full power commercial broadcast television stations; 7.8 percent of commercially licensed AM radio stations; and 5.8 percent of commercially licensed FM radio stations. Racial minorities collectively or individually held a majority of the voting interests in 2.2 percent of full power commercial broadcast television stations; 6.2 percent of commercially licensed AM radio stations; and 3.5 percent of commercially licensed FM radio stations. The bleak report led to the recharter of the FCC's Diversity Committee in March 2013 and drew attention within the agency to the lack of minority ownership.

During this time the Howard Media Group, based in Howard University (a historically Black university), began challenging the empirical basis of FCC research on media ownership and argued for the agency to employ specific research methods, such as ethnography, which may help provide a much broader array of evidence than methodologies that only aim to assess economic efficiency (see Howard Media Group, 2013, 2017). The inclusion of expert knowledge and research about culture and content would better inform the FCC's decision-making about media ownership and counter the dominant neoliberal economic paradigm. FCC Commissioner Mignon Clyburn, the first and (to date) only African-American woman to ever serve as a commissioner on the FCC, has continued to push the agency to promote the principle of diversity (Radio Ink, 2017, January 26). Moreover, Clyburn (2017, p. 3) has expressed dismay that despite the acute lack of ownership diversity and financial barriers for women and minorities to own and operate broadcast facilities, "the only advocacy of many is for the elimination of rules that were created to prevent the concentration of station ownership into the hands of a few large media conglomerates." The concern is that ownership matters; and one should look no further than the dominance of politically conservative talk radio programming and the absence of other voices as an example of the impact of radio ownership consolidation.

Clear Channel (now iHeartMedia) amassed over 1,200 radio stations in the decade following the TCA and along with Cumulus and Citadel owned the bulk of U.S. stations by 2009 (Pew, 2009). During this time, right-wing talk show hosts Rush Limbaugh, Michael Savage, Michael

Reagan, Glenn Beck, Neal Boortz, and similar syndicated programs saturated the U.S. airwaves, as conservatives commanded over 90 percent of the weekday news/talk programing among the top five radio owners. Such right-wing radio jocks impressed neoconservative political and social ideals, and neoliberal economic philosophy upon their audiences, and at worst, deteriorated into "hate speech" as program hosts routinely demonized political opponents through sophistic discourse (see Bill Moyers Journal, 2008, September 12). Research by Noriega and Iribarren (2012) also documented the systematic use of hate speech in widely broadcast conservative talk-radio programming.

While there is a correlation between the consolidation of radio ownership and the growth of right-wing radio, it is not necessarily the cause. Rather, the expansion of white male conservative talk shows since mid-1990s was part and parcel of the so-called "Republican Revolution" after the 1994 midterm congressional elections, and its growth has been fostered by media ownership consolidation that allowed a handful of powerful radio operators to leverage syndicated programs across their networks featuring hosts that advocated neoliberal economic policies and cultural politics consistent with their world view. For instance, shortly after Mark Lloyd was appointed as Chief Diversity Officer of the FCC in 2009, radio hosts Glenn Beck and Michael Savage dismissed him as a "Marxist" and "Communist vermin" that would threaten broadcasting (Bogado, 2009, November 1). A study of the 10,506 commercially licensed U.S. radio stations found that outlets owned by racial minorities and women were less likely to air conservative talk programming, while group-owned stations were more likely to air conservative-oriented programming (Center for American Progress & Free Press, 2007). The lack of minority ownership in radio broadcasting intensifies the problem, as targeted minority groups do not have equal access to the medium to present opposing views (see Blevins & Martinez, 2010, p. 232). Stimulating more diverse broadcast ownership is one way to counterbalance the plethora right-wing voices on the radio. Utilizing online media platforms, including social media, is another.

The Battle for Broadband

The Broadband Technology Opportunities Program (BTOP) was part of the American Recovery and Reinvestment Act of 2009 (ARRA) and provided over $4 billion in federal grants to be administered by the U.S. Department of Commerce and National Telecommunications and Information Administration to help facilitate broadband Internet access and adoption in unserved and underserved areas of the United States, including rural and urban regions. BTOP presented an opportunity for media reformers to connect their digital justice efforts to the broader social justice movement. For instance, the Detroit-based Allied

Media Projects and Philadelphia's Media Mobilizing Project used the occasion to build coalitions among media reformers and social justice groups focused on an array of concerns, including urban housing, workers' rights, and environmental issues, among other causes (see Breitbart, 2016). However, long-term efforts to sustain broadband access and media diversity in the FCC were cut short by Republicans in the U.S. House of Representatives in 2011 when they passed an amendment to their spending bill defunding Chief Diversity Officer Lloyd's salary at a time when he was working to spread broadband Internet access to low-income people (Eggerton, 2011, February 17). The BTOP funding was a one-time occasion, but as Breitbart (2016, p. 113) observed:

> it provided an opportunity for an enduring impact on broadband in the United States. In Philadelphia and Detroit, we were able to use the grant-seeking process as a vehicle for visioning and organizing, and for bringing new voices and audiences into the conversation about our shared digital future.

Long-term social justice movements playing out on social media should take note that their efforts should not be divorced from the media reform movement. As Freedman and Obar (2016, p. 7) recognized:

> [W]e cannot rely on mainstream media to adequately represent our lives as they are lived, to hold power to account and to reflect honestly on the media's own interconnections with established power; we are forced to make our own media.

In today's media-saturated world, social justice depends on communication platforms that allows for access by all and to all.

Social Media Power in St. Louis and Cincinnati

The power of social media to help drive social justice movements was, perhaps, first recognized in Guatemala in 2009 after the killing of Rodrigo Rosenberg, as social media provided a forum for Guatemalans to organize and mobilize while expressing their concerns about violence in their country (see Harlow, 2012). Two years later, social media helped bring the 2011 Arab Spring to the global stage as waves of protests against repressive regimes swept across parts of the Middle East and North Africa (see Howard et al., 2011).

In the United States, the role of social media in social justice efforts was first noticed in the Occupy Wall Street movement (see DeLuca, Lawson, & Sun, 2012), but became prominent in the development of the Black Lives Matter phenomenon after George Zimmerman was acquitted in 2013 for the murder of Trayvon Martin, and then in the events following the shooting death of Michael Brown in Ferguson during the summer of 2014 (see Freelon, McIlwain, & Clark, 2016). Social media provided instantaneous imagery and commentary in the civil unrest that followed. As the hashtag #Ferguson trended on Twitter, national news outlets followed social media activity in covering the protests, looting, and militarized police response.

Similar disturbances occurred in Cincinnati's Over-the-Rhine neighborhood in 2001 after an unarmed Black teenager, Timothy Thomas, was shot and killed by Stephen Roach, a white police officer. Despite the similarity, the turmoil in Cincinnati lasted four days, while disquiet in Ferguson went on for weeks. However, Facebook and Twitter were not in existence then, and the use of mobile technology and social media platforms seems to have been a significant factor in drawing attention to more recent events. Social media appeared to change the relationship between news media and the public, as tweets and posts did more than just reiterate the images and messages from traditional news outlets about the events in Ferguson. Rather, social media was the platform for people in Ferguson to document what was happening to a global audience and the primary venue for public commentary.

Using the hashtag #IfTheyGunnedMeDown, individuals juxtaposed two dissimilar images of themselves: one, a wholesome picture of the individual, perhaps attired in cap and gown at a high school graduation; the other, the same person in street attire, maybe holding an alcoholic beverage or cigarette. The question being: if the police killed me, which picture would be in the news—the wholesome high school graduate or the menace to society? By featuring two contrasting images of the same person, these posts demonstrated that one picture alone doesn't tell the whole story of a person, and questioned the tendency of news media to focus on the one image that contributes to the 'menace to society' narrative.

In reaction to eyewitness accounts that Brown was surrendering with his "hands up" before being shot, several posts on Twitter using the hashtag #HandsUpDontShoot featured images of people holding their hands up. One of the most potent was a video of kids on a school bus chanting: "hands up, don't shoot." The message suggested that Michael Brown "could have been me" and engages concern about police officers overestimating the threat posed by Black suspects and too quickly responding with deadly force.

Social media provided a forum for a community in Ferguson, and the public at large, to tell its own stories in the aftermath of the shooting and challenge the images that tend to pervade national news. In a mediated world dominated by national outlets, social media allowed the public to exercise its First Amendment rights in a way that changed the balance of communicative power and enhanced everyone's ability to relate the meaning of the events in Ferguson to their own personal lives.

Papacharissi (2015, p. 309) explained this kind of phenomenon as affective expression in the form of networked publics that "want to tell their story collaboratively and on their own terms." Moreover, these "affective publics" tend to "produce disruptions... of dominant political narratives by presencing [sic] underrepresented viewpoints" (Papacharissi, 2015, p. 19). For social justice movements, social media has presented significant opportunities for the disturbance and redirection of dominant and oppressive narratives.

Making Affective Social Justice Movements Effective Media Reformers

Social media appeared to change the relationship between mainstream news media and the public, as tweets and posts didn't just reiterate the images and messages from traditional news outlets about the events in Ferguson. Rather, social media was the platform for people in Ferguson to document what was happening to a global audience and the primary venue for public commentary. For instance, the conversation from (and about) Ferguson reached as far as the Middle East, where Palestinians tweeted in solidarity about racial injustice (see Goldstein, 2014, August 15). Several players for the then St. Louis Rams attracted international attention when they came on to the field before a National Football League game imitating the #HandsUpDontShoot thread on Twitter (McCormack, 2014, November 30). Social justice advocates were able to help drive the local, national, and international conversation through social media.

Similarly, in Cincinnati, social justice organizations @BlackLivesCincy and @theIRATE8 utilized multiple social media platforms in a sustained effort that involved a broader array of social justice issues beyond the Sam DuBose shooting. For instance, "theIRATE8" group name refers to the percent of University of Cincinnati's student body that are Black. The organization launched a website (www.theirate8.com/) and social media accounts on Twitter (@theIRATE8) and Facebook (www.facebook.com/theirate8/). Although, the shooting death of an unarmed Black man during a traffic stop by a white university police officer was the initial focusing event for the group, their scope of concern quickly broadened to include reforming policies on University of Cincinnati's campus, including retention of Black students and increasing faculty diversity. TheIRATE8 keeps a log of media coverage of the organization by legacy news outlets (see www.theirate8.com/in-the-media.html), which also provides a record of their impact on civil discourse about social justice issues. The DuBose shooting was also a focusing event for @BlackLivesCincy, but the group has also addressed a much broader range of social justice issues on its Twitter account and Facebook page (www.facebook.com/BlackLivesMatterCincinnati/), including transgender rights, support for rape survivors, refugee and immigration policy, poverty, healthcare, environmental justice, and many others. Certainly, the organizational acumen of these groups was a primary reason for their successes, but their engagement with social media and utilization of digital media resources to tell their own stories was also an instrumental factor.

The use of mobile streaming video technology (MSVT), such as Facebook Live and Periscope, which can be used with Twitter, have also emerged as important tools for broadcasting and documenting events of interest to social justice movements.

> In sum, MSVTs are best understood as something akin to live broadcast television with two major differences. First, their use of mobile phones to capture and stream good, quality video means that anyone, anywhere, has the ability to become a live video broadcaster so long as they have a capable smartphone, and this represents a significant change in the barriers for entry to live streaming. Second, dissemination of this video is highly decentralized along social network lines, meaning the power to capture audience attention for events such as news has shifted away from the singular format of the television channel such that it now includes distribution along social networks.
>
> (Stewart & Littau, 2016, p. 316)

The development of MSVTs on social media networks represent an important shift away from an audience-based media model, such as television broadcasting in which a limited number of stations distribute programming for mass consumption, to a user-created content model where everyday citizens are their own storytellers. These citizen-storytellers are not only generating their own content, but they are also reframing stories that used to be in the more exclusive domain of professional media.

While social media have proven to be valuable platforms for social justice movements, it is important to keep in mind that these outlets and MSVTs depend upon broadband telecommunication networks that are subject to the same forces of neoliberal economic philosophy and cultural politics that affected broadcasting. Just as broadcast ownership deregulation limited program diversity, there could be a similar effect upon free expression taking place on Internet platforms as the FCC repeal of its network neutrality rules take effect on April 23, 2018. This alters the model that previously classified Internet Service Providers (ISPs) as common carriers, so that Comcast, Verizon, AT&T, and other providers do not block or degrade access to specific sites and services or charge customers extra fees for using sites and services that may compete with their own. Doing away with these important consumer protections allows ISPs to act as an editor of our online experiences and potentially limit the interconnectivity of user-centric platforms and services that have proven useful in social justice activism.

Access to mobile consumer technologies and high-speed broadband services may already be constrained based upon one's financial wherewithal; and, because Blacks and other racial minorities are more likely than whites to rely on mobile broadband services for access to social media applications, they are also more prone to discriminatory marketing practices based upon predictive analytics of their personal data through pay-for privacy plans or service tiers required by their broadband providers (see Blevins, 2016, p. 26). Consequently, social justice efforts toward media reform must encompass the principle of network neutrality to provide better access to information and call for greater privacy protection online to help ensure that social justice advocates are not sanctioned for their choice of online activities or left on the wrong side of the digital divide.

Social justice groups in St. Louis, Cincinnati, and elsewhere should include media reform in their broader agendas for social justice following the examples set out in Detroit and Philadelphia. Those committed to media reform for social justice will also need to bear in mind that they will face "formidable challenges," including

> entrenched commercial interests and media conglomerates;... neo-liberal governments; a general public often disenfranchised, digitally illiterate and not focused on issues of media reform; and always, the uphill battle of organization, mobilization, and influence.
>
> (Freedman & Obar, 2016, p. 3)

Still, the "struggles for communication rights are part of a wider challenge to social and economic inequalities and an essential component of a vision for a just and democratic society" (Freedman & Obar, 2016, p. 5). Free expression and the means of free expression are worth struggling for, and they are an essential component of social justice in the digital age. As Bill Moyers said in his keynote address to the 2007 Media Reform Conference in Memphis: "freedom begins the moment you realize someone else has been writing your story, and it's time you took the pen from his hand and started writing it yourself."

Freedom of expression is essential to the pursuit of social justice, and social media has proven to be a valuable platform to raise concerns and represent underrepresented voices. However, it does not galvanize action in and of itself. In each of the cases discussed in this chapter, from the Arab Spring to Occupy Wall Street and Black Lives Matter, it took boots-on-the-ground activism to keep the social justice narrative alive.

While social media is an important part of empowering social justice advocates as storytellers, we would do well to remember that as a medium of expression, it also empowers hate groups and others who use these digital tools as form of intimidation through trolling, cyberbullying, and social media mobbing (see Blevins, 2016, August 28). Social media mobs relentlessly barrage their targets with insults, threats, and vulgar memes intending to drown out more respectful voices in the process.

Although social media may provide a venue for civic disruption for both the advocates and detractors of social justice, it is nonetheless a more equal platform for individual expression and public discussion. Furthermore, as this political economic analysis has shown, social media has demonstrated its usefulness in advancing the cause of social justice and has potential for further application in future efforts, so long as mobile telecommunication networks remain neutral carriers of content and services.

References

American Recovery and Reinvestment Act of 2009, Pub. L. No. 111–5, 123 Stat. 115). 2009.

Bill Moyers Journal. (2008, September 12). Rage on the Radio, Bill Moyers Journal (PBS). www.pbs.org/moyers/journal/09122008/profile.html

Blevins, J. L. (2016). Panoptic missorts and the hegemony of U.S. data privacy policy. *Political Economy of Communication, 4*(2), 18–33.

Blevins, J. L. (2016, August 28). Social media mobbing diminishes the quality of public discourse. *The Cincinnati Project.* Retrieved from http://thecincyproject.org/2016/08/28/social-media-mobbing-diminishes-the-quality-of-public-discourse/

Blevins, J. L., & Brown, D. H. (2010). Concerns about the disproportionate use of economic research in the FCC's media ownership studies from 2002–2007. *Journal of Broadcasting & Electronic Media, 54*(4), 603–620.

Blevins, J. L., & Martinez, K. (2010). A political-economic history of FCC policy on minority broadcast ownership. *The Communication Review, 13*(3), 216–238.

Bogado, A. (2009, November 1). Right-wing witch hunt reaches FCC: Glenn Beck and friends attack diversity officer Mark Lloyd. *FAIR: Fairness & Accuracy in Reporting.* Retrieved from http://fair.org/extra/right-wing-witch-hunt-reaches-fcc/

Breitbart, J. (2016). A victory for digital justice. In D. Freedman, J. A. Obar, C. Martens, & R. W. McChesney (Eds.), *Strategies for media reform: International perspectives* (pp. 107–114). New York: Fordham University Press.

Center for American Progress & Free Press. (2007). *The structural imbalance of political talk radio.* Retrieved from https://cdn.americanprogress.org/wp-content/uploads/issues/2007/06/pdf/talk_radio.pdf

Clyburn, M. L. (2017). Prepared remarks of FCC commissioner Mignon L. Clyburn for the capital assets conference: Financing minority and women ownership in broadcasting, National Association of Broadcasters, Washington, D.C. (2017, January 25). Retrieved from https://apps.fcc.gov/edocs_public/attachmatch/DOC-343198A1.pdf

DeLuca, K. M., Lawson, S., & Sun, Y. (2012). Occupy wall street on the public screens of social media: The many framings of the birth of a protest movement. *Communication, Culture & Critique, 5*(4), 483–509.

Eggerton, J. (2011, February 17). Update: House OK's amendment to defund FCC chief diversity officer. *Broadcasting & Cable.* Retrieved from www.broadcastingcable.com/news/news-articles/update-house-oks-amendment-defund-fcc-chief-diversity-officer/111640

Federal Communications Commission. (2012, November 14). Report on ownership of commercial broadcast stations. Retrieved from www.fcc.gov/document/report-ownership-commercial-broadcast-stations

Fowler, M., & Brenner, D. (1982). A marketplace approach to broadcast regulation. *Texas Law Review, 60,* 207–257.

Freedman, D., & Obar, J. A. (2016). Media reform: An overview. In D. Freedman, J. A. Obar, C. Martens, & R. W. McChesney (Eds.), *Strategies for media reform: International perspectives.* New York: Fordham University Press.

Freelon, D., McIlwain, C. D., & Clark, M. D. (2016). *Beyond the hashtags: #Ferguson, #BlackLivesMatter, and the online struggle for offline justice.* Center for Media and Social Impact, School of Communication, American University, Washington, D.C. Retrieved from http://cmsimpact.org/wp-content/uploads/2016/03/beyond_the_hashtags_2016.pdf

Goldstein, A. (2014, August 15). Palestinian and Ferguson protestors link arms via social media. *Yes! Magazine.* Retrieved from www.yesmagazine.org/peace-justice/palestinians-and-ferguson-protesters-link-arms-via-social-media

Harlow, S. (2012). Social media and social movements: Facebook and an online Guatemalan justice movement that moved offline. *New Media & Society, 14*(2), 225–243.

Herman, E. S., & Chomsky, N. (1988). *Manufacturing consent: The political economy of mass media.* New York: Pantheon Books.

Howard, P. N., Duffy, A., Freelon, D., Hussain, M. M., Mari, W., & Maziad, M. (2011). Opening closed regimes: What was the role of social media during the Arab spring? Social Science Research Network (SSRN). Retrieved from http://ssrn.com/abstract=2595096

Howard Media Group. (2013). Comments on the research design for the multi-market study of critical information needs (FCC Docket 12–30). Retrieved from https://ecfsapi.fcc.gov/file/7520932711.pdf

Howard Media Group. (2017). Retrieved from www.howardmediagroup.org

McChesney, R. W. (2008). *The political economy of media: Enduring issues, emerging dilemmas.* New York: Monthly Review Press.

McChesney, R. W. (2016). Preface. In D. Freedman, J. A. Obar, C. Martens, & R. W. McChesney (Eds.), *Strategies for media reform: International perspectives.* New York: Fordham University Press.

McCormack, D. (2014, November 30). St. Louis Rams players stage 'hands up, don't shoot protest' at NFL game in solidarity with Ferguson protestors. *Daily Mail* (United Kingdom). Retrieved from www.dailymail.co.uk/news/article-2855253/Five-St-Louis-Rams-players-field-arms-raised-hands-don-t-shot-gesture-solidarity-Ferguson-protesters.html

Mosco, V. (2009). *The political economy of communication* (2nd ed.). Los Angeles: Sage.

Moyers, B. (2007, January 12). *Life on the plantation*. Transcript of address to the Media Reform Conference, Memphis, TN. Retrieved from http://billmoyers.com/2007/01/12/life-on-the-plantation-january-12-2007/

Noriega, C. A., & Iribarren, F. J. (2012). Social networks for hate speech: Commercial talk. *Radio and New Media*. Chicano Studies Research Center Working Paper, No. 2. Retrieved from www.chicano.ucla.edu/files/WP02_Social-Networks.pdf

Papacharissi, Z. (2015). Affective publics and structures of storytelling: Sentiment, events and mediality. *Information, Communication & Society, 19*, 307–324.

Pew Project for Excellence in Journalism. (2009). The State of the Media. Retrieved from www.stateofthemedia.org/2009/audio-intro/ownership/

Prometheus Radio Project v. FCC, 373 F.3d 372 (2004).

Prometheus Radio Project v. FCC, 652 F.3d 431 (2011).

Radio Ink. (2017, January 26). Clyburn: CBS radio should consider offers from minorities. *Radio Ink*. Retrieved from http://radioink.com/2017/01/26/clyburn-cbs-radio-consider-offers-minorities/

Stewart, D. R., & Littau, J. (2016). Up, periscope: Mobile streaming video technologies, privacy in public, and the right to record. *Journalism & Mass Communication Quarterly, 93*(2), 312–331.

Telecommunications Act of 1996, Pub. L. No. 104-104, 110 Stat. 56. 1996.

Torres, J., & Turner S. D. (2013, December 20). A sorry moment in the history of American media. *Free Press*. Retrieved from https://viewsweek.com/a-sorry-moment-in-the-history-of-american-media/

12 Science and Online Construction of Identity among the African Diaspora

Gado Alzouma

Since the advent of the Internet, online spaces have become some of the most important platforms for identity construction. Social networks like Facebook or YouTube, online discussion forums, online newspapers and magazines, national or diasporic websites of all kinds, Internet-supported radio and television stations, blogs by influential intellectual or political figures who act as identity entrepreneurs, platforms of ethnic artists, and online social media platforms are all invested and used in countless ways to promote identity themes or create, nurture, and maintain online communities, often across borders and even continents. On the other hand, the widespread use of the latest generation of mobile phones (3G or 4G devices known as smartphones), even in the poorest countries, coupled with the convergence of technical objects, is making it possible to access the Internet and its associated networks by an ever-increasing number of actors who use them to send or receive images and messages, coordinate the actions of social movements, and/or represent collective identities and identity performances.

Thus, in Africa, but especially in the Diaspora of Black descent like elsewhere in the world, identity entrepreneurs are using these technical tools for similar communication purposes. (Alzouma, 2008, 2013; Nakamura, 2002; Wright, 2005). However, within the African or Black diaspora, some of the most important trends in digital activism are related to science and technology and how these fields are being used on different websites and social networks to promote a Black transnational identity. These science-related activities or social or ideological representations of science are part of a long tradition that goes as far back as the 19th century, when certain Black identity activists such as Anténor Firmin (Firmin, 2005) or W. E. B. Du Bois (Du Bois, 2008) felt compelled to counter the Eurocentrist nationalistic discourses that relied on certain disciplines (like biology or psychology) to lend scientific support to the European identity myths. Indeed, it is well known that, in line with the ideology of the civilizing mission, the dominant European powers and some of the greatest European thinkers often presented Europe's scientific and technological advances as a difference of kind, not a difference of degree, and as proof that there was something special to be found in the European spirit and a mental line of demarcation between the European peoples and the colonized peoples.

While today we agree that most of these discourses were pseudoscientific elucubrations, beliefs masqueraded as science, they have, nevertheless, contributed to defining a certain form of humanity, one kind which one was given to understand that some of us could not be part of because of the absence, among their nations, of civilizational or scientific achievements or because of certain natural or genetic intellectual limitations.

From this perspective, the so-called European singularity, the object of many treaties or essays that always start with the same questions or premises ("why is it in Europe and nowhere else that science has been invented?" "Why is it in Europe and nowhere else that capitalism was born?", etc.), has always been associated with the ability to invent science. This ability in turn was conceived as the most definitive answer to the following question: what does it mean to be human, i.e., fully human, or at least to have the opportunity to enjoy a certain form of differential, exclusive humanity? In view of this context, it then can be argued that Black identity activities that are undertaken online regarding science are a reaction to the hegemonic definition of Black identity. Some of the aspects of that hegemonic definition of Black identity are for example those which, still today, tend to associate Black people with sporting or musical performances, or those which, within the African-American community itself (especially among some young Black people), tend to present any scientific prowess or performance in science, or even the love of science or mathematics for example, as attitudes or aspirations far removed from those of Blacks: an attitude known in the United States under the pejorative expression of Acting white (See Buck, 2010; Fryer, 2006).

In view of these issues, this chapter examines the place that science and technology occupy in today's Black identity discourse as it is being expressed online on the websites of the Diaspora of African descent.

Some of the questions this study asks are the following: What are the tools and symbols associated with science or civilization that are being used online to express Black identity? What representations of Black scientists and Black inventors are offered? What are the representations associated with the scientific or technological achievements of Black people and their relationship to Black identity? Is the identity discourse developed online by the Diaspora being reappropriated by Africans so as to contribute to the creation of a transnational or even transcontinental Black online community? What are the barriers to the existence of such a transcontinental online community?

Our main argument is that the representations associated with the scientific and technological inventions of Black people on the websites of the Diaspora of African descent take on their meaning in a context that is perceived as that of a white or European cultural hegemony, which is then countered by developing an identity discourse that seeks to shows not only the contributions of people of African or Black descent to scientific and civilizational progress, but also to reintegrate them into the known historically constituted scientific communities or even to re-affirm, in so doing, their full humanity. This counter rhetoric is based on the supposed ability of technology and particularly the Internet to (re) negotiate the different meanings attached to Black identity.

Theoretically, this research effort takes place within the structuralist-constructivist framework that was designed by Bourdieu (1990). It apprehends identity constructions as the outcome of symbolic struggles whose purpose is to "determine the (mental) representation that others may have of us" (Bourdieu, 1980a, p. 65). In this case, it can also be noted that among the many symbolic resources that dominated groups are generally dispossessed of is the very possibility of defining their own identity, the opportunity to tell others who they (the dominated) are and what they are. Dominated groups always see themselves through the eyes of the dominating groups and what the dominant culture says about them. In other words, it is the dominant group who has the power to name and give authority and recognition to this naming. According to Bourdieu, the symbolic power of naming is also an institutional act because it assigns properties (physical or intellectual) through which the group so named is then perceived. However, it should be noted that this naming power of the dominant groups is not total. It sometimes comes up against the opposing discourse of certain dominated groups who refuse to allow themselves to be trapped within the confines of any stigmatized identity. The dominated groups are themselves endowed with agency and, as in the example we examine here, they have the capacity to develop an identity discourse that seeks to impose a new vision of identity-related divisions imposed upon society.

Methodologically, this study is based on an analysis of ten websites: five Black anglophone websites and five Black francophone websites chosen in accordance with their design, their content, and their relationship to the central topic of this work. In selecting these ten websites, the author used an initial list provided by the Library of Congress's website platform (Science, Technology, and Business Division) that is devoted to African-Americans in Science and Technology (Selected Internet Resources). From a list of 18 identified websites, the author selected only those that appeared to have a Pan-African content (i.e., those that appeared to target a Black audience outside the United States). Five other francophone websites were then obtained using a similar search on Google.fr, based on the first 100 results provided by that search engine. The resulting list was of course intuitive, interpretative, and arbitrary, and the author is duly aware of its limitations. This list does not claim to be exhaustive or representative in the statistical sense, but based on the author's own experience and observations, there is no doubt that the analysis of those websites provides a sufficiently accurate picture of the identity construction-related activities of the websites' builders. The complete list of the websites is provided here in the Appendix.

With regard to the plan adopted for this work, it should be noted that the first part is devoted to a brief review of the literature related to online Black identity. Second, the design and functionalities that those websites offer in terms of visitor interactivity are analyzed, as well as site images and symbols that are related to science, technology, and Black people. The content of the websites is also critically reviewed, in particular for themes related to the Black counter-discourse and the images of Black scientists and Black inventors as presented online. Finally, in the last part, we analyze some of the assertions made on these websites and critically examine the presuppositions of Black digital activism as related to science popularization and the impact of that activism on the Black transnational community, particularly in continental Africa.

Literature Review

How the Internet contributes to the construction of individual and collective identity has been a major theme in the literature devoted to cyberspace. Some of the first scholars who addressed these questions (Chandler, 1998; Donath, 1999; Turkle, 1995) focused on the analysis of self-presentation or the way that individuals, including those of different ethnic or "racial" origin, build an image of themselves either on the online discussion forums or on their own personal web pages. In general, these early works have taken an irenic approach to ICTs, by contending that the World Wide Web is a space of freedom and an a-racial space, where ordinary divisions and related conflicts between human groups can be transcended because evaluative categories related to the body (skin color, physical appearance, ethnicity, etc.) can be concealed, neutralized, or even denied, leaving all users free to adopt all imaginable identities. However, certain other authors (Burkhalter, 1999; Ebo, 1998; Nakamura, 2002; O'Brien, 1999) highlighted the limitations of these early analyses by stressing that racial divisions or even racism do not suddenly disappear simply because of any use of the Net. As Burkhalter (1999) was to point out, although the characteristics of these users do not appear online, racial identification does not disappear because perceptions of racial categories are not solely based on the phenotype. These categories are mainly the result of a mental construct that creates a "typical profile" of "the Black man/woman" through stereotypes, modes of reasoning, and reactions, whether as written or oral communication. Consequently, Burkhalter said, "the resources of the medium are sufficient for participants' determinations of racial identity" (1999, p. 62). Thus, while online discussion groups, for example, are set up on the basis of common interests, they are also set up on the basis of certain other characteristics, such as "race," which is of particular importance in this instance. Similarly, the themes of discussion (e.g., sport, music, or dance) and the perspectives according to which they are debated are designed with a view of being linked to racial identity.

While the work of the group of authors Burkhalter belongs to is largely a continuation of ethnic or "racial" interactions studies in the United States, they also take place, without identifying themselves with it, within a long tradition inaugurated by Erving Goffman (1959). Consequently, the methods of analysis that have proven their worth in studies of face-to-face interactions initiated by Goffman also apply, to some extent, to studies of online interactions, i.e., the relationships between individuals or groups of individuals that are formed and dissolved online on a daily basis. As such, these studies are microsociological or psychosociological analyses that focus on the internal dynamics of groups. However, they do not tell us much about how the Internet contributes to the formation of large groups like diasporic communities or transnational organiza-tions and movements that are formed based on common ethnicity or even a common "race."

However, that is precisely the issue that some other authors, such as Rheingold (1993), Castells (1997), Watson (1997), or Schwartz (1996), tackled by showing how individual citizens, interest groups, or per-secuted and dispersed communities around the world are using the Internet to create, maintain, or consolidate their identity and culture, or internationally promote their daily struggles. To that end, these authors have focused on the processes by which transnational online ethnic communities, for which the Internet and its associated networks are instruments for the production of identity, are creating online cultural goods (texts, symbols, ideologies) conceived as a shared intangible heri-tage. It should, nevertheless, be stressed here that by the time these works were being developed, the large-scale use of the Internet and the expan-sion of the Internet on a global scale were still in their early stages. By that time, most of the technical devices we know today as social media (Facebook, YouTube, WhatsApp [actually a messaging application], blogs, or even online TV) did not yet exist and mobile phones were scarce in many parts of the world, including Africa. Notwithstanding this sit-uation, the growing awareness of the potential offered by the Internet in the construction of collective identities quickly helped to orient ethnic or "racial" mobilization studies in a new direction.

Thus, authors such as Lisa Nakamura (2002) mainly focused on how the Internet helps shape our perceptions or our notions of race and eth-nicity; in other words, how identity entrepreneurs mobilize images, sym-bols, and ideas to act on what Bourdieu (1980) calls our schemes of perception and action. Studies like Nakamura's constitute a break with the past in that they focus on the activities of social agents organized in online communities who use the Internet for political, cultural, or identity-related purposes. These online activities, in Nakamura's words, are grouped under the name of *cybertyping*, which she defines as "the distinctive ways that the Internet propagates, disseminates and commodifies images of race and racism" (2002, p. 3). As for *cybertypes*, they correspond to all the images or stereotypes produced online by these same agents. More generally, what Nakamura describes in her work takes place within a literature that is now abundant—a literature in which the central theme is known as cyberactivism, digital activism, Internet activism, online activism, web activism, or all the forms of activism that these technical objects make possible, among which, of course, are various activities of an identity (and notably a "racial" identity) nature.

In this respect, until the 2000s, very few studies have specifically focused on Black identity entrepreneurs and how they use the Internet to build a transnational racial identity. Indeed, studies devoted to Black identity representation on the Internet by Black people, a problematic known as *Black agency in cyberspace* (Eberling, 2003), are relatively recent. Defined as a kind of self-determination of Black people in cyberspace (Eberling, 2003), this problematic has been examined from several perspectives by various authors. However, in most studies, the authors have mainly emphasized "the community life of Blacks" as it appears on the Internet, particularly on associative sites, commercial sites, leisure sites, social networks, online discussion forums, etc.

We find a typical example of this focus in an article that Byrne (2007) wrote, which is devoted to the study of *BlackPlanet*, a Black social network, that includes online discussion forums (on religion and spirituality, women, political and social news, etc.), entertainment platforms, mobile applications... in fact, all aspects of Black life. Byrne examines how the participants view their community life as Blacks, how they participate in public discussions, and whether those discussions focus on issues that are considered important to the Black community, and especially if the social network they use allows them to promote a certain level of civic engagement. It goes without saying, however, that the answer to these questions tells us a lot about how social network participants define their identity and how they relate to others. Other authors (Warren, Hect, Jung, Kvasny, & Henderson, 2010) have tried to answer the same question by examining the Web navigation and information retrieval habits of Black people on the Net and what these habits reveal about Black identity and Black self-perception. In so doing, they have been able to show that ethnic or class identities are important predictors of the type of information sought by users. For his part, Matthew Hughey (2008) analyzed the online communities of Black "fraternities and sororities," in particular the way in which "online authenticity" (i.e., the expression of a sense of belonging in its spontaneous nature) is accomplished in these communities through what Hughey calls « the making of "brothers" and "others" based on the symbolic boundaries of exclusion and inclusion ». (2008, p. 258). Here the role of the Internet is examined in relation to the constraints and advantages it provides in the ongoing quest and formation of a Black identity. Thus, it appears that in an environment so strongly marked by institutionalized racism, these online communities, by their very existence, function as valuable spaces where a counterculture or a counter-discourse that actually manifests a resistance to oppression is organized. This is also what Carmen Kynard (2010) demonstrates in an article written in the first-person singular and dedicated to the analysis of a Black female site where participants make a return to the dominant discourse (or more specifically "the dominant narrative"), which they have "bathed" in all their lives to elaborate a counter-discourse, which she calls the "sista-cipher," and which is intended to restore their denied identity.

The first worthiness of all these works is that they show that the Internet is no longer a monolithic or exclusively "white" environment, but rather a universe marked by ethnic or "racial" diversity, whether in its representations of identity, cultural productions, consumer habits, or protest discourses for which the Web serves as a viable platform. The second, and perhaps the most important, merit of these works is that they see Black online communities as being endowed with agency—that is to say, the ability to act or to have an autonomous determination capacity—in that they focus on what Black people actually do when they go online. Also, these studies helped orient Black identity research in new directions, in particular the examination of the relationship that exists between the Internet and Black transnationalism or the way in which the Internet facilitates or provides a better means for interconnection between Blacks across continental barriers. In other words, these studies helped us investigate and understand how the Internet is contributing to the creation and the consolidation of a common identity and a common consciousness among Black people.

From this point of view, most current works emphasize the specificity of the Internet compared to the old information and communication technologies, in particular radio, television, cassettes, and compact discs. They emphasize the fact that the Internet allows for the interconnection of users, but also a coordination of action made possible by its strong interactive nature. As Eberling earlier explained,

> it is Internet technology's transnational character—globally networked, media-rich computers unfettered by national or geographic boundaries—that allows for multiple users in multiple locations to communicate, organize, and access data and transcend time and space by meeting in cyberspace.
>
> (2003, p. 96)

Thus, there is a parallelism or even a possible convergence between Pan-African or Pan-Black identity consciousness and the Internet. This manifests an adequation of the object (the Internet) to function (building a Pan-Black or a transnational Black identity consciousness). While Black online discussion forums and Black websites once had a narrow national character, it is now possible to federate identity energies so as to build or consolidate a common and intercontinental sense of belonging.

How do Pan-African websites actually tackle this task? What are the identity referents that they mobilize for this purpose? To answer these questions, this chapter examines how the interpretation and reinterpretation of scientific discoveries and technological inventions made by Black people contribute to the expression of a transnational Black identity that is centered on science and technology as their marks of a collective identity. This identity construction is reflected, first and foremost, in the very way in which the websites that are the subject of this chapter were designed.

Nature of the Websites: Design, Images, and Symbols

The ten websites we examine here are different in many respects. Some, such as *The Faces of Sciences: African Americans in Sciences*, are static websites, i.e., their interactive character is very limited. Their web pages and all the texts, images, and audio and video content stored on them are not subject to modification by their users. However, in many cases, content and special links can sometimes be added to allow visitors to react by sending emails, as in the case of *Ankhonline.com*. Some other websites, such as *Afrikhepri.org,* allow users to share links on Facebook, LinkedIn, YouTube, Twitter, or Google+. This particular website (*Afrikhepri.org*) even makes it possible for visitors to access videos, Black radio, and TV programs that are devoted to science and technology, and audio eBooks and movies. Some others like Ankhonline.com again allow visitors to download documents and even scientific articles.

It is also worth noting the old version of *Africamaat*'s website,[1] which always had each article it posted accompanied by a section that was dedicated to comments from users who could react and engage in lively debate or provide feedback on the scientific questions being raised. Likewise, *Blackinventor.com* and *Mathematicians of the African Diaspora* websites both solicit texts or information from their visitors about Black scientists or inventors with the intention of adding them to the list of those already in existence. Thus, one can find on the *Blackinventor. com (Black Inventor Online Museum)* website the following statement: "Please let us know if there are more inventors who should be included or if you have any comments or suggestions." However, in terms of the Pan-African democratic ideal which has led to the creation of these websites, some of them appear to be partially limited in their ability to serve as viable platforms for the international exchange of ideas and opinions. Thus, on the *Ankhonline.com* website, with the notable exception of the contact address and an email address, there is no link that gives visitors the opportunity to add content or react to it. However, on the *Rekhet Academy Club*, it is possible to leave comments and also take tests on one's knowledge of Africa.

On all of these websites, however, one can access images of dozens of Black scientists (notably on The Faces of Sciences: African Americans in the Sciences [Black Inventors Online Museum] or on Afrikhepri.org: Inventeurs et savants noirs, etc,). In other cases, biographies of Black historical figures, like Martin Luther King or Nelson Mandela, who have distinguished themselves in fields other than science can also be found. Also found are figurative representations of Black pharaohs and numerous Egyptian iconographies (notably on Ankhonline.com), of African queens and kings (on Rekhet Academy Club). Also found are images of African historical sites or objects or inventions made by Blacks (such as an image of Benjamin Banneker's clock, a sketch of Alexander Miles's elevator, or a sketch of Norbert Rillieux's evaporation tank), which can be found on Lawaan.com (contribution des noirs à la civilization [les inventions]).

It should be noted as well that access to these websites is free and public and does not require any registration or subscription. These are nonprofit websites, which are sometimes linked to organizations that claim to defend a cause seen as universal (the rehabilitation of the role of people of African or Black descent in the history of science and technology; the fight against racism, etc.). Although the majority have country-specific content (especially those in the United States), their target audience is actually the Black transnational community, i.e., all Black people everywhere. With the exception of *Black Scientists and Inventors*, which has a Nigerian Internet country code top-level domain (*.ng*) and a contact page located in the UK, all the sites we examine here are based either in the United States or France. This detail indicates the centrality of the Black Diaspora (people of African descent, who for historical or migratory reasons live outside Africa) in this study. Quite surprisingly, we did not find a significant number of similar websites based in Africa; indeed, if such websites do exist, they are still much less numerous than the diasporic websites. This situation can be attributed as much to the lack of equipment and the absence or numerical weakness of African online communities than the need for a rooted Black identity, which is more present among the Black Diaspora on the other side of the Atlantic than it is in Africa.

Content and Major Themes

In terms of ideological or symbolic productions that these platforms support, it is first and foremost the names of the websites and their domain names (e.g., *www.Blackinventor.com*) that are seen as evoking both Black identity and the historical depth of the relations between the Black world and science. Thus, some of the websites have names that are evocative of ancient Egypt, such as *Ankhonline.com* (*ankh* meaning, as represented by the corresponding sacred hieroglyph, life) or *Rekhet* (*Rekhet Academy Club*) which refers to the rigorous knowledge of the real or *Africamaat* (*maat* meaning truth, justice, etc.). Both *Ankhonline* and the *Rekhet Academy club* reproduce Egyptian hieroglyphs that correspond to those notions in the upper part of the website above the browser window. The other websites are characterized by a certain sobriety (in terms of colors, visual representations, iconographies, etc.) but all do evoke the Black world, Africa, or the Diaspora, as for example, Black inventors, Mathematicians of the African Diaspora, *Savants et inventeurs noirs* (Black Savants and Inventors), etc. Moreover, the list of pages (what is found on these websites) gives one a clear indication of the structure and the nature of these websites. These are websites whose content allows the users or the online community to discover common interests or even build a common awareness, without necessarily allowing them to build relationships like those made possible on social networking sites such as Facebook or the messenger WhatsApp conversation groups. Social networking sites allow users to share comments, texts, videos, and photographs and create conversation groups or other kinds of groups of sociability that are active and that engage in lively debates and exchanges. By contrast, the websites we are describing here mainly have an information provision function. In other words, they provide information to an audience that can be characterized as a relatively passive receptor. The possibilities for this audience to exist as an interactive online community, an interconnected group, are quite limited.

Rather, in the creation of discussion groups or online communities, some form of popularization or dissemination of scientific knowledge seems to be the central goals of these websites. However, that aspect also poses a difficulty in analyzing these platforms. First, it is clear that these are not didactic websites—namely, websites only designed to educate visitors in a given area of science. These websites do not always offer scientific content in specific scientific fields, such as mathematics or oceanography. If this were the case, they would belong to the field of science communication or science popularization (dissemination). That is apparently not the case here, although these sites do share a common characteristic with ordinary scientific websites—namely, using the Internet as a platform for visitor information. However, while the visitors to a scientific website will find scientific explanations on specific natural phenomena, here the emphasis is mainly on the contributions, discoveries, and historical performances of Black scientists and inventors. In fact, very little scientific information is given about these Black scientists and inventors' discoveries, what they consist of, and their scientific explanations. It is clear that we are not dealing here with purely scientific websites but instead much more with identity websites. However, like all websites, they do have specific functionalities, designs, and contents and can be analyzed as actual cultural productions.

Thus, the identity aspect of these websites can be seen in their texts; a common feature of all these platforms is what can be called their "statement of principle," which indicates the purpose of the website or what one might call its mission.

On each website, there are always two major ideas constantly proclaimed. On the one hand, the initiators of the website want to make known what they believe is a concealed or a negated aspect of the history of the Black world—namely, the important contributions of people of African descent to scientific development, technological discoveries, and the advancement of human civilization. On the other hand, the aim of the websites is said to educate present generations of young Black people by raising in them more awareness of the scientific role played by Blacks throughout history. These missions, as can be seen, have an identity component in the sense that it is not only a matter of revealing and restoring a "concealed" scientific truth, but even more a matter of strengthening the self-esteem of Black people by making them rediscover the still unknown parts of their history. *Blackinventor.com* for example presents Black scientists and inventors as "unknown pioneers" in the fields of invention and innovation. Similar to that situation, *Rekhet Academy Club* has set as its objective of "studying and disseminating Africa's intellectual, historical and cultural heritage" (http://rekhet-academy-club.blogspot.com.ng/). In this way, the site intends to work toward an awakening of African consciousness to help Black people face the challenges of their contemporary world. However, above all, it is on the *Mathematicians of the African Diaspora* website that this philosophy is most clearly stated. According to the creators of this website, it is in the field of mathematics more than in any other that Blacks are said to be incapable of success. According to them, however, the earlier and current achievements of Blacks contradict these statements, which is why this website intends to demonstrate the inaccuracy of that point of view by presenting the achievements of scholars from Africa and the African Diaspora in the mathematical sciences.

The second type of texts found on these websites consists of fairly detailed biographies of Black scientists and inventors and, in certain cases, the history of their discoveries and inventions. *Blackinventor. com* highlights Black pioneers who have distinguished themselves in the sciences, Black scientists who are no longer living, and contemporary Black scientists. On *Mathematicians of the African diaspora*, we can find profiles of dozens of Black mathematicians divided into three categories: the earliest Black mathematicians, today's Black mathematicians, and Black female mathematicians. Until a few years ago, the list of Mathematicians in the African Diaspora was constantly updated by a census of new Black PhDs in mathematics. Profiles of Black computer scientists and physicists can also be found on this same website. While former Black mathematicians are the subjects of biographies, for today's mathematicians, the site generally refers to their own web pages at the universities and research centers where they work. Similarly, on the *Faces of Sciences: African Americans in Sciences*, the achievements of Black scientists and inventors are presented in terms of the past, present, and future while also highlighting the role that Black women have played in science. The website states that "Profiled here are African American men and women who have contributed to the advancement of science and engineering. The accomplishments of the past and present can serve as pathfinders to present and future engineers and scientists" (https:// webfiles.uci.edu/mcbrown/display/faces.html). These are also sites that can (or are) constantly enriched by new information.

Again, from the point of view of the types of texts found on these sites, *Ankhonline.com* and *Africamaat.com* are different from the other websites because the first site publishes scientific articles written by Black Egyptologists and an important place is given to the works of Cheikh Anta Diop and some of his disciples, i.e., Théophile Obenga or Bilolo Mubabinge. *Africamaat.com*, until the old version was deleted, mainly published texts related to scientific news, in particular articles about discoveries related to the history of science in Africa or the central role that Africa plays in these discoveries. Thus, *Ankhonline* is a scientific journal that is centered on Egyptology and its relationship to the Black world, while *Africamaat* is a site for science popularization but still centered on the Black world. The first publishes articles by African scientists, while the second summarizes, in language accessible to the general public, the scientific discoveries that highlight the role of the African continent in the development of the sciences and the history of civilizations.

So, while the identity aspect of these websites can be noted in their design and content, it can also be analyzed in terms of the type of ideas, representations, and ideologies they each disseminate.

Science, Ideology, and Identity

From that perspective, one should recall that the production of scientific knowledge is embedded in everyday day cultural and social practices; ideological and philosophical conceptions of the world shape the basic orientation of scientific research. Social representations of science do contribute to how people see themselves and how they see others. They may, therefore, participate in the definition of their identity. Using this perspective, scientific discoveries, technological inventions, and famous scientific figures may all be mobilized by various groups or communities when framing their identities.

Thus, in the case we examine here, there is a parallel between the history of Black people (a history of oppression, discrimination, and resistance) and the history of Black scientists and Black inventors, and how that history contributes to framing Black identity.

This parallel appears first in the fact that Black scientists and inventors are presented as heroes of the Black world in every sense of that word because they have had to face and overcome formidable obstacles. As Jenkins says, "Consistent in all their lives was the fact that each endured hardships and deprivations that were imposed upon them because of their impoverished economic status and because of their race" (1984, p. 477). Jenkins then adds: "Each case presented a story of triumph over formidable social, economic, and political obstacle" (1991, p. 314). It is from that perspective that the struggles of Black scholars and inventors to overcome obstacles are often remembered, notably during the commemorations marking Black History Months, wherein the achievements of Black inventors and scientists are associated or integrated into the history of the struggle and resistance of Black people against slavery. Thus, in a 2008 speech celebrating Black History Month, Turner notably stated, "It's important to pause and reflect on how African Americans and our ancestors have helped to further scientific and technological progress—often overcoming great odds in the process" (Turner, 2008). Moreover, in biographies that are published online, the itineraries of these savants-heroes and their social experiences are strangely similar, even when we cross the Atlantic and find ourselves in Francophone Africa. The biographers of Cheikh Anta Diop, for example, never fail to emphasize the "ostracism of the white scientific world" he was confronted with during all his life. More importantly, apart from the constant racism that Black scientists and inventors have faced, many of them, born in misery and ignorance, had in their very beginnings an improbable destiny. On the *Blackinventor.com* website, there are many examples of such edifying biographies. There is the case of the biography of Daniel Hale Williams (1856–1931), a pioneer in cardiac surgery, the son of an extremely poor and large family, who was orphaned very early in life, and who worked in several trades, including as a cobbler and barber, before enrolling in Northwestern University Medical School and later opening his own medical practice. There is also the case of Benjamin Banneker (1731–1806), an astronomer, farmer, inventor, and scientist, born the son of a slave, who owed his salvation to the Quakers, who noticed his exceptional gifts early on and enrolled him in school. Jack Jonson (1878–1946) can also be listed. He practiced various trades in his childhood before becoming a boxing champion and the inventor of a key used to loosen nuts.

To all these obstacles that Black scientists and inventors faced, we can add the fact that these websites often highlight the refusal, by the scientific community during their times, to acknowledge the authorship of their inventions or to attribute to them a patent for a technological invention. In most cases, it was the very scientific character of their work that was often held in doubt. According to Jenkins, "Generally, historians of science have not recognized the contributions of Black scientists and inventors. The National Inventors Hall of Fame has, so far, rejected the nominations of Black inventors for membership" (1991, p. 313). On the *African Americans in the Sciences* website, Blacks are shown as having contributed to all fields of science in all possible ways, even though this contribution is generally still unrecognized. On the *Rekhet Academy Club* the goal is to "rediscover" African scientific history by "unveiling" a reality that has too long remained hidden.

It appears, therefore, that the biographies of Black scientists and inventors are conceived of as offering histories of sufferance, resistance, and victory that echo the epic struggles of Black people, indeed struggles that are a part and parcel of how they see and define themselves.

However, although the online biographies of Black scientists and inventors always mention the obstacles they have been confronted with, among which is racism, they also sometimes appear as characters who were the children of those who can be considered as the Black petty-bourgeoisie of their times. Some were sons of pastors (such as Garrett Morgan, inventor of traffic lights, 1877–1963); sons of engineers (Jan Metzliger, inventor of automatic shoelaces, 1889); sons of teachers (Ernest Just, a pioneer in marine biology, 1883–1941); or sons of postal workers (Piercy Julian, a pioneer in synthetic chemistry, 1899–1975). It thus appears that the origins, social situations, and paths of these scientists and inventors, far from being homogeneous, reflect a certain diversity. The obstacles they encountered are, therefore, part of a narrative of which the aim is to give an epic character to destinies that were, in some cases, predictable or even banal. In some cases, we can say that they are a posteriori reconstructions that are intended to illustrate the epic narrative and make the individual the icon of a group. Therefore, this narrative says less about science than about the scientist and his/her relations with others, i.e. the confrontation of identities. Indeed, here science is used to build identity.

Impact of the Websites: Transnationalism and Black Identity Construction

What then is the impact of these websites on their target audiences, including the transnational online community, or what can then be called the Pan-African online community? In other words, what can be said about the "reverberation effects" of the Black Scientific Websites' project on its target audience, namely, potentially all Blacks and particularly the Black Diaspora and the African populations? To offer an answer (albeit partial), to this question, it is necessary to refer to the number and characteristics of the visitors of these websites to learn who their users are and their national or ethnic origins. On the Internet, there are many tools (softwares) that are capable of providing such information, including websites that provide data (usually for commercial purposes) on traffic and user characteristics. This is true of Alexa, a toolbar that collects data on the browsing habits of website users, which we decided to use for the purpose of this study. The main question that guided our research is the geographical origin of the visitors to these websites. For this purpose, we selected one single website from the ten we studied: *Mathematicians of the African Diaspora*.

The reason why is that it is the only website featuring both living Diaspora and continental African scientists and which, therefore, can be expected to be of interest to both Africans living on the continent and Black diasporic populations. Thus, the information provided about the visitors of this website allows us to get a fairly clear idea of its visitors and draw certain conclusions regarding their transnational character. For example, in terms of the geographical origin of visitors to this website as of May 25, 2014, Alexa reported that 59.8 percent came from the United States, followed (surprisingly) by India (8.2 percent), the United Kingdom (2.5 percent), China (1.8 percent), Canada (1.6 percent), and a few other countries, such as Germany, Australia, etc. The most remarkable detail is that no African countries are included in the list that was provided. This finding indicates that the online traffic from this continent is too low to be taken into account. However, it can also be said that the vast majority or at least a significant proportion of the visitors to this website come from the African Diaspora. Either way, it is clear that the continental African users of this website are almost absent, and nearly 60 percent of visitors to the website come from the United States. Therefore, it cannot be inferred from these statistics that this website is contributing to the creation of a Black transnational online mathematician community to which those Africans residing on the Continent are actively connected.

As far as *Mathematicians of the African Diaspora* is concerned, if this online community does exist, it is essentially diasporic, and nothing allows us to say that the referents associated with science as built on the Internet are being reappropriated by young Africans now living in Africa. However, it must be recognized that this is partly so because many obstacles, both economic (such as the cost of Internet access in African countries) and cultural (low literacy rates and linguistic barriers in particular), make it difficult to create online Black transnational communities in Africa.

Conclusion

It is important to note, before concluding this study, that the digital counter-discourse that we have analyzed here is part of a long tradition that goes as far back as the 19th century when Black activists, Black writers, and Black scientists felt compelled to counter the European-centric nationalist discourses that were using science as an appendix in the construction of European identity myths. Indeed, it was during the period from the second half of the 19th century to the end of the Second World War that science was called upon and used in many European countries with a view toward differentiation and to contribute to the construction of national identities and even to the construction of a European or "white" identity. In France, as in other European countries, it is during these years that racial anthropology was institutionalized with the creation of scholarly societies, schools, chairs, and journals, thereby giving rise to racialist and essentialist theories (wherein Gobineau [1816–1882], Lapouge [1854–1936], Maurras [1868–1952], etc., are now the most known contenders). These culminated a few years later in scientific anti-Semitism, then Nazism, an ideology built on the Aryan myth, which was backed by pseudo-scientific and "biologizing" theories (See Taguieff, 1986; and/or Reynaud-Paligot, 2006, 2011), the native peoples in the colonies thus became a privileged field of experimentation for "raciology," the "science of races." During these years, the different human groups, classified as peoples, races, or tribes, were assigned moral and intellectual characteristics, so-called innate predispositions, and distinct ranks in a hierarchy that was based on material or civilizational achievements or scientific or technological prowess. These identities thus forged will be reappropriated by the groups they designate, which will then use them to define themselves in their relationship to others. In this regard, it is not indifferent to recall that Senghor's assertion that "Emotion is Negro, as reason is Hellenic" or Césaire's reference to "those who have invented neither the powder nor the compass" are undoubtedly echoes of these distant debates that nevertheless profoundly affected our representations of identity and are until today still perceptible in unspoken ways for how national pride is exalted in the public discourse and both scientific and technological competition at the international level.

However, these classifications made in the 19th century, as much as the exclusive association of science with the European identity, never imposed themselves definitively. They have always been confronted with what Bourdieu (1980b) calls the "dominated groups' strategies of subversion," aimed at opposing a competing vision of identity to the actions of inculcation of the dominant discourse. Thus, as early as the 19th century, some of the first Black thinkers challenged the idea that science was a distinctive mark of the sole European spirit.

One of the very first of those pioneer identity thinkers was Anténor Firmin, a Haitian, who, in order to answer Gobineau's theses and question the science of races or racial anthropology, set for himself a goal that was totally similar to the one we find on the Pan-African websites dedicated to science today. Firmin wrote:

We will investigate whether among the peoples who have contributed most to the evolution of the human species, in the most remote epochs of human history, there are no nations of nigritic origin in any region of the world. Wouldn't the existence of such a fact, whatever the time of its manifestation, be enough to completely overturn the theory of racial inequality?

(2005 (1885), p. 203)

As can be seen, Firmin's project to evaluate the contributions of Blacks to science and technology was an ideological as well as a purely scientific approach because it comes at a time when science had replaced religious dogmas as a source of truth and was participating in the definition of European or "white" identity itself, or as an embodiment of the values or the ideas that Europeans had about themselves. In this context, to show the achievements of Blacks in science was somehow to contribute to their "re-humanization." It is, therefore, clear for Firmin as much as for the initiators of the websites that are the subject of this article that the use of science (or rather the use of the representations of science) is part of identity politics. Above all, what is at stake is a reappropriation of the "confiscated word" by elaborating on a discourse that goes against the hegemonic vision of the history of science in which Blacks have no place. That is why these websites are primarily designed as identity production tools. Here the Internet is invested with all sorts of expectations, notably its supposed ability to (re) negotiate the meanings attached to Black identity. However, this discourse also faces many obstacles, including those related to Internet access and the sociocultural characteristics of African users. Nevertheless, the identity referents elaborated online still do have an impact on the representations of African Black youth because many other channels also exist through which these concepts can be conveyed and reappropriated.

Science and Technology-Related Black Diasporic Websites

1　**Black History Inventors - Black History Month**
　　http://inventors.about.com/od/Blackinventors/a/Black_History.htm
2　**The Black Inventor Online Museum**
　　www.Blackinventor.com/
3　**The Faces of Science: African Americans in the Sciences**
　　https://webfiles.uci.edu/mcbrown/display/faces.html
4　**Mathematicians of the African Diaspora**
　　www.math.buffalo.edu/mad/
5　**Black Scientists and Inventors**
　　http://Blackscientistsandinventors.blogspot.com.ng/
6　**Contribution des noirs à la civilisation moderne (les inventions)**
　　www.laawan.com/fr/science/868-contribution-des-noirs-a-la-civilisation-moderne-les-inventions.html

7 Inventeurs et savants noirs
http://afrikhepri.org/category/inventeurs-et-savants-noirs/page/2/
8 Egyptologie, histoire de l'Afrique et sciences exactes
www.ankhonline.com/
9 Africamaat
www.africamaat.fr/accueil.php
10 Rekhet Academy Club
www.Rekhet-academy-club.blogspot.com.ng/

Note

1 The MENAIBUC/EDILAC website, on which the *africamaat* site lodged, was closed in August 2011 by Court decision due to unpaid rents. It has since been replaced by another *Africamaat* site (http://africamaat.com/), which no longer seems as rich as the previous one.

References

Alzouma, G. (2008). Identities in a 'fragmegrated' world: Black cyber-communities and the French integration system. *African and Black Diaspora: An International Journal, 1*(2), 201–214.

Alzouma, G. (2013). Blacks in France: A minority or a community? In J. O. Adekunle & H. V. Williams (Eds.), *Converging identities: Blackness in the modern African diaspora* (pp. 27–48). Durham, NC: Carolina Academic Press.

Bourdieu, P. (1980a). *Le sens pratique*. Paris: Editions de Minuit.

Bourdieu, P. (1980b). L'identité et la représentation [Éléments pour une réflexion critique sur l'idée de région]. *Actes de la Recherche en Sciences Sociales, 35*(1), 63–72.

Bourdieu, P. (1990). *In other words: Essay towards a reflexive sociology*. Cambridge: Polity Press.

Buck, S. (2010). *Acting white: The ironic legacy of desegregation*. New Haven, CT: Yale University Press.

Burkhalter, B. (1999). Reading race online: Discovering racial identity in Usenet discussions. In A. A. Smith & P. Kollok (Eds.), *Communities in cyberspace* (pp. 60–75). London: Routledge.

Byrne, D. N. (2007). Public discourse, community concerns, and civic engagement: Exploring Black social networking traditions on BlackPlanet.com. *Journal of Computer-Mediated Communication, 13*(1), 319–340.

Castells, M. (1997). *The power of identity*. Oxford: Blackwell.

Chandler, D. (1998). *Personal homepages in the construction of identities on the web*. Paper presented at Aberystwyth Post-International Group Conference on Linking Theory and Practice: Issues in the Politics of Identity, 9–11 September, University of Wales. Retrieved from www.aber.ac.uk/media/Documents/short/webident.html

Donath, J. (1999). Identity and deception in the online community. In A. A. Smith & P. Kollok (Eds.), *Communities in cyberspace* (pp. 29–59). London: Routledge.

Du Bois, W. E. B. (2008). *The souls of Black folk*. New York: Oxford University Press.

Eberling, M. F. E. (2003). The new dawn: Black agency in cyberspace. *Radical History Review, 87*(1), 96–108.

Ebo, B. (Ed.). (1998). *Cyberghetto or cybertopia? Race, class, and gender on the internet.* Westport, CT: Pareger.

Firmin, A. (2005). *De l'égalité des races humaines – Anthropologie positive, 1st Edition 1885.* Paris: Ed. Mémoire d'Encrier.

Fryer, R. G. (2006). "Acting white": The social price paid by the best and brightest minority students. *Education Next, 6*(1), 53–59.

Goffman, E. (1959). *The presentation of self in everyday life.* New York: Anchor Books.

Hughey, M. W. (2008). Online (Br) others and (Re) sisters: Authentic Black fraternity and sorority identity on the internet. *Journal of Contemporary Ethnography, 37*(5), 528–560.

Jenkins, E. S. (1984). Impact of social conditions. A study of American Black scientists and inventors. *Journal of Black Studies, 14*(4), 477–491.

Jenkins, E. S. (1991). Bridging the two cultures: American Black scientists and inventors. *Journal of Black Studies, 21*(3), 313–324.

Kynard, C. (2010). From candy girls to cyber sista-cipher: Narrating black females' color-consciousness and counterstories in and out of school. *Harvard Educational Review, 80*(1), 30–53.

Nakamura, L. (2002). *Cybertypes: Race, ethnicity, and identity on the internet.* London: Routledge.

O'Brien, J. (1999). Writing in the body: Gender (Re)production in online communication. In P. Kollok & M. A. Smith (Eds.), *Communities in cyberspace* (pp. 76–104). London: Routledge.

Reynaud-Paligot, C. (2006). *La République raciale 1860–1930. Paradigme racial et idéologie républicaine.* Paris: PUF.

Reynaud-Paligot, C. (2011). *De l'identité nationale. Science, race et politiques en Europe et aux Etats-Unis, XIXe-XXe siècles.* Paris: PUF.

Rheingold, H. (1993). *The online community: Homesteading on the electronic frontier.* Reading, MA: Addison-Wesley.

Schwartz, E. (1996). *Net activism: How citizens use the internet.* Cambridge, MA: O'Reilly.

Taguieff, P. A. (1986). L'identité nationale saisie par les logiques de racisation. Aspects, figures et problèmes du racisme différentialiste. *Mots, 12,* 91–128.

Turkle, S. (1995). *Life on the screen: Identity in the age of the internet.* New York: Simon and Schuster.

Turner, J. M. (2008). African-American technological contributions: Past, present, and future. Retrieved from www.nist.gov/speech-testimony/african-american-technological-contributions-past-present-and-future

Warren, J. R., Hect, M. L., Jung, E., Kvasny, L., & Henderson, M. G. (2010). African American ethnic and class-based identities on the World Wide Web: Moderating the effects of self-perceived information seeking/finding and web self-efficacy. *Communication Research, 37*(5), 674–702.

Watson, N. (1997). Why we argue about online community: A case study of the Phish.net Fan community. In S. G. Jones (Ed.), *Identity and communication in cybersociety* (pp. 108–111). London: Sage.

Wright, M. M. (2005). Finding a place in cyberspace: Black women, technology, and identity. *Frontiers: A Journal of Women Studies, 26*(1), 48–59.

13 'Prime Time' Geographies

Dancehall Performance, Visual Communication, and the Philosophy of 'Boundarylessness'

Sonjah Stanley Niaah

The first time I heard of British *Link-Up* events[1] was in the late 1990s. Eventually I found my way to one of the sessions branded then as one of the most prestigious dancehall events. They sometimes featured red carpets for celebrities and aspirants to strut their proverbial stuff, and attracted patrons from within Jamaica and outside. By the time I began formal study of dancehall performance geography, it became clear that I had to engage with this category of events. But there was something different. They were most indicative of the way dancehall provided a platform for the deployment of techniques of visibility, and this required multidisciplinary analytical lenses for engaging with dancehall as spectacle.

It was a two-tiered site that had multiple sections and significant permanent infrastructure such as balconies and bars unlike many of the others around Kingston where I had based my study. I could see the dancehall celebrities lining the balconies, taking their rightful positions to be most visible. The celebrities 'in the house' were the likes of Winston Powell,[2] Bounti Killa and Lexus (DJs), members of the British Crew, Dancehall Queen Stacey, dancing crews, media personalities, videographers, and selectors. The popular hip-hop drink *Pimpjuice* was a sponsor for the event, something which was not the norm for regular events. By 3:30 a.m., three video cameras had started to capture images of the red-carpet rebirth of British Link-Up. Patrons from Canada, Jamaica, Britain, and the United States were attired in dancehall regalia of a semi-formal or formal nature, including gowns and suits, often adorned with glitter and expensive shiny jewelry, also known as *cargo*, *ice*, or *bling*. As the event heightened in intensity, around 4:30 a.m., video cameras could be seen tracking the dancers, who were performing popular moves at the time such as the '*tek weh yu self.*' I had been used to seeing video cameras in dancehall events, but the atmosphere changed from a mere session to something out of Hollywood, at least for the patrons involved.

What is dancehall and how does it employ visual technologies? Dancehall is not just a musical genre. It is Jamaica's *premier popular street theatre*, a celebration of the entire spectrum of life from birth to death around events that combine dance and music where consenting adults leave their troubles behind for just a moment to revel in the deep and old rhythmic structures that transport them into scapes beyond the urban, beyond the inner city, into spaces of fulfillment. Scholarly inquiry into dancehall has centered on studies of Jamaican popular music/culture from ethnomusicological analyses and sound system technology, practice, and culture. Cultural and Gender Studies explorations including studies of dancehall masculinities, violence, and lyrical analyses, as well as the business practices around copyright and distribution as key examples, also exist.[3] Visual cultural studies analyses are sparse. In responding to the dearth of critical analysis of dancehall's rich visual landscape, I engage the idea of *'prime time geographies'* here in continuation of work I began in the late 1990s. I seek to locate local dancehall community practice in a broader landscape of visual circuits while distinguishing the unique ways in which mobility and agency are achieved, sometimes beyond the very people who are creators into new mainstreams.

I use *prime time geographies* to signal a certain way that embodied practices and lifestyles are thrust into a visual domain that accords *prime time* luminosity for working-class perpetuators (purveyors of the culture) of dancehall who wouldn't otherwise receive a taste of mainstream media attention, audience, or placement but for dancehall. It is usual for performances originating inside local Jamaican dancehall events to be broadcast within dancehall circles at home and abroad where niche cable transmissions bring dancehall content to audiences across the Caribbean diaspora, especially in the New York tristate area. It is also usual that local dancehall performances receive local media attention once a hit dance, dancer, DJ, song, or other performance attribute of interest captures the attention of the masses and demands attention from local entertainment programs including CVM's 'On Stage' and Television Jamaica's 'Entertainment Report.'[4] This chapter highlights the way dancehall moves beyond local boundaries to international loci. It is in this sense that I seek to locate this chapter in the deliberations consistent with cultural studies, cultural geography, and mediated geographies in particular[5] to highlight analysis of the way images or other media productions occupy and shape various landscapes through time. In such analyses, we are able to see otherwise obscure sites usually outside the domain of prime-time visibility.

The global impact of urban dancehall music and practice is largely attributable to the performances by dancehall and reggae artists at stage shows and festivals, with Bob Marley's global prominence as a significant contributing factor. Celebrations of Marley aside, various persons consume Jamaican music, in particular, dancehall on various continents in multiple ways. To put this sharply into perspective, Jamaican music occupies pride of place in the global circulation of music matched only by American and British pop music. While in Jamaica, dancehall occupies the precarious liminal place between mainstream and the margin, there has been increased popularity beyond its home shores since the early 1990s. Not to be underestimated in the scheme of distribution and popularity, however, is the early traffic and sale of dancehall live audiotapes, CDs, videotapes, and DVDs from within the urban ghettoes of Kingston to the Jamaican Diaspora, as well as the countries that have large populations of reggae/dancehall fans across North and South America, Europe, and the Caribbean. From the circulation of dancehall audiotapes of Sound System Stone Love's performances of the 1980s among college students in the United States and Canada, the presence of dancehall videos in Brazil and Kenya, to dutty wine and daggering features on YouTube, dancehall culture (visual and oral) has secured a prominent place in the global traffic of popular culture and performance aesthetic. The video camera, or the more popularly used term 'videolight,' forms part of the popular mechanism for channeling images and messages of/from Jamaican popular culture into 'prime-time' visibility, both inside and beyond Jamaica, into a realm of boundarylessness.

Using boundarylessness as a theoretical frame, this chapter explores the videolight, the making of dancehall celebrities, and the evolution of the dancehall performance aesthetic afforded by the spectacle of, and for, the videolight. Premised on over 15 years of scholarly research, which examines over 60 years of performance, and using a combination of participant observation, case studies, visual ethnography, and content analysis, this chapter establishes that dancehall celebrities of urban Kingston are produced and catapulted into the global domain on their own terms using creative performance modes that communicate first at the community level as they simultaneously establish a world wide web of performance practice beyond the inner city. Ultimately, this chapter analyses the unique ways in which this music and its videoscape provide agency for largely disenfranchised youth, their messages, lifestyles, and main players behind and in front of the videolight.

While a focus on urban visualscapes characterized by reggae and dancehall has been largely underrepresented in the scholarship on communication and visual culture studies broadly, this chapter positions the context of amateur dancehall video creation in contemporary debates about visual culture, as well as media/film studies. I examine these videos as products that reinforce the ways in which new media requires new analytical, multidisciplinary tools with contextual emphases and vernacular specificity.

With digital technology marking a shift in media/film studies, dancehall community videos (especially since 2000) and their use of and transmission through such technologies help reinforce arguments about the ways in which such phenomena would fall outside Media Studies 1.0. whose emphasis has been on the "broadcast-era of media in a specific time around media production, distribution and consumption" (Merrin, 2009, p. 17). By virtue of differential production, consumption, and distribution strategies, dancehall videos therefore fall squarely within the context of what the digital revolution has seen to be "fluid, connected, always on," with "personalised, individually and immediately available content," which is "manipulatable at will, and feeding into, promoting or giving rise to personal production, content and meaning creation" (Merrin, 2009, pp. 17–18).

The late 20th-century phenomenon of the 'videolight,' and its distinct 21st-century expanded mobilization through dancehall performativity, is notably in geopolitical opposition to dancehall's site of origin. The arguments herein build on my earlier work while being aware of more recent interventions[6] on material and historical conditions of visuality among the mostly subaltern Jamaican dancehall community. In seeking answers to 21st-century questions about the Black Atlantic circulation of the visual as commodity, one has to engage first with the self-reflexivity in the visual, a power in which lies the ability of dancehall creators and perpetuators to determine modes of consumption and engagement. It is where street theatre constructs a hybrid form of the 'fourth wall' using the video camera held by mostly amateur videographers with the attendant light allowing patrons to reflect 'optically' on themselves, their re-/ presentations of self, and in which they participate as consenting adults in an arena of the spectacular, of hyper/visibility. This chapter therefore highlights distinct ways in which Jamaicans, who are mostly people of African descent (estimates suggest 99 percent) living in the postcolonial present, deploy visual technologies where they themselves, their lifestyles, and aesthetic practices are mobilized in the advancement of a visual economy in which many sit at the lowest financial rung. But, the videolight "has the power to bring geographic transcendence and social ascendance" (Thompson, 2015, p. 6).

Performing Boundarylessness in a Visual Landscape

The world-wide visual web is replete with evidence regarding the globalization of dancehall performance practice. Dance moves appear in pop music videos (the 'rock away' dance was featured in an Usher music video), songs feature in ad campaigns for telecoms (a Sean Paul recording was used in a Verizon ad), and countries like Argentina boast some 300 reggae/dancehall bands. There are Japanese dancehall queens and major sound systems such as Mighty Crown, which celebrated its 25th anniversary in 2016, and legendary dancehall events such as Passa Passa had migrated beyond local shores into the wider Caribbean and beyond. Other compelling examples regarding the globalization of dancehall performance practice include the high degree to which top music charts featured a strong circulation of hit songs which either sampled dancehall 'riddims' or were recorded in the dancehall musical genre.[7]

It is well worth theorizing this global phenomenon through a reading of developments in mediated as well as transgressive geographies. Dancehall today demands analysis of a global sense of 'placement' with its movement across various personal, local, media, and national boundaries to occupy a global place.[8] One might consider the traction in movement of dancehall content across various media landscapes to be an example of out-of-place-ness and ultimately to be read as a practice of transgression. I begin with de Certeau's assertion, though, that cities are products of strategies by state governments and their apparatuses. In contrast, a different view of the city, at street level, reveals people whose moves in 'walking' the city are 'tactical' and often outside the conventions intended by the state. For de Certeau (1984), everyday life becomes a means of creating space inside, yet outside hegemonic culture. The dancehall cultural landscape in a postcolonial setting reveals transgressive[9] tendencies, transgressing and rebutting hegemonic discourses in contrast to conceptions of spatial use, practice, one's place, being in place and knowing your place, liberation, and agency. The creators and perpetuators of performance cultures such as dancehall make statements about agency in their daily existence, their 'tactics of consumption' that subvert the hegemonic uses of devices such as video cameras inside the socioeconomic uses stipulated by producers, and mock the oppressive forces that prepare for and predict their demise.

In the dilemma of margin versus center, visible versus invisible, prime time versus trivial time, expression versus repression, the videolight is controlled by consumers who construct different narratives often woven into the performance for the videolight. For example, Figure 13.1 shows a Japanese patron who occupies the dancehall spotlight inside Jamaica only within a momentary sojourn through dancehall's visual economy.

The *dancing* dancehall Japanese patron became more prominent after her entry into the International Dancehall Queen competitions and Junko Kudo won the title of Dancehall Queen in 2002. After two years of training and grounding in classical ballet, Kudo wowed the audience at Pier One during the contest. In real ways, therefore, the dancehall operates as a space of mobility for not just Jamaican patrons but Japanese and others who consume and position themselves strategically within the democratized dancehall visual product and are thrust into visual landscapes outside Jamaica.

Dancehall queens emerged as informal community celebrities in the 1970s, but Carlene Smith (proclaimed a dancehall queen by the media in 1992), Denise Cumberland, also referred to as Stacey (winner of the International Dancehall Queen Contest in 1999), and subsequent winners are significant contributors to the rise of the image, style, and appeal of such queens who are expected to demonstrate certain attributes of attitude and style as well as dancing skill. This international event has also spawned contests in the contestants' home countries, many

Figure 13.1 Japanese Dancehall Patron at a Passa Passa event being filmed by Cameraman.

of which have an established presence on the web, with, for example, social media accounts. A survey of the international scene revealed dancehall queen contests in at least six locations in the United States (Atlanta, Brooklyn, Charlotte, Chicago, Detroit, and Florida) and in four countries in Europe (Italy, Germany, Belgium, and Poland), as well as in Australia and Japan. The Australian Dancehall Queen Contest has been a national event featuring heat rounds in cities such as Melbourne, Sydney, Perth, Brisbane, and Adelaide before the national finals. This has been one way in which dancehall crossed borders through media images consumed by aspiring women. Videos of dancehall events captured mostly on Jamaican streets circulated inside distant locations such as Japan and became the tools which were used to teach reggae/dancehall/bashment classes to aspiring queens.

There is a strong degree to which 'boundarylessness'[10] can be used to classify the dancehall phenomenon. I expand 'boundarylessness' beyond its use in organizational theory as blurring "turf distinctions and established territories or cultures" (Halley, 2004, p. 6) to incorporate an expanded conception of boundaries. Therefore, the transcendence of boundaries is not only turf, but also categories, hierarchies, walls, styles, states, borders—created or inherited±evidenced in the way especially categories and hierarchies are pushed beyond the ordinary to new levels of style, prestige, and values.

It is important to acknowledge that my advocacy for an application of the term 'boundarylessness' to dancehall is not blinded to the complex ways in which an understanding of dancehall's material and cultural production has to also acknowledge its 'boundedness.' Several factors converge in dancehall: the centrality of Kingston as national urban capital, the marginality (geopolitically and aesthetically) of dancehall's creative ethos within Kingston's poverty traps and in many cases uninhabitable spaces, and dancehall's simultaneous centrality to national identity. Further, when Browning's analysis of African Diasporic performance cultures vis-à-vis Western culture is applied to dancehall, we appreciate that it is a 'war zone' as much as a party, with 'infectious rhythms' and 'contagious dances, often characterized as dangerous' (Browning, 1998, pp. 1–6). She explained that "the conflation of economic, spiritual, and sexual exchange…has allowed for the characterization of diasporic culture as chaotic or uncontrolled force which can only be countered by military or police violence" (Browning, 1998, p. 7). Numerous raids on dance events since the 1960s, alongside 'sufferation' traps, political banditry, 'donmanship,' gangs, and the constant struggle to articulate identity, as part of the psychoscape,[11] highlight the level of state policing and futility within a bounded urban experience. This boundedness then is not just a consideration of place, but psychic, national, and social space.

Browning's point of reference, while not entirely applicable, is one part of the profile, especially considering patron's encounters with police brutality and violence. However, dancehall has evolved and maintained itself outside the state apparatus even while in tension with it; its locus of creativity is at once the very marginality of its citizenry. This betwixt and between place, this liminality, is the source of its power. But, I don't wish to dwell on this liminality, except to highlight that an appreciation of dancehall necessitates understanding its multiple spaces, relationships, its marginality, and its centrality. In other words, there is no place/space erasure here, no 'cartographic non-existence.' Rather, boundaries exist, but within a philosophy of boundarylessness held by key dancehall participants that can arguably be understood within yet outside the context of 'spatial tactics' (Lefebvre, 1991) in the way that the disenfranchised could be seen to use space as a means to power, dwelling within and simultaneously evading the discipline of urban planning, strategies that camouflage the contradictions of social production.

'Prime Time' Geographies

I use the phenomenon of the 'videolight' as a central organizing force around which boundarylessness becomes evident and excavate 'prime time' as constructed through amateur dancehall videography. The dizzying phenomenon of the 'videolight' is an under-theorized aspect of dancehall in terms of its role in the creation and maintenance of spectacle, but also the way in which it features prominently in the dance space and holds a degree of responsibility for the transmission of dancehall images beyond its nation of origin. By spectacle, I am highlighting here the attempts to achieve striking public appearance that is beyond the normative visual appearance for the onlooker in some instances associated with what is superficial and distracting. One can envision the stage lights of Broadway, the cityscape of Las Vegas, or the bejeweled religious/festival dress of India for examples of the spectacular. Dancehall operates as a space of spectacle through attempts by patrons to have light shine on their finest performative offerings outside traditional mass media, the modern city, and mainstream consumer/celebrity culture.[12]

What is this videolight? This special light forms part of the apparatus for recording visual images, an intense spotlight for lighting an object or event to be recorded by a video camera. There is a powered camera (electric or battery), accompanied by the video light, which shines on its target. Essentially a video light is turned on or off on the basis of the detected current value. Within dancehall, the phenomenon of the video light came to prominence because of early dancehall videographers such as Jack Sowah, seen in Figure 13.2, who stood alone in the late 1980s as one who recorded the happenings at large and small dancehall events. Today the videolight is a phenomenon present at many dance events—large, small, at home, and abroad (see typical images of video camera men in Figure 13.3).

The recorded images from local events were mostly sold as amateur video productions, while others generated by prominent videographers, such as Knight Rider and Scrappy among others, are packaged for distribution in the local sphere and metropolitan centers such as London and New York. Generally, dancehall videos circulated within countries where reggae and dancehall have been popularly consumed, such as Germany, Brazil, South Africa, Kenya, Canada, and Japan. Videos have become much more available globally since the digital age, information technology advances in the World Wide Web, and with websites such as DancehallTV.com, YouTube, and Google. Dancehall videos/DVDs have

Figure 13.2 Jack Sowah, notable Dancehall videographer.
Source: Author.

fetched prices internationally ranging on average between US$5.00 and $25.00.

From cursory mention in song to treatises on the videolight by artists such as Frisco Kidd, T.O.K, Elephant Man, Lexxus, Macka Diamond, and Mad Cobra, the dancehall massive (or family) is encouraged into certain norms and rules governing readiness for and consumption of the videolight. These discourses are linked to mature debates about economic security, 'prime time' focus or center stage appearance, female sexuality, and performance. For example, in chastising the woman who has not taken enough care of the health and strength of her vagina, those of the 'tired body' variety for instance, in the single 'Likkle and Cute' DJ Frisco Kidd advances a discourse about the "good body gyal" who has no need to use alum to reduce the elasticity of her pudenda like those

Figure 13.3 Typical images from a Dancehall scene including dancers and amateur.

who engage in too much sexual activity. He further lauds the woman whose pudenda has not stretched to the capacity of an elastic band:

> "Certain gyal ah walk inna video light crew
> And every man dun know she nah no glue
> She coulda have AIDS cause she no stop catch flue
> And tek man like Burger King drive-thru"
> [Certain girls are walking in the videolight crew
> but every man knows she has no glue
> she might have AIDS because she always catching the flue
> and takes men like the Burger King drive-thru]

In 'Make it Clap (remix),' Busta Rhymes, Sean Paul, and Spliff Star highlight the role of the videolight as an apparatus for achieving prime time visibility: "Dawn and Karyn or Angie and Patsy inna di videolight just like a big sunday matinee." In the single 'Taxi Fare,' Lexxus and Mr Vegas (2006) explain that walking from Asylum to Papine after clubbing is not right. All hot girls must have their taxi fares to get home after partying. Girls shouldn't have to walk or solicit rides to get to the dance either, as they should have the means to support reliable and secure transportation. All the girls with their own taxi fare can take center stage. He is talking here about the independent woman.

> "A who mi hear seh come a dancehall and a hype
> And don't even have a fifty fi buy a sprite
> Gal, yuh have yuh money then tek di videolight
> And nuff a dem don't know how dem a reach home tonight"

Mad Cobra (2005) adds to the lyrical database on the videolight in talking about the independent and fashionable dancehall woman. In 'Last Year Clothes' the DJ talks of those women who "nah fi find di video man di video man find yuh [don't have to find the video man because he will find you]":

> "Cut inna face gal nuh ready fi di video yet
> Two color face gal nuh ready fi di video yet
> Nuh watch yuh mate she nuh ready fi di video yet
> She nuh ready she nuh ready fi di video yet
> Beer bokkle shape nuh ready fi di video yet
> Borrow clothes gal dem nuh ready fi di video yet
> Repeat clothes gal nuh ready fi di video yet
> Dash wey belly gal dem nuh ready fi di video..."

In 'Grindacologist' by Beenie Man (2004, feat. Kymberli) the DJ commands: "Gimme some a dem gal weh ever look bright, face ever ready, coochie ever tight, always ready wah! fi di videolight, hotty hotty girl a fi mi type..." 'Hotta' by TOK (feat. Maestro) is another single which highlights the videolight as an important dimension of dancehall performance. The song speaks to the woman whose skin is full of scars, has a big belly, with worn out shoes: "Gal yuh hotta, step out inna di videolight yuh run Passa Passa, some gal a fi go stay behind di camera like Kassa, yuh man still in love like Sean Paul and Sasha..."

How does this videolight operate in the dance? Cameramen typically enter the dance space at or around the moment of transition from the 'early dance' to periods of most intense concentration of dance and presence of celebrity dancers, promoters, dons, DJs, and other dancehall notables. Once the cameraman determines that there is something to be captured, the lights are turned on and patrons vie through performance for the spotlight. The video determines the space of activity, and accomplished or celebrity dancers often command the spotlight while others compete sometimes violently to stay in its focus or be rendered as spectators. Many patrons attend events having employed various devices of adornment before the event and during the event, such as engaging the camera with emotionally charged vocalizations ('bigging up' one's baby father or mother, for example) and other performance modes such as dancing and 'profiling' command attention from the videographer and his spotlight.

A typical dancehall event (community or commercial) can have one to four cameras, depending on the scale of the performance. It is such an integral part of the performance that finding an event in the Kingston Metropolitan Area without a camera might be near impossible. Discussion fora[13] have documented some of the anxieties over the introduction of the video camera into the performance space. For example: girls get pretty at night to attract the videolight but not men; they have stopped dancing because they don't want to look disheveled for the camera; women go to great lengths to compete with their competition for access to the videolight, including getting x-rated and into fights because they want to be visible internationally; females leave their partners to dance with experienced dancers who can capture the videolight; and the videolight, though adding hype, is thought to have contributed to killing the 'vibes' in dancehall. Even more concretely, nightclub owners attest to the fact that in instances where fights occur they are sometimes between women who are competing for the 'videolight,' seeking publicity or their proverbial 'five minutes of fame' (Wright, 2004, p. 47).

An important dimension is the role of the mostly male videographer, his gaze, and the narratives produced in the recorded events and images. It is mostly women, their fashion, bodies, and dance moves that are captured to excessive proportions. The woman in dancehall is queen, and without her there would be no dancehall, according to many perpetuators and creators of dancehall. Taking into consideration the vantage point of the videographer with that of those whose performances (verbal, dance, etc.) are recorded, the videolight is both technology that has utility as well as a figure, a personality, an instigator, that creates the need/desire for recognition, while preserving images of performers who can later be consumed by those who are far removed from their material ontologies. There is a relationship between the videographer, the spectacular subject/object, and the spectator who views the process or final product. All are authors in the process or final product taking control of their image, representation, and ultimate marketing. There is a sense in which the product is constructed by the community and belongs to that community: there is joint participation and ownership, common identities around common interests that build on each other.

The 'erotic art' of making these 'community music videos' or 'docuvideos,' according to Wright (2004), with the participation of mostly women who freely partake in the display of intimate body parts and emotions in this visual culture, centralizes the dancehall woman's agency in scripting her role in dancehall as 'queen.' Even as males have gained access to the mostly female-dominated videolight since 2003, their place as dancers is fragile in a society where narratives of the construction of normative masculinity is centered around very little display of the dancing male body. That male dancing body is stigmatized as homoerotic versus the female dancing body, which is accepted for the assumed heterosexual gaze.

In the context of the joint production and ownership of dancehall docuvideos, there is a transcendental dimension—a crucial aspect of the way it operates to shape boundarylessness for the dancehall phenomenon that has to be highlighted. Wright (2004) first argued for the way in which the videolight afforded the flow of dancing female energy in particular through the communication of unabashed subjectified freedom in the display of sexuality. Here is where cameramen, camera, spectators, and dancers participate in the transmission of a sexuality so powerful and simultaneously elusive so as to construct what Wright (2004, p. 45) refers to as a "theory of wholeness for the black female body." She argues that not only are the women using the dancehall as stage to gain visibility, but

> ...by manipulating the conventional scopophilic gaze, that is the desire to see and through their erotic performances, women perform a communication ritual of sorts with their audience, where elements of the past and indeed present are re-thought and re-membered in an attempt to create ultimate spiritual and psychological change.
>
> (Wright, 2004, p. 46)

So as audiences abroad want to see the latest happenings in the dancehall scene, and "Jamaicans at home want to see themselves on camera and remember their dance experiences" (Wright, 2004, p. 46), such recordings step outside of the conventional production schemes and present as hybrid scripts, old yet new, material yet spiritual, local yet global, powerful yet simple, timeless yet everyday. Crucially, they also fall outside the schemes of production and transmission for music videos as well as documentaries, argues Wright, and in this sense their narratives have to be read with different lenses, taking account of their improvisatory, unscripted, unchoreographed, mostly unedited nature, depicting nonfictional material conditions of an ethnographic nature.

The Videolight and a Psychology of Unbounded Urban Stardom

The videos produced could be considered community 'music videos,' and there's a way in which the videolight has become a community-building strategy occasioned by its role in the projection of community life within and outside dancehall. When Patterson (1974) stated that every community should have its own sound system because he saw it as part of the systematic construction of 'bonds of solidarity' or economic potential for especially men who occupied themselves gainfully rather than engaging in deviant behavior, the videolight did not exist. But today it forms part of the sound system culture as a feature used excessively by patrons. Being a result of this culture, it forms part of the mechanism for projecting communities and their citizenry beyond community/national/geographical boundaries in concrete ways.

The entrance of the video camera has assisted in the transformation of the ordinary into the fantastic through adopting masks more ready for the screen. The videolight has played a significant role in shining selves, often with bleached skin,[14] into stardom and the celebration of personhood vis-à-vis the urban phenomena of "sufferation," political banditry, "donmanship," and gangs, the constant struggle to articulate identity, as part of the psychoscape. The aforementioned alter egos, which are enacted through the wearing of masks, are defined by the dress (new outfit, new hairdo, no borrowed clothes), hairstyles (wigs, braids), and behaviors adopted (language, profile) within the social celebration. Masks have to be contextualized therefore as self-aggrandizing tools, a tradition with antecedents such as the 19th-century Set Girls and Jonkonnu performances. The wearing of a different mask at each dance event is a criterion for attending the event and is seen to guarantee the eventual broadcast of a well-worked out visual product, a spectacular one.

The videolight shines people into recognition within and outside their communities as dance videos circulate within the local, national, and international communities. It affords a 'prime time visibility' as well as status and access to resources (gained outside the mainstream). Linked to the manifestation of the videolight in dancehall therefore is the idea of the celebrity, in some instances created but certainly maintained as a result of the video camera's light. Constructions of certain types of celebrities within the videolight are noteworthy, and distinctions about the traditional media/cultural studies definition of celebrity and the mechanisms for production within the dancehall context can be made. Who is the star or celebrity? Wernick (1991) defined the star:

> A star is anyone whose name and fame has been built up to the point where reference to them, via mention, mediatized representation or live appearance, can serve as a promotional booster in itself.
> (in Turner, 2004, p. 9)

Taken in its most general sense, the terms star and celebrity are used synonymously by those who ascribe greatest importance to celebrity as a mechanism which functions within the ambit of the mass media.

The celebrity is one who is 'famous for being famous' and arguably gains this status based on no special achievements. Usually found in the sporting or entertainment industries, and mostly represented by the film star, this particular cultural figure has a public life that is of more interest than their professional life (Turner, 2004, pp. 3–4). The mass appeal and therefore consumption of facts and images about the celebrity's life defines the excessiveness around the development of this figure. This figure is about representation, attracting attention which is strongly linked to the mass media.[15] Chris Rojek (2001) and John Frow (1998) offer that "the cultural function of the celebrity today contains significant parallels with the functions normally ascribed to religion" (Turner, 2004, p. 6). Various figures and effects on their audiences have been ascribed godlike qualities or fame (see also Chevannes, 1999). Even as these views are held, others critique the celebrity for their fickle nature, faddishness, and "constructedness." It is important to note the media's role in the production of celebrity—for example, the manufacture, trade, and marketing of celebrity is the result of strategic commercial plans.

There are important differences in the way celebrity is produced and consumed in the Jamaican popular performance space, especially around dancehall culture. Many dancers, DJs, producers, promoters, and other dancehall celebrities hail from the margins rather than the mainstream, and their rise to prominence has been outside the mass media, existing on a smaller scale of technological and financial input for production, access, marketing, and distribution of news and images often centered in the small communities they hail from and later transcending them. At a local level, community celebrities erupt into prominence, unlike the star who takes time to develop. For example, a dancer can reveal a new dance move and overnight achieves community fame and celebrity status facilitated in no small way through the videolight. The achievement of such a dancer brings attention to the self, the dance, and the community. S/he is tied to a wider network of not merely fans, but through community media and international circulation, a diasporic aesthetic community. Here there are no strategic commercial plans backed by marketing and trade innovations of the celebrity product. There is also no corporate sponsorship. Though the sphere of entertainment remains the arena for celebrities in the dancehall context, the mode by which they are created is different. There are distinctions to be made in respect of the role of alternative media in the production of celebrities, the traditional role of the performances by local celebrities, their connection and relationship to audiences and fans, the incorporation and differential use of technology (especially the camera) and capital, the way they articulate constructions of national, gender, class, and sexual identities, and how they function as local, regional, and international brands and identities.

Jamaican culture is replete with examples of how ordinary people create and maintain the status of hero, star, and actor, and produce and consume celebrities, in such areas as film, sports, music, rebellion, and community activism or leadership. Visual representations of Jamaicans in the 21st century have not come from Hollywood, Broadway, or the French Riviera, even though they might have been influenced by these spaces. Rather, they are more localized, fashioned by the people for the people. Perhaps one of the most profound statements about celebrity in Jamaica comes from the song lines, "I'm broad, I'm broad, I'm broader than Broadway" (from Barrington Levy, 2006). The simultaneous use, transgressive rejection, and gigantic leap beyond Broadway in the lines is corroborated in Jamaicanisms such as 'wi likkle but wi tallawah,'[16] larger than life when necessary, powered on the engine of ancestral struggle and memory.

Jamaica's place on the music video production scene is now secure—some two dozen music videos are shot in Jamaica each month, and commercial cable channels such as Hype TV and Reggae Entertainment TV feature videos often including acts filmed at local dance events, which are popular locations for filming music videos. It is in these events that dancers, for example, gain exposure in order to enter the sphere of music videos that are broadcast locally, regionally, and internationally. With such visibility of the video production process and the constant need for local acts, it is no wonder that females and males go to extremes to capture the attention of any willing videographer to achieve presence during the 'prime time' spotlight. Temporal and performative boundaries are also traversed when these images are deployed in performance cultures beyond dancehall (for example, reggaetón), and images of past events, music videos, or dance moves such as the 'limbo' or 'hoola hoop,' which both have iterations prior to their 21st-century appearance, are rebroadcasted or repurposed.

'New World' Visual Landscapes: The 'Unbounded' Red Bull Culture Clash

In this section, I analyze the fragile context of luminosity using dancehall's relationship with the transnational corporation Red Bull. Not only is Jamaica's place on the music video production scene secure, but Jamaican aesthetic practices have populated the commercial performance and video production landscapes around sound clashes staged for global appeal. A popular dancehall performance mode, the sound system became prominent in the 1960s around sound system owners such as Arthur 'Duke' Reid (the Trojan sound system and Treasure Isle label) and Clement 'Sir Coxone' Dodd (Downbeat sound system and Studio One recording studio), who played in sometimes incendiary clashes across Kingston's landscape. Clashes were sources of heightened engagement with indigenous Jamaican music and resulted in symbolic as well as real violence. By the 1980s and 1990s, sound systems such as Stone Love, Kilimanjaro, and Bass Odyssey, among many others, ruled the Jamaican nightscape, and sound system clashes became popular beyond Jamaica to occupy 'outernational' terrains. Violent clashes produced a damper on the sound system scene in Jamaica, but they gained popularity abroad in the 1990s when the World Clash events organized by 'Irish and Chin' began in New York.[17] Even though there have been attempts to revive the practice through the Jamaica Sound System Festival (see Figure 13.4),[18] clashes remain as rare aspect of Jamaica's dancehall scene. However, as the sound system clashes at home subsided, they increased on a global scale, especially in metropolitan centers such as New York, Atlanta, London, Lisbon, and further afield in Johannesburg.

Most importantly, for those who are not resident in such cities, the spotlight has been casted on sound system clashes within the global videoscape inside primary visual repositories such as YouTube where Jamaican dancehall aesthetics are paraded in such events as the Red Bull Culture Clash. Red Bull has been explicit about its transnational commercialization of the dancehall performance mode usually staged in indoor venues (a departure from the typical Jamaican scene where events are usually outdoors). Originating in 2010, the Red Bull Culture Clash series (see Figure 13.5) is hailed as "the world's biggest musical battle" and has featured Artistes, Disc Jocks, MCs, Rappers, and Sound Systems such as Metalheadz, Skream & Benga, Channel One, Major Lazer, Federation Sound, Wiz Khalifa, Stone Love Movement, Disturbing London, David Rodigan, Unruly (featuring Popcaan seen in Figure 13.6), African Storm, Durban Massacre, and Tinie Tempah, among many others. The modus operandi is similar to the typical Jamaican sound clash with four sounds (sometimes referred to as crews) compete in series of four or five clash rounds and success in each round is determined by crowd response. The events have seen up to 25,000 persons in attendance, making them some of the most successful one-night events staged around sound system culture globally.

Following the first Red Bull Culture Clash in 2010, the England Riots of 2011 spotlighted Jamaica as accusations circulated about the role Jamaicans, and more specifically, the Jamaican language,[19] played in the successful spread of the riots. Beyond these years, I argue that the consumption of Jamaica as a product and personality reached a high point in 2013, a saturation point in a sort of boundaryless hegemonic dissolution, and Louise 'Miss Lou' Bennett's poem 'Colonization in Reverse' captures this idea well.[20] As Red Bull Culture Clashes sought to cement Jamaican aesthetic practices in specific sites, by 2013 we saw a critical increase in the consumption of Jamaica as a brand, made visible through a different sort of 'videolight' in a global landscape. Highlights of 2013 as a year of critical consumption contained the following representations of Jamaica, occupying various forms of visual media, and

Figure 13.4 Flyer of Bass Odyssey's sound system festival.

Figure 13.5 Flyers for Red Bull culture clash events – Manchester and Johannesburg.

their spotlight: the Volkswagen commercial at the Super Bowl Sunday featured a Caucasian male speaking Jamaican and cajoling his coworkers to be happy;[21] Beyoncé performed her hit song featuring Grammy-winning act Sean Paul to millions at the same Super Bowl; the BET Awards featured dancehall performances Beenie Man and Elephant

Figure 13.6 Popcaan dropping Drake's track 'One Dance' at the 2014 culture clash.

Man, among others; the Saturn Ad which featured the highest symbolic representation of hegemonic dissolution with the burning of the Jamaican flag earned the ire of Jamaicans at home and abroad so much so the that the ad was pulled in short order; Jamaican songster Tessanne Chin won the Voice competition; the 'No Woman Nuh Drive' video remixing Bob Marley's 'No Woman Nuh Cry' bringing attention to advocacy for Saudi women to be allowed to drive circulated around the globe; and Major Lazer's release of dancehall productions has contributed to him becoming one of the top paid DJs globally, featuring such acts as Sean Paul, Busy Signal Chronixx, and Protojé.

By way of context, therefore, the preceding outline regarding the explicit consumption of Jamaican popular culture highlights the 'cool factor' which Jamaica embodies. I use cool here arcing back to Farris Thompson's (1973) articulations, and subsequent analyses, on 'an aesthetic of the cool' to engage with the translation of a self-conscious confidence seen in attitude, determination, pleasure in the self, bodily carriage, dress, and performance, which manifests not only from a *certain* mental state but also in a performance aesthetic as 'cool as water' linked to ancestral histories. Moreover, the clash, mobilizing the seriousness of competition and pleasure of play around music, is one of the cool aspects of Jamaican performance which has gained new visibility through the clash. What is arguable, however, is that this visibility is muted by virtue of Red Bull's marketing in an arena of unbounded global media consumption that can easily occlude sites of origin and make way for interpretations of cultural appropriation.

Of the Red Bull Culture Clashes which have been staged, I highlight the September 2017 clash, which travelled for the second time to Johannesburg, South Africa. Dubbed the 'Jozi installment' by Red Bull, it featured four artists and their crews vying to win support and be crowned winners. They included AKA and Top Boyz Sound System, Patoranking (Nigerian Afrobeat star with heavy dancehall-influenced tunes) and Red Hot Sound System, DJ Tira and Durban Massacre Sound System, and Admiral and Jahseed (longstanding kwaito and dancehall selector/DJ duo) with African Storm Sound System (see Figure 13.7).[22] In typical clash style, the featured acts played dubs and featured surprise guests to metaphorically kill their opponents amidst delight of participants, with the hype of featured artists such as Patoranking introducing tunes. Notably, it has been the playing of dubs made specifically for sound systems that seek in a clash to distinguish their musical arsenal from that of their opponents based on special customized artiste recordings that became the gravitas of a real clash.

Figure 13.7 Admiral and Jah Seed playing on African storm sound system, Johannesburg.

The consumers of the sound clash content transmitted through Red Bull's site, among others, can be gleaned from online comments. They are youth music lovers generally, Red Bull Academy/Culture Clash fans, and music aficionados of all ages beyond the jurisdiction of the clash. Specifically, the online video teasers[23] for the culture clash engaged viewers in the international spread of sound clashes with videos advertising the culture clash event featuring the competitors ('The enigma and career of patoranking'), South African music ('The oral history of durban kwaito music'), and the art and culture around dubs.[24] Mention of Jamaica which holds centrality as a nation-state to the emergence and proliferation of dubs was only sparse (it was mentioned only once in the article on dub previously mentioned). However, there was no doubt that Jamaica's solid musical innovations received global visibility in spite of Red Bull's crafty marketing strategies at the intersection between authentic dancehall culture and the corporate power brokering in ownership of the mega successful music events featuring local music in multiple locations that have often gained new notoriety because of cross-fertilization with Jamaican musical aesthetics. In pushing its brand, Red Bull used Jamaica contradictorily as a 'backdrop' with cursory mention as sight of origin and producer of the cool. However, onstage in the midst of dubs being hurled in musical battle, Jamaica was central, inside the 'videolight' of infectious musical landscape seeing a revival through such sound clashes. Jamaican sound system clashes have transcended national borders to occupy transnational soundscapes with Red Bull sound clashes at the contemporary center providing another dimension for analysis of dancehall culture in the context of boundarylessness beyond the visions of dancehall creators and perpetuators who do not own the means of production in a visual economy.

Conclusion

Using dancehall visual culture, specifically the videolight and political economy of visuality as a primary framework for thinking, I have contributed a view of dancehall which includes an unexplored philosophical terrain of boundarylessness applied beyond the context of organizational behavior to performance practice centered around the phenomenon of the videolight. Immersed outside the traditional production and broadcast mediascape in a digital age of immediacy, dancehall videographers inscribe in their recordings practitioners' needs for immediate gratification, in the context of pre- and post-broadcast alternatives of production, narrative, scripting, audience involvement, and transmission.

With the examples before, I have highlighted that even as dancehall culture is situated in a field of boundaries, its key participants have created several unbounded dance and soundscapes through everyday street events around music and dance that transcend the street, their travel across geopolitical borders allowing for the articulation of an urban dancehall transnation, and in the way transnational corporations have deployed dancehall performance culture in a global landscape. These events, and with 'videolight' within them, have allowed for transcendence at various spatial, psychic, and material levels.

As an aesthetic community, dancehall adherents imprint themselves on regional and international cityscapes, breaking boundaries that open the flow to other sites and even fertilizing other aesthetic communities. Ultimately, this chapter widens the map of dancehall, specifically its visual culture, and continues work on a grossly underexplored terrain that can yield important insights about how disenfranchised citizens create and recreate spaces of celebration, renewal, and transgression.

Notes

1 See Stanley Niaah (2010), especially pp. 110–114, for further discussion of British Link-Up dance events.
2 Owner of Stone Love sound system, otherwise known as 'Wee Pow' or 'Father Pow.'
3 For this range of studies, see for example Cooper (2004), Stolzoff (2000), Stanley Niaah (2010), Hope (2010), Henriques (2011), Hitchins (2014), Thompson (2015), and Howard (2016).
4 On Stage and Entertainment Report are longstanding entertainment review programmes in Jamaica that regularly feature developments in dancehall.
5 See for example recent compilations of works on mediated geographies in Mains, Cupples, and Lukinbeal (2015).
6 Thompson (2015).
7 I argue that by the first quarter of 2017 when the Billboard top/hot 100 charts began to show the significant impacts from 2013 as a year of saturation for the consumption of Jamaican popular culture. Jamaican music's presence and influence on the Billboard Hot 100 charts have been inspiring to say the least. Tracks like Sia's "Cheap Thrills" feat. Sean Paul (nominated for a 2016 Grammy in the Pop Duo/Group Performance category), Drake's "Controlla" and "One Dance," Justin Bieber's "Let Me Love You," Rihanna's "Work" (also nominated for a 2016 Grammy in the Pop Duo/Group Performance category), Nicky Jam's "Hasta El Amenever," Enrique Iglesias's "Duele El Corazon," and Torey Lanez's "Luv" are obviously dancehall-inspired if not sampled. One could also argue that Shawn Mendes' "Treat You Better" also has a bit of dancehall flavor. The Luis Fonsi/Daddy Yankee mega hit "Despacito" with Justin Bieber remix is another example. See Marshall (2017) for expert guidance on how the Jamaican influence pans out for such mega hits as Despacito.
8 See Massey (1994).
9 In the trajectory of a Foucauldian reading, see Cresswell (1996).
10 Boundarylessness has been used in the context of systems research (see for example Dempster, 2002) and organizational culture (see for example Halley's application of boundary theory at www.pamij.com/halley.html [accessed June 2004]). It is important to note that boundary theorists have

emerged within economics, mathematics, law, philosophy, political geography, political science, public administration, psychology, among other disciplines, to establish an interdisciplinary framework.

11 After the idea I first read in Lipsitz (1994, p. 5; introduced by Appadurai, 1990), which delimits the importance of reorganizing space beyond the local experience, especially those of urban areas, beyond landscapes to talk about concurrent ethnoscapes, mediascapes, technoscapes, finance scapes, and ideoscapes. This entails development of a new vision of world cultural economy based on the active travel of images, techniques, ideas, and capital that can occupy different places and spaces simultaneously, rather than one continent or country. Thus, I use this term with the recognition that all inner-city urban settings breed certain conditions that make them more susceptible to instability and varied recreative responses.

12 It is worth highlighting here that the attempts to achieve striking spectacular appearance has theoretical association with analyses of the '"psychogeography" of the modern city' counterposed with the contending models such as 'societies of surveillance' from Foucault. For further discussion of this, see Crary (2005, pp. 335–336).

13 For an example of such forums, see www.dancehallreggae.com/forum/archive/index.php?t-3861.html (accessed July 23, 2007). Also see Evans (2007).

14 See Thompson (2015) for a discussion of how the videolight operates as a 'technology of race' with patrons often reinscribed in a political history and economy of white privilege: cameras and camera lights privilege whiteness, mediascapes propel images of whiteness, and the circulation of images fuel aspirations to achieve whiteness.

15 See for example pioneering works by Turner (2004), Boorstin (1971), Richard Dyer (1979, 1986), Gamson (1994), and more recent studies by Rojek (2001), Marshall (1997) and Turner, Bonner, and Marshall (2000), among others.

16 This is a Jamaican saying/proverb which translates to "we are little but strong" (not to be taken for granted, formidable).

17 See Macleod and Chamberlain (2016) for a succinct history of sound system activity.

18 It is important to note that attempts at reviving the sound system landscape in Jamaica have resulted in the staging of the Sound System Festival or SoundFest initiated by Bass Odyssey, which converted its annual anniversary event (2017 saw the 28th anniversary) into a major festival event now in its 3rd staging. Similarly, Sumfest incorporated the Heavyweight Sound System clash in the 2017 staging of the longstanding festival.

19 The fusion between British street lingua franca and Jamaican is sometimes referred to as London Metropolitan English.

20 See text of Louise Bennett's poem here http://louisebennett.com/colonization-in-reverse/ (accessed October 19, 2017).

21 See more on the Get Happy Volkswagen commercial 2013 here www.youtube.com/watch?v=09JTtVxztv4 (accessed October 20, 2017).

22 For more details, including teasers on the Johannesburg sound clash, see http://ewn.co.za/2017/09/24/durban-massacre-steals-the-shows-at-red-bull-culture-clash and www.redbull.com/za-en/events/Red%20Bull%20Culture%20Clash%202017 (accessed October 20, 2017).

23 See teasers for Red Bull Culture Clash - South Africa, in particular Red Bull's tweet of the culture clash 101 teaser https://twitter.com/RBMA/status/911167962257678336 which I commented on here https://twitter.com/SonjahStanley/status/911185704075612161 (accessed October 20, 2017).

24 See for example Bradley (n.d.).

References

Aitken, S. C. A., & Zonn, L. E. (Eds.). (1994). *Place, power, situation and spectacle: A geography of film.* Lanham, MD: Rowman & Littlefield.

Alleyne, M. (1998 March). "Babylon makes the rules": The politics of Reggae crossover. *Social and Economic Studies, 47*(1, Reggae Studies Issue), 65–77.

Appadurai, A. (1990). Disjuncture and difference in the global cultural economy. *Public Culture, 2*(2), 1–24.

Beenie Man (2004). *'Grindacologist' single on the album Back to Basics.* Los Angeles, CA: Virgin Records America.

Boorstin, D. (1971). *The image: A guide to pseudo-events in America.* New York: Athenium.

Bradley, T. (n.d.). 'What the hell are dubs?' Retrieved November 12, 2017 from https://www.redbull.com/za-en/everything-you-need-to-know-about-dubs

Browning, B. (1998). *Infectious rhythm: Metaphors of contagion and the spread of African culture.* New York and London: Routledge.

Busta Rhymes (featuring Sean Paul & Spliff Star) (2002). *Make it clap [single].* New York: J Records

de Certeau, M. (1984). *The practice of everyday life.* Berkeley, CA: University of California Press.

Chang, O. K., & Chen, W. (1998). *Reggae routes: The story of the Jamaican music.* Philadelphia, PA: Temple University Press.

Chevannes, B. (1999). Between the living and the dead: The apotheosis of Rastafari hero. In J. Pulis (Ed.), *Religion, diaspora, and cultural identity* (pp. 337–356). Amsterdam: Gordon and Breach.

Cooper, C. (2004). *Sound clash: Jamaican Dancehall culture at large.* New York: Palgrave Macmillan.

Cooper, C. (Ed.). (2013). *Global Reggae.* Kingston: University of the West Indies Press.

Crary, J. (2005). Spectacle. In T. Bennett, L. Grossberg, & M. Morris (Eds.), *New keywords: A revised vocabulary of culture and society* (pp. 335–336). Malden, MA: Blackwell.

Cresswell, T. (1996). *In place/out of place: Geography, ideology, and transgression.* Minneapolis, MN: University of Minnesota Press.

Cresswell, T. A., & Dixon, D. P. (Eds.). (2002). *Engaging film: Geographies of mobility and identity.* Lanham, MA: Rowman & Littlefield.

Davis, G. (2016). Dancehall and crime: Is there really a link? Jamaica Observer, July 13.

Dempster, B. (2002). *Boundarylessness: introducing a systems heuristic for conceptualizing complexity.* Paper presented at Toward a Taxonomy of Boundaries Conference, Kansas, June.

Dyer, R. (1979). *Stars.* London: BFI Revised Edition.

Dyer, R. (1986). *Heavenly bodies: Film stars and society.* London: BFI Macmillan.

Evans, T. (2007). Women get x-rated for video light. The Jamaica Star, March 24.

Frisco Kidd (1997). *'Little and cute' [single] on Dancehall Queen – Original motion picture soundtrack.* Kingston: Island Jamaica.

Frow, John (1998). Is Elvis a god? Cult, culture, questions of method. *International Journal of Cultural Studies, 1*(2), 197–210.

Gamson, J. (1994). *Claims to fame: Celebrity in contemporary America*. Berkeley, CA: University of California Press

Halley, A. (2004). Applications of Boundary theory to organizational and inter-organizational culture. Retrieved May 13, 2009, from www.pamij.com/halley.html

Henriques, J. (2011). *Sonic bodies: Reggae sound systems, performance techniques and ways of knowing*. New York: Continuum.

Henriques, J. (2014). Rhythmic bodies: Amplification, inflection and transduction in the dance performance techniques of the "Bashment gal". *Body and Society, 20* (3 and 4), 79–112.

Hitchins, R. (2014). *Vibes merchants: The sound creators of Jamaican popular music*. Farnham: Ashgate Publishing Limited.

Hope, D. (2010). *Man vibes: Masculinities in the Jamaican Dancehall*. Kingston: Ian Randle Publishers.

Howard, D. (2016). *The creative echo chamber: Contemporary music production in Kingston Jamaica*. Kingston: Ian Randle Publishers.

Lefebvre, H. (1991). *The production of space* (H. Nicholson-Smith, Trans.) Oxford: Blackwell Publishers.

Levy, B. (2006). Here I come (Broader than Broadway), *The Best of Barrington Levy: Broader than Broadway*, [LP] Time 1 Jamaica.

Lipsitz, G. (1994). *Dangerous crossroads: Popular music, postmodernism and the poetics of place*. London and New York: Verso.

Macleod, E., & Chamberlain, J. (2016). A beginner's guide to Jamaica's greatest musical sport: Soundclash. Retrieved November 12, 2017, from http://daily.redbullmusicacademy.com/2016/10/a-history-of-soundclash

Mad Cobra (2005). *'Last year clothes', single on the compilation album The Biggest Ragga Dancehall Anthems*. Huddersfield: Greensleeves.

Mains, S. P. (2015). From bolt to brand: Olympic celebrations, tourist destinations and media landscapes. In S. P. Mains, J. Cupples, & C. Lukinbeal (Eds.), *Mediated geographies and geographies of media*. Rotterdam: Springer.

Mains, S. P., Cupples, J., & Lukinbeal, C. (Eds.), (2015). *Mediated geographies and geographies of media*. New York and London: Springer.

Marshall, P. D. (1997). *Celebrity and power: Fame in contemporary culture*. Minneapolis, MN and London: University of Minnesota Press.

Marshall, W. (2017). Everything you ever wanted to know about despacito. Retrieved January 13, 2018 from www.vulture.com/2017/08/everything-you-ever-wanted-to-know-about-despacito.html

Massey, D. (1994). A global sense of place. *Marxism Today* (38) 24–29.

Merrin, W. (2009). Media studies 2.0: Upgrading and open-sourcing the discipline. *Interactions: Studies in Communication and Culture, 1*(1), 17–34.

Mr Vegas feat. Lexxus, 2017. 'Taxi Fare' [Single]. *Hot it Up*, Delicious Vinyl

Noxolo, P. (2016). *Caribbean in/security and creativity: A working paper*. Retrieved November 18, 2017 from http://epapers.bham.ac.uk/2208/1/CARISCC-Working-Paper-Noxolo.pdf

Patterson, O. (1974). *The condition of the low-income population in the Kingston metropolitan area*. Kingston: Office of the Prime Minister.

Rhiney, K., & Cruse, R. (2012). Trench town rock: Reggae music, landscape inscription and the making of place in Kingston, Jamaica. *Urban Studies Research Journal*. www.hindawi.com/journals/usr/2012/585160/

Rietvald, H. (2013). Journey to the light? Immersion, spectacle and mediation. In B. Attias, A. Gavanas, & H. Rietvald (Eds.), *DJ culture in the mix: Power, technology and social change in electronic dance music*. London: Bloomsbury.

Rojek, C. (2001). *Celebrity*. London: Reaktion.

Stanley Niaah, S. (2004). Kingston's dancehall: A story of space and celebration. *Space and Culture*, 7(1), 102–118.

Stanley Niaah, S. (2010). *DanceHall: From slave ship to Ghetto*. Ottawa: University of Ottawa Press.

Stewart, K. (2002). "So Wha, Mi Nuh Fi Live to?": Interpreting violence in Jamaica through Dancehall culture. *Ideaz*, 1(1), 17–28.

Stolzoff, N. (2000). *Wake the town and tell the people: Dancehall culture in Jamaica*. Durham, NC: Duke University Press.

Thompson, K. (2015). *Shine: The visual economy of light in African diasporic aesthetic practice*. Durham, NC and London: Duke University Press.

Thompson, R. F. (1973). An aesthetic of the cool. *African Arts*, 7(1, Autumn), 40–43, 64–67, 89–91.

Turner, G. (2004). *Understanding celebrity*. London: Sage.

Turner, G., Bonner, F., & Marshall, P. D. (2000). *Fame games: The production of celebrity in Australia*. Melbourne: Cambridge University Press.

Wernick, A. (1991). *Promotional culture: Advertising, ideology and symbolic expression*. London: Sage.

Wright, B. S. (2004). Speaking the unspeakable: Politics of the Vagina in Dancehall docu-videos. *Discourses in Dance*, 2(2), 45–59.

List of Contributors

Adedayo 'Dayo' Abah, Ph.D. is a Professor in the Department of Journalism and Mass Communications at Washington and Lee University, Lexington, Virginia. She teaches courses in law and communications, news media and society, public relations, and global communication. Her research interests include the First Amendment, digital media and the law, and media and pop culture in Africa. Her work has appeared in media and communications journals such as *Communication, Culture & Critique, Media Culture & Society, Journal f Media Law and Ethics, International Communication Gazette, Interactions: Studies in Communication and Culture*, and an edited book.

Valerie N. Adams-Bass is an Assistant Professor of Youth and Social Innovation, a faculty affiliate of the Youth-Nex Center to Promote Effective Youth Development in the Curry School of Education at the University of Virginia and a faculty affiliate of The Racial Empowerment Collaborative at the University of Pennsylvania's Graduate School of Education. Dr. Adams-Bass is most interested in examining how racial/ethnic socialization experiences are related to the process of identity development, the social and the academic experiences of Black children, and the effects of exposure to racial media stereotypes on interpersonal interactions and the self-concept of Black youth. Dr. Adams-Bass regularly trains youth development professionals to use culturally relevant and inclusive practices when working with African-American children and youth.

Gado Alzouma obtained his undergraduate and graduate degrees from the University of Bordeaux II and University of Strasbourg, in France, and later proceeded to the Southern Illinois University, in the USA for a Ph.D. in Anthropology. Before joining AUN, Dr. Alzouma was at the Abdou Moumouni University of Niamey, Niger, where he taught Sociology and Anthropology courses for 12 years. He has worked as Coordinator, Evaluation and Learning Systems in the Africa and Information Society Program of the International Development Research Center (IDRC Dakar, Senegal) and as Research Fellow in the Global Media Research Center of Southern Illinois University, Carbondale.

Godfried Asante is an Assistant Professor of Rhetoric, Media and Social Change at Drake University. He earned his BA in Communication, Media and Rhetoric from the University of Minnesota, Morris and his MA in Communication Studies from Minnesota State University, Mankato. Godfried has a Ph.D. in Intercultural Communication from the University of New Mexico. His research interests focus on social identities such as race, class, gender, and sexuality in transnational contexts. The primary goal of his research is to use communication to explore how social inequalities and human rights violations are enacted and reproduced. Specifically, how social actors are positioned in systems of power relations to create subjugated subject positions. Godfried's approach into these research areas is to examine the relationship between language use and social disparities. He has published essays in journals including Howard Journal of Communications, Communication Theory, and the Journal of International and Intercultural Communication.

Omotayo O. Banjo, PhD (Penn State University, 2009) focuses on representation and audience responses to racial and cultural media. Her work has been published in peer reviewed journals including *Journal of Broadcasting and Electronic Media, Communication Theory, Journalism and Mass Communication Quarterly, Journal of Media and Religion,* and *Race and Social Problems.* She has also presented her research at regional, national, and international conferences. She is also coeditor of Contemporary Christian Culture: Messages, Missions and Dilemmas. Dr. Banjo teaches courses related to media theory, identity, and race.

Jeffrey Layne Blevins (Ph.D., Ohio University) is an Associate Professor and Head of the Journalism Department at the University of Cincinnati, where he also holds courtesy appointments in the Department of Communication and the Department of Political Science. His research examines media law and the political economy of media industries. The study presented here was made possible with the support of The Cincinnati Project at the University of Cincinnati and follows his service as a federal grant reviewer for the Broadband Technology Opportunities Program created under the American Recovery and Reinvestment Act of 2009. The $4.7 billion dollar grant program targeted "unserved and underserved" areas of the United States, such as rural and minority communities.

Christopher Brown (PhD, University of New Mexico, 2009) is an Associate Professor and Chair of the Department of Communication Studies at Minnesota State University, Mankato. His scholarly research explores the discourses of white supremacist groups and white male elites' constructions of race. His work appears in such journals as the *Communication Monographs*, *Howard Journal of Communications*, *Departures in Critical Qualitative Research*, *Media Psychology*, *Journalism and Mass Communication Quarterly*, and *Journal of Advertising Education*. He is currently coauthoring a book examining the intersection between race and sensorial experiences.

Godfried Daniels is currently an Assistant Professor at Western Washington University, and her research emphases are Intergroup Communication (specifically, issues related to gender and cultural identities) and Organizational Communication. She is interested in the notions of gender that are encouraged, accepted, and deeply woven into the social fabric and how these notions influence the identity of individuals in varied communication contexts. She is also interested in the processing and use of messages between and within organizations, and how people from different cultures communicate and form intercultural relationships.

Judy L. Isaksen is a Full Professor of Media & Popular Culture Studies and Women's & Gender Studies at High Point University in North Carolina, teaches courses at the intersection of critical/cultural theory and media studies focusing on issues of race, gender identity, and sexual orientation. She has published two articles on Barack Obama, the latest in a special legacy issue of the *Howard Journal of Communications*. Her work also appears in *Communication Studies*, *Legal Studies Forum*, and the *Journal of Popular Culture*, along with a variety of anthology chapters.

Justin T. Gammage is an Assistant Professor in the Department of Africana Studies at California State University, Dominguez Hills. He earned a B.A. in Africana Studies from CSU, Dominguez Hills. He holds a Masters and Ph.D. degree in African American Studies from Temple University. Dr. Gammage's research interests are African-American political economy with a focus on the history of social movements, past and present, that address factors challenging the social, political, and economic security of people of African descent. In addition, his research explores models of economic development in African-American communities.

Marquita Marie Gammage is an Associate Professor in the Africana Studies Department at California State University, Northridge. She earned her PhD in African American Studies from Temple University. Her research interest focus on overt and covert representations of racism and sexism as it pertains to media generated images of Black womanhood. Marquita Gammage was raised in the 9th ward community in New Orleans, LA, and her experiences led her to yield an unwavering commitment to researching issues impacting the Black community. Dr. Gammage first began researching the representations of Black women in the media as an undergraduate student at Howard University. Since then she has diligently researched media portrayals of Black women. Her highly anticipated text, "*Representations of Black Women in the Media: The Damnation of Black Womanhood*," uses the Afrocentric paradigm to critically analyze contemporary media portrayals of Black women and argues that these images have damned Black women to an inferior position in society. Through this work, Dr. Gammage offers a thought-provoking critique of the racist assault on Black womanhood and African humanity. In addition to contesting such portrayals, she affirms the dignity of Black womanhood and challenges media, and Black media in particular, to do the same.

Brandon McCasland (MA, University of Alabama, 2014) is a doctoral student and teaching assistant in the Department of Communication Studies at the University of Iowa. His scholarship examines mediated constructions of queer visibility, resistance, and acquiescence in the subcultural context of punk rock music.

Sonjah Stanley Niaah is the inaugural Rhodes Trust Rex Nettleford Fellow in Cultural Studies (2005) and is Senior Lecturer in Cultural Studies at the University of the West Indies' Mona Campus. She is the author of *Dancehall: From Slave Ship to Ghetto* (University of Ottawa Press, 2010) and editor of "'I'm Broader than Broadway': Caribbean Perspectives on Producing Celebrity" (*Wadabagei*, Vol. 12: 2, 2009). With research interests around Black Atlantic performance geographies, ritual, dance, as well as popular culture and the sacred, Stanley Niaah is a leading author on Jamaican popular culture, and Caribbean cultural studies more broadly, having published articles and book chapters in numerous journals and edited collections locally, regionally, and internationally. She is an Associate Editor of *Wadabagei: A Journal of the Caribbean and its Diasporas* and serves on the editorial boards of *Cultural Studies, Social and Economic Studies, Tout Moun*, and *Dancecult*, among others.

Tokunbo Ojo teaches at the Department of Communication Studies, York University, Toronto, Ontario, Canada. His teaching and research expertise include journalism studies, international development and communication, geopolitics of global communication, political economy of global media industries, diasporic media, and political communication.

Mandy Paris (MA, Minnesota State University, Mankato, 2016) is a doctoral student and a teaching assistant in the Department of

Communication Studies at the University of Minnesota. Her work explores disability justice and identity.

Gloria Nziba Pindi (PhD, Southern Illinois University Carbondale) is an Assistant Professor in the Department of Communication at California State University San Marcos. Her research lies in the area of Black feminism, critical intercultural communication, and performance of the self in transnational context. Her scholarship focuses on African immigrants' process of identity negotiation in diasporic context with a critical approach to diversity and social justice.

Sachi Sekimoto (PhD, University of New Mexico, 2011) is Associate Professor in the Department of Communication Studies at Minnesota State University, Mankato. She is a coeditor of *Globalizing Intercultural Communication: A Reader* (Sage, 2016). She writes in the areas of phenomenology, embodiment, identity politics, and sensory studies. Her work has appeared in *Journal of International and Intercultural Communication*, *Communication Quarterly*, *Departures in Critical Qualitative Research*, and *Critical Philosophy of Race*. She is currently coauthoring a book examining the intersection between race and sensorial experiences.

Catherine R. Squires is Professor of Communication Studies and Director of the Race, Indigeneity, Gender & Sexuality Studies Initiative (RIGS) at the University of Minnesota. Dr. Squires' work investigates the interactions between social identities, media discourses, and publics. She is the author of Dispatches from the Color Line (SUNY, 2007) and African Americans and the Media (Polity, 2009). Her most recent book, The Post-racial Mystique (NYU Press, 2014), explores how a variety of media—the news, network television, and online, independent media—debate, define, and deploy the term "post-racial" in their representations of American politics and society.

Mark Ward Sr. (PhD, Clemson University) is Associate Professor of communication at the University of Houston-Victoria, Texas, USA. He has authored two histories of religious broadcasting, *The Lord's Radio* (2017) and *Air of Salvation* (1994), and edited the multivolume series *The Electronic Church in the Digital Age* (2016), for which he received the 2017 Clifford G. Christians Ethics Research Award. His studies of evangelical culture and media have appeared in the *Journal of Communication and Religion, Journal of Media and Religion, Journal of Religion, Media and Digital Culture, Journal of Radio and Audio Media, Interdisciplinary Journal of Research on Religion, Intercultural Communication Studies, Voluntas*, and other venues. He serves on the Executive Council of the Religious Communication Association, which named his ethnography of evangelical media its 2014 Article of the Year. His interest in institutional and organizational cultures is also seen in the book *Deadly Documents* (2014), which examines the Holocaust through discourse analyses of everyday Nazi bureaucratic documents, and the coauthored textbook *Organizational Communication: Theory, Research, and Practice* (2015). Before entering academe, Dr. Ward was communications director and journal editor for several national and international nonprofits and industry trade associations, and worked as a broadcaster in roles ranging from local announcer to national syndication.

Index

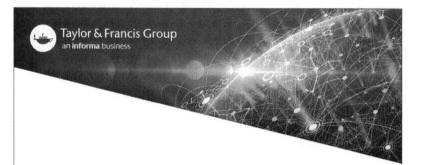

Taylor & Francis eBooks

www.taylorfrancis.com

A single destination for eBooks from Taylor & Francis
with increased functionality and an improved user
experience to meet the needs of our customers.

90,000+ eBooks of award-winning academic content in
Humanities, Social Science, Science, Technology, Engineering,
and Medical written by a global network of editors and authors.

TAYLOR & FRANCIS EBOOKS OFFERS:

A streamlined
experience for
our library
customers

A single point
of discovery
for all of our
eBook content

Improved
search and
discovery of
content at both
book and
chapter level

REQUEST A FREE TRIAL
support@taylorfrancis.com